GW00672121

BENET'S

ARTEFACTS OF ENGLAND & THE UNITED KINGDOM

CURRENT VALUES

Fourth Edition 2021

Published by Greenlight Publishing

Written and Compiled by Aaron Hammond

BENET'S ARTEFACTS OF ENGLAND & THE UNITED KINGDOM CURRENT VALUES 4th EDITION

Written and compiled by Aaron Hammond (COO)
TimeLine Auctions Ltd
The Court House, 363 Main Road,
Harwich, Essex CO12 4DN, UK
Tel. +44(0)1277 815121
Email: enquiries@timelineauctions.com
www.timelineauctions.com

Published by:
Greenlight Publishing
Unit E5 East Gores Farm, Coggeshall CO6 1FW
Tel. 01376 521900
www.greenlightpublishing.co.uk

Cover by Damir Radić

ISBN 978-1-897738-66-5

ii

INTRODUCTION TO THE FOURTH EDITION

Welcome to the fourth edition of Benet's Artefacts, a handy visual guide to objects from the United Kingdom dating from the Stone Age (Paleolithic period) to post–medieval times.

Benet's Artefacts has now been in print for over twenty years, and has come to be trusted as the standard visual encyclopedia for UK metal detectorists and collectors. It has been consulted and studied by thousands of users in this time, who rely on its clear photographs and concise descriptions for assistance in identifying their finds.

The first edition, issued in 2000, sold out quickly and became a very sought-after title. The second edition was issued in 2003, and had twice as many colour photographs of artefacts included. The third edition of 2014 was about 25% larger again and widened its scope with over 3,000 images.

The present fourth edition contains over 500 new objects and still totals over 3,000 images. It will, we believe, become the standard reference work for years to come as the quality of images has been improved and the market-related price information has been brought up to date in line with present conditions.

Benet's Artefacts has always been from the outset a handy guide to current achievable prices, based on our detailed knowledge of the market for antiquities in the United Kingdom. Obviously such prices vary over time according to a number of factors, including the object's physical condition, its rarity, and the number of collectors who are likely to want to buy it. For these reasons, a complete revision of the book's published price ranges has been made based on current market trends and recent actual sale prices.

One factor that can affect the price is accurate identification. Objects recorded with the Finds Liaison Officers of the Portable Antiquities Scheme are studied by professionals who have access to years of experience and large libraries of reference books. Obviously, the more objects recorded with the scheme, the more comprehensive its records become and thus items which appear rare and mysterious can be more easily identified.

The items photographed for this book have been chosen as a good cross-section of the material that can be found in the United Kingdom, but we have not aimed at publishing a full range of any particular object-type nor the range of items from any period. There are specialist books and magazine articles on most artefact types, and the reader should consult these for detailed information. The number of examples published in these pages does not relate directly to rarity in the market.

Thank you for choosing Benet's Artefacts. We hope you find it useful and enjoyable!

iii

CONTENTS

ACKNOWLEDGEMENTS

This is the fourth edition of a work that has become a standard reference, building on the success of the previous versions. It is, of course, the product of many contributors since the editor and his team have called on the skills and specialist knowledge of a number of people in compiling the final text and images.

First I wish to thank the TimeLine Auctions team for their long-term assistance in all aspects of the project. Special thanks are due to Christopher Wren for sharing his detailed knowledge of Stone Age and Bronze Age material, and for his advice regarding the post-medieval section. I am grateful to Stephen Pollington who assisted with the Saxon and Viking sections, to Michael Healy for his photography, to Brett Hammond and to Heather Godfrey for their helpful input.

Images have been sourced from the archives of TimeLine Auctions whose photographic and data-processing assistance has been invaluable.

My most profound thanks are due to my greatest mentor, the late David M. Miller, the leading coin and artefact specialist.

Aaron Hammond, editor
Harwich, 2021

ARRANGEMENT AND REFERENCES

The arrangement of artefacts within these pages follows a single pattern to help the user find things quickly. The overall arrangement is chronological, from Stone Age to post-medieval, with the last entries relating to the 18th century AD. Every item is prefixed with an alphanumeric reference. The historical periods are assigned a letter according to the following system:-

S	STONE AGE	V	VIKING
B	BRONZE AGE	M	MEDIEVAL
I	IRON AGE		(including Tudor)
R	ROMAN	P	POST-MEDIEVAL
A	ANGLO-SAXON		

Immediately after the period-letter is a two-digit number which shows the artefact type, as follows:-

01	AXES	15	HORSE HARNESS & RIDER FITTINGS
02	ARROWHEADS		
03	SPEARS	16	SEALS
04	SWORDS, DAGGERS & KNIVES	17	KEYS & LOCKS
		18	WEIGHTS & MEASURES
05	OTHER WEAPONRY	19	WRITING IMPLEMENTS
06	PINS	20	BELLS & WHISTLES
07	BROOCHES	21	FOOD, DRINK & DOMESTIC WARES
08	PENDANTS & BADGES		
09	MOUNTS	22	MEDICAL IMPLEMENTS
10	RINGS & JEWELLERY	23	TOKENS, JETTONS & PLAYTHINGS
11	STATUES & FIGURINES		
12	STRAP ENDS & BUCKLES	24	PILGRIM & RELIGIOUS ITEMS
13	CLOTHES FASTENERS		
14	COSMETIC IMPLEMENTS	25	THIMBLES & PURSE BARS
		99	MISCELLANEOUS ITEMS

Objects in these classes appear in numerical order within their respective sections, so that S02 signifies a Stone Age arrowhead, R07 a Roman brooch, M10 a medieval ring, and so on.

After the alphanumeric prefix there is a hyphen followed by a four-digit number, which is provided for identification purposes but has no further significance (i.e. item 0001 will not necessarily be the earliest in date nor the most valuable of the objects in that section).

VALUES

The price ranges indicated in this book represent what a collector or purchaser might be prepared to pay at auction in present market conditions, not what a dealer might offer.

PLEASE NOTE that the price ranges indicated in these pages refer to the illustrated objects in the condition shown. If you have a similar artefact in better or worse condition, the achievable price will vary accordingly. The valuations are affected by four principal criteria:

1. Condition of the item
2. Quality of the workmanship
3. Rarity
4. Demand

Quality of workmanship is often the single most important factor. Items produced to a high standard from quality materials are exceptional in any age and are therefore most sought-after by collectors.

STONE AGE BRITAIN

Human history is a continuum. Every dawn brings a new day, the days in succession weeks, months, years, centuries and millennia. For the purpose of study, it is convenient to divide the passage of time into sections and to characterise them by their dominant technologies.

Since stone tools are the oldest objects relatable to human activity, the first periods of human history are collectively known as 'The Stone Age' although this masks a range of developing cultures. That labelled the 'Eolithic' is the foundation, the earliest men whose tools are barely recognisable as such. The 'Palaeolithic', the 'Old Stone Age', lasts for hundreds of thousands of years during which time whatever advances in technology were made have left no record in the worked stones which are the only remains of the period. The following 'Mesolithic' or 'Middle Stone Age' lasts from about 8,000 BC to 3,500 BC when smaller stone tools ('microliths') were created and there is evidence for wooden components in the form of handles and shafts; it is only from around 6,000 BC that we can really speak of 'Britain' as an island, since before that time a single landmass extended from present-day Ireland to Asia.

The 'Neolithic' or 'New Stone Age' from 3,500 BC to 2,500 BC marks the transition from the old hunter-gatherer societies to new forms of organisation involving fixed settlements, agriculture, the use of wheeled vehicles, boats, horse-riding and the development of textiles and ceramics. Stone tools from this period are often polished and include arrowheads, axes, drills, chisels, awls and picks. Antler and other materials survive, indicating a wide range of resources in use.

Stone Age material may be found widely in the modern landscape but it takes a practiced eye to determine the difference between a worked stone axe and a randomly chipped pebble. Because of this, it is advisable to consult an expert when assessing Stone Age material.

S01-0101
Palaeolithic Hand Axe
175mm
Large and perfect example with a provenance.
£300 - £400

S01-0105
Palaeolithic Axe
225mm
Complete and undamaged. Scarce.
£100 - £150

S01-0106
Palaeolithic Axe
200mm
Very large, perfect condition and rare.
£400 - £600

S01-41048
Axe
180mm
Neolithic type, knapped and polished flint.
£200 - £300

S01-92441
Polished Axe
125mm
Neolithic type,
knapped and
polished with inked
collector's findspot.
£400 - £600

S01-92437
Polished Axe
130mm
Neolithic polished
'Cuttlefish' type.
£400 - £600

S01-135260
Axehead
133mm
Finely polished
diorite, convex
edge.
£200 - £300

S01-131475
Handaxe
190mm
Mesolithic type,
river valley
gravels patination.
£500 - £700

S01-0207
Jadeite Axe
Polished
165mm
Perfect example.
Smooth surface.
Undamaged.
From £2,000

S01-0108
Palaeolithic
Hand Axe
132mm
Pretty colour. Pear shape.
£200 - £300

S01-0109
Palaeolithic Ovate
Hand Axe
90mm
Nicely worked.
£80 - £100

S01-0116
Palaeolithic Axe
95mm
Well worked.
£80 - £100

S01-0114
Palaeolithic Axe
185mm
Very rich colour.
£150 - £200

S01-0201
Neolithic Polished
Axehead
250mm
Finest example. Superb
colour. Very large.
£600 - £800

S01-0202
Neolithic Polished
Axehead
90mm
£50 - £70

S01-0203
Neolithic Polished
Stone Axe
145mm
Highly polished.
£150 - £200

S01-0204
Neolithic
Polished
Axehead
155mm
Slight chip to
the cutting edge.
£150 - £200

S01-0211
Neolithic Axehead
102mm
Grainy surface.
£60 - £80

S01-0212
Neolithic Axehead (Greenstone)
95mm
Complete and undamaged.
£60 - £80

S01-0213
Axehead
135mm
Well worked. Dark flint.
£120 - £180

S01-0214
Neolithic Polished Axe
98mm
Highly polished and
complete.
£200 - £300

S01-0215
Neolithic Polished
Axe
100mm
Nicely polished and
complete.
£200 - £300

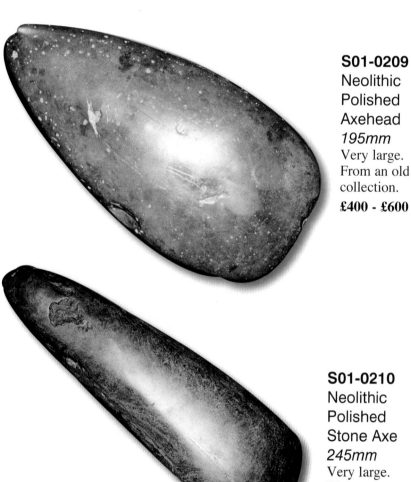

S01-0209
Neolithic
Polished
Axehead
195mm
Very large.
From an old
collection.
£400 - £600

S01-0210
Neolithic
Polished
Stone Axe
245mm
Very large.
Rich green
colour.
£300 - £400

S01-0317
Neolithic Flint
Axe
155mm
Smooth brown
patinated flint.
£200 - £300

S01-0223
Neolithic Polished
Axehead
132mm
Pretty. Rich colour
and perfect.
£300 - £400

S01-0319
Palaeolithic
Flint Axe
210mm
Small loss to the
tip, some cortex
remaining.
£200 - £300

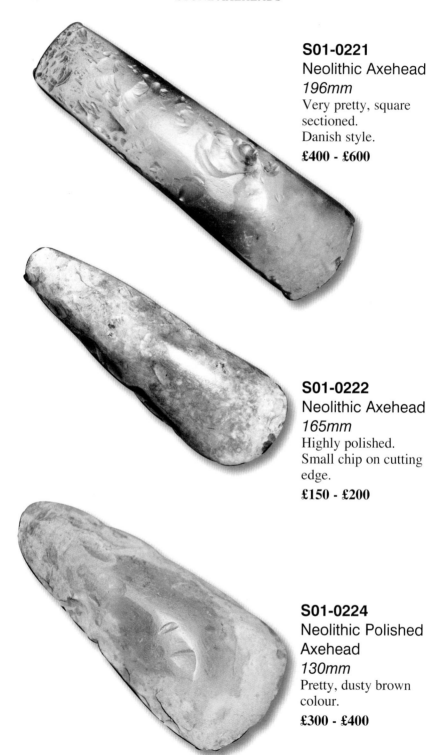

S01-0221
Neolithic Axehead
196mm
Very pretty, square
sectioned.
Danish style.
£400 - £600

S01-0222
Neolithic Axehead
165mm
Highly polished.
Small chip on cutting
edge.
£150 - £200

S01-0224
Neolithic Polished
Axehead
130mm
Pretty, dusty brown
colour.
£300 - £400

S01-0301
Neolithic Hand Axe
120mm
Standard type.
£50 - £80

S01-0220
Neolithic Axe
220mm
Very large. Damage
to cutting edge.
£200 - £300

S01-0303
Neolithic Flint Axehead
132mm
Sharp cutting edge. Polished.
£200 - £300

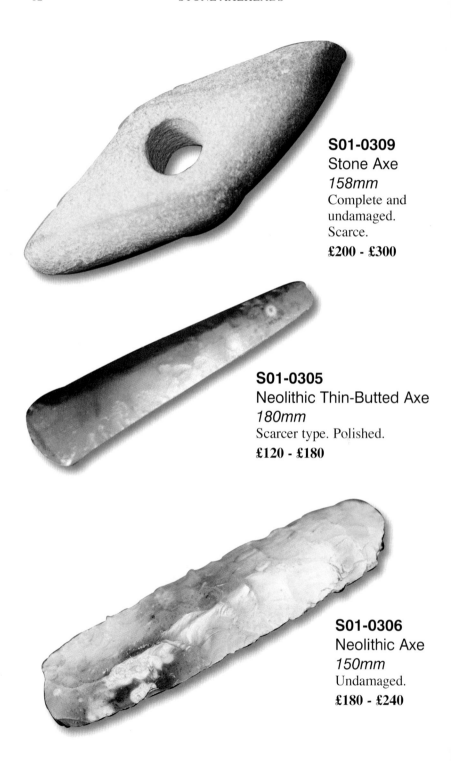

S01-0309
Stone Axe
158mm
Complete and
undamaged.
Scarce.
£200 - £300

S01-0305
Neolithic Thin-Butted Axe
180mm
Scarcer type. Polished.
£120 - £180

S01-0306
Neolithic Axe
150mm
Undamaged.
£180 - £240

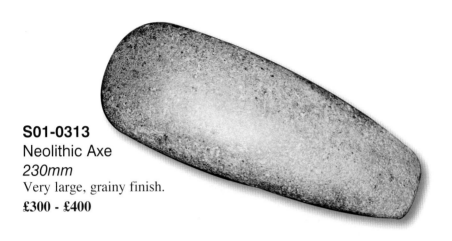

S01-0313
Neolithic Axe
230mm
Very large, grainy finish.
£300 - £400

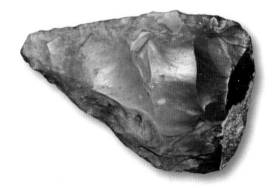

S01-0320
Palaeolithic Flint
Axe
110mm
Remnants of the cortex
on the upper end
£200 - £300

S01-0315
Palaeolithic Flint
Axe
120mm
Orange-brown
patination from river
gravels.
£80 - £100

S01-0310
Stone Axe or
Chopper
190mm
Large example.
£150 - £200

S01-0311
Neolithic Flint
Axehead
(Splayed)
138mm
Perfect in every
respect and
provenanced.
£300 - £400

S01-0316
Neolithic Flint
Axe
120mm
Speckled flint.
£150 - £200

S01-0321
Palaeolithic Flint
Axe
150mm
With some original
cortex.
£150 - £200

S01-0322
Palaeolithic Flint
Axe
160mm
Typical river terrace
patination.
£120 - £180

S01-0323
Palaeolithic
Flint Axe
125mm
With some
original cortex to
the butt.
£100 - £150

S01-0324
Palaeolithic Flint Axe
190mm
With yellowish river-gravel patination.
£150 - £200

S01-0325
Mesolithic Flint Axe
100mm
Square cutting edge.
£120 - £180

S01-0326
Neolithic Sandstone Axe-Hammer
130mm
Abrasion to butt and edge.
£150 - £200

S01-0327
Mesolithic Flint Hand Axe
125mm
Mottled white and tan flint, finely knapped.
£80 - £100

S01-0328
Neolithic Polished
Axe
120mm
Finely polished,
brown-orange flint
with river gravel
patination.
£200 - £300

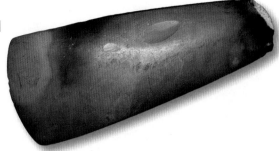

S01-0329
Neolithic Polished
Axehead
110mm
Double-curved profile,
drilled in the centre.
Dark green diorite.
£800 - £1,000

S01-0330
Neolithic Axe-
Hammer
83mm
Finely ground and
polished basalt, drilled.
£600 - £800

S01-0331
Palaeolithic
Hand Axe
179mm
Rounded butt, pointed
working surface.
£200 - £300

S02-0101
Neolithic
Arrowheads
Basic
examples.
£15 each

S02-0102
Neolithic
Arrowheads
Basic
examples.
£10 each

S02-0103
Neolithic Leaf-Shaped
Arrowhead
40mm
Point broken.
£20 - £30

S02-0204
Bronze Age Barbed
& Tanged Arrowhead
37mm
Large and perfect. Provenanced.
£80 - £120

S02-0308
Bronze Age Flint Arrowhead
22mm
Barbed and tanged form.
£50 - £70

S02-0104
Neolithic Leaf-Shaped
Arrowhead
50mm
Standard type.
£30 - £40

S02-0109
Neolithic Leaf-
Shaped Arrowhead
43mm
Large size.
£50 - £70

S02-0110
Neolithic Arrowhead
35mm
Standard type.
£40 - £60

S02-0111
Neolithic Arrowhead
42mm
Standard type.
£40 - £60

S02-0112
Neolithic Tranchet
Arrowhead
27mm
Scarcer type.
£40 - £60

S02-0113
Neolithic Arrowhead
30mm
Beautifully worked.
£60 - £80

S02-0201
Bronze Age Barbed &
Tanged Arrowhead
32mm
Complete and undamaged.
£80 - £120

S02-0202
Bronze Age Barbed
& Tanged Arrowhead
23mm
Perfect and undamaged.
£80 - £120

S02-92432
Bronze Age Barbed
& Tanged Arrowhead
32mm
Complete and undamaged.
£50 - £70

S02-0305
Bronze Age Flint
Arrowhead Group
21-32mm
Four barbed and tanged
types.
£50 - £70 each

S02-0306
Bronze Age Flint
Arrowhead
36mm
Carefully knapped from a thin
flake.
£50 - £70

S02-0307
Neolithic Flint
Arrowhead
52mm
Thinned at the butt for
attachment to the shaft.
£120 - £180

S02-0309
Mesolithic Chert
Arrowhead
20mm
Triangular form.
£30 - £40

S03-0301
Neolithic Flint Halberd
130mm
Carefully knapped with some retouching.
£200 - £300

S03-0302
Neolithic
Javelin Head
95mm
With tapered tang and
shoulders.
£100 - £150

S04-0101
Neolithic Knife
110mm
Undamaged.
£20 - £30

S04-0102
Neolithic Flint
Knife
105mm
Slight damage.
£30 - £40

S04-0103
Neolithic Knife
95mm
Nicely worked and
undamaged.
£80 - £100

S04-0104
Neolithic Knife
80mm
Perfect and
undamaged.
Some cortex.
£100 - £150

S04-70350
Neolithic Sickle Knife
110mm
Transluscent grey-brown flint.
£150 - £200

S04-64834
Neolithic Sickle Knife
170mm
Showing considerable polish.
£200 - £300

S04-0301
Neolithic Sickle Knife
130mm
Formed on a large flake with bulbar scar still evident.
£150 - £200

S04-0302
Neolithic Sickle Knife
115mm
Retouched edges, light patination.
£200 - £300

S04-0304
Neolithic Flint
Knife
65mm
Extensive usage
polish to tip.
£60 - £80

S04-0305
Neolithic Flint
Dagger
170mm
Retouched edges.
£150 - £200

S04-0306
Neolithic Sickle
Knife
160mm
Light wear polish
from use.
£200 - £300

S04-0307
Neolithic Flake
Dagger
167mm
Tip damaged and
repaired.
£300 - 400

S04-0308
Neolithic Flint Dagger
150mm
Portion of cortex
remaining.
£200 - £300

S04-0309
Flint Dagger
217mm
Large bifacial, finely
worked.
£300 - £400

S04-0310
Flint Knife
150mm
High quality knapping.
£100 - £150

S05-0101
Neolithic
Mace Head
58mm
Light grey
quartzite, pecked
spherical form.
£50 - £70

S05-0102
Neolithic
Mace Head
93mm
Partial perforation
to upper and lower
faces.
£80 - £100

S05-0103
Neolithic
Mace Head
75mm
Dark grey basalt,
partial perforation
to upper and lower
faces.
£60 - £80

S05-0104
Neolithic Mace
Head
90mm
Scarcer item.
£80 - £100

S05-0105
Neolithic Mace
Head
77mm
Doughnut type.
£60 - £80

S05-0106
Neolithic Mace Head
(Round)
75mm
Round with indentations.
£80 - £100

S99-0101
Neolithic Leaf-Shaped
Point
44mm
Basic type.
£10 - £20

S99-0102
Neolithic Leaf-Shaped
Point
50mm
Basic type.
£10 - £20

S99-0103
Neolithic Leaf-Shaped
Point
52mm
Basic type.
£15 - £20

S99-0104
Neolithic Leaf-Shaped
Point
50mm
Nicely worked.
£20 - £30

S99-0201
Neolithic
Scrapers
Worked edges.
£5 each

S99-0202
Neolithic
Chisel
175mm
Large and
rare.
£300 - £400

S99-0301
Neolithic
Boring Tool
130mm
Scarcer item.
£60 - £80

S99-0404
Bone Fish Hook
57mm
Carved from an
animal's long
bone, pierced for
suspension.
£40 - £60

S99-0405
Paleolithic Flint
Cleaver
170mm
With some original
cortex to the butt.
£120 - £180

S99-0406
Flint Scraper
Group
37-50mm
Five convex scrapers
formed on flakes.
£80 - £100

S99-0407
Mesolithic Flint
Pick
105mm
Curved profile,
rounded cutting edge
and pointed butt. Iron
salt staining to white
patina.
£100 - £150

BRONZE AGE BRITAIN

Metalworking in Britain begins with the creation of bronze from copper and tin, a technology which began in western Asia and spread across Europe, reaching these shores by 2,500 BC. Copper is not abundant in Britain (although it is found in Ireland), but the island's western reaches were identified as a source of tin and a cross-Channel trade in metals began which involved the spread of new knowledge and ideas.

The introduction of bronze was a game-changing moment. The new material could be worked into any shape desired by casting – creating a master out of wax, coating it in clay, melting the copper and tin to make a quantity of bronze and pouring it into the mould. This innovation would probably not have been possible if the Neolithic farmer ancestors had not already worked out how to get very high temperatures in their kilns when making pottery. New forms of tool immediately became possible: axeheads with flared blades and a socket to attach to the wooden handle; leaf-shaped spearheads; swords and daggers; gouges, scythes, chisels and razors. Gold ornaments made their first appearance, in the form of bracelets and finger rings, cups and jewellery items.

Burials from the Bronze Age include many of the 'barrows', gravemounds which are clustered in certain areas of the country. Many of these were later re-used, but the mounds often contain jewellery, flint arrowheads and ceramic vessels – perhaps to be taken into the afterlife by the deceased.

Despite the invention of the new technologies based around casting bronze, the old knapping techniques did not die out and there are countless examples of stone arrowheads from Bronze Age contexts.

Bronze Age artefacts are heavily collected, and they are not especially rare as a whole. Many artefacts are known from 'founder's hoards', stashes of scrapped or unfinished objects which were probably intended for melting down and recycling. Swords are sometimes found deposited in rivers, a custom which continued in some areas into the later Iron Age.

B01-0101
Looped & Socketted Axe
65mm
Plain axehead, slight pitting
and a little damage to blade.
Small size.
£120 - £180

B01-0102
Looped & Socketted
Axe
100mm
Plain axehead, very little
pitting on surface. Blade a
little ragged.
£180 - £240

B01-0103
Looped & Socketted
Axe
102mm
Plain axehead, undamaged,
slight pitting on surface.
Large size.
£200 - £300

B01-0104
Looped & Socketted
Axe
90mm
Very lightly decorated
axehead, single band near
the top, slight pitting.
£180 - £240

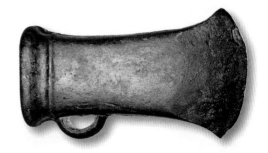

B01-0105
Looped & Socketted Axe
101mm
Lightly decorated axehead with single band near the top. Blade a little ragged.
£150 - £200

B01-0106
Looped & Socketted Axe
95mm
Decorated with a single band near the top. Very little pitting. Flared blade.
£150 - £200

B01-0110
Looped & Socketted Decorated Axe
107mm
Light decoration, blade undamaged, small scuff on surface.
£180 - £240

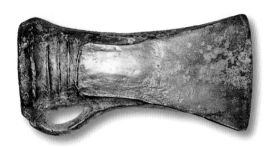

B01-0108
Looped & Socketted Axe
92mm
Decorated axehead of typical European style. Light pitting.
£180 - £240

B01-0111
Looped & Socketted
Decorated Axe
110mm
Flared socket, linear
decoration. Pitted. Blade
a little ragged.
£150 - £200

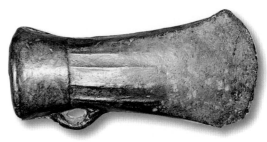

B01-0115
Looped & Socketted
Decorated Axe
102mm
Decorated axehead.
Slight tin content.
Corrosion around the
blade.
£150 - £200

B01-0113
Looped
& Socketted
Decorated Axe
102mm
Short linear decoration.
Blade a little ragged.
£150 - £200

B01-0114
Looped & Socketted
Decorated Axe
102mm
Decorated axehead.
Slight tin content.
Corrosion around the
blade.
£120 - £180

B01-0112
Looped & Socketted
Decorated Axe
140mm
Perfect axehead. Linear
decoration. Very large with
superb patination.
£300 - £400

B01-0204
Palstave Axe
165mm
Centre rib. Good,
smooth surface.
Even patina.
Undamaged.
£400 - £600

B01-41087
Looped & Socketted
Axehead 'Sompting'
Type.
145mm
£600 - £800

B01-41080
Looped & Socketted
Axehead 'Wilburton'
Type.
95mm
£200 - £300

B01-41092
Palstave Axe
140mm
Looped with square butt
and median stop.
£250 - £350

B01-149574
Palstave Axe
180mm
From the Manston hoard
pit deposit.
£300 - £400

B01-0202
Palstave Axe
142mm
Superb blade. Shield decoration.
Lovely brown patina.
£250 - £350

B01-0414
Palstave Axe
130mm
With square butt end.
£100 - £150

B01-0415
Copper Axe
110mm
Small casting flaw.
£80 - £100

B01-0416
Copper Axe
150mm
Flat in section with
small flare to the
blade.
£100 - £150

B01-0206
Palstave
Looped Axe
151mm
Superb condition.
Fine blade. Even
patina.
£300 - £400

B01-0207
Palstave
Looped Axe
171mm
Complete
example.
Very large.
Slightly
raised central rib.
£250 - £350

B01-0208
Palstave Axe
155mm
Shield decoration.
Patina a little
ragged. Some
pitting.
£200 - £300

B01-0301
Flanged Axe
90mm
Pitted surface.
Patina flaking.
£100 - £150

B01-0303
Flanged Axe
110mm
Good, even patina.
Blade undamaged.
£400 - £600

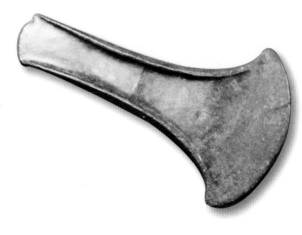

B01-0304
Decorated
Flanged Axe
131mm
Flared blade. Even
patina.
£400 - £600

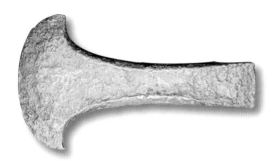

B01-0305
Flanged Axe
100mm
Pitted and uneven
surface.
£120 - £180

B01-41072
Flanged Axe
145mm
'Balbirnie' type .
£500 - £800

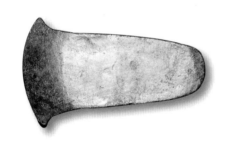

B01-0402
Flat Axe
75mm
Very nice example.
Smooth, even
surface. Good
cutting edge.
£150 - £200

B01-0403
Flat Axe
110mm
Plain example.
Surface a little
rough.
£100 - £150

B01-0404
Socketted Axe
118mm
With small side loop,
even patination.
£120 - £180

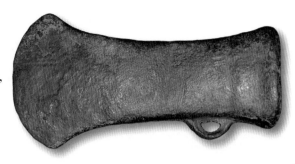

B01-0405
Socketted Axe
83mm
Five raised ribs to each
face.
£100 - £150

B01-0406
Looped &
SockettedAxe
99mm
Crescent-shaped
blade.
£150 - £200

B01-0407
Palstave Axe
131mm
Lateral flanges.
Smooth
patination.
£250 - £350

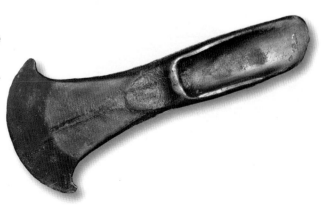

B01-0408
Palstave Axe
175mm
Minor casting flaws.
£200 - £300

B01-0409
Palstave Axe
165mm
Keyed surface and
flared blade.
£300 - £400

B01-0410
Axe
100mm
Substantial size
with decoration.
£200 - £300

B01-0411
Palstave Axe
155mm
Y-shaped ribs
before the socket.
£300 - £400

B01-0412
Looped &
Socketted Axe
50mm
Collars to the socket.
£100 - £150

B01-0413
Axe
230mm
Keyed and textured
surfaces.
£150 - £200

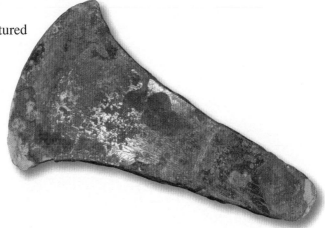

B03-0101
Socketted Spearhead
200mm
Pitted surface. Late type,
maybe into Iron Age. Large
example.
£120 - £180

B03-0102
Socketted Spearhead
190mm
Sound patina. Good blade.
£150 - £200

B03-0103
Socketted Spearhead
120mm
Point broken and restored.
Leaf-shaped blade.
£100 - £150

B03-41028
Spearhead
99mm
Side-looped and socketted,
narrow profile.
£500 - £800

B03-0105
Socketted Spearhead
330mm
Very long example. Surface a
little patchy.
£300 - £500

B03-0106
Socketted
Spearhead
185mm
Good, large example. A
little pitting in places.
£150 - £200

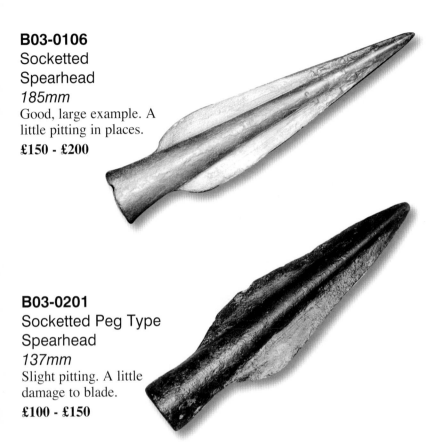

B03-0201
Socketted Peg Type
Spearhead
137mm
Slight pitting. A little
damage to blade.
£100 - £150

B03-41026
Socketted Spearhead
105mm
Side-looped and socketted,
broad edges.
£250 - £350

B03-0203
Socketted Spearhead
(Peg Type)
90mm
Short and stocky. Light
crack along the fins.
£120 - £180

B03-0301
Looped & Socketted
Spearhead
118mm
Scarcer type. Even patina.
Undamaged.
£200 - £300

B03-0303
Lugged & Socketted
Spearhead
164mm
Smooth surface. A little
damage on the blade.
£300 - £500

B03-134838
Spearhead
130mm
Blade with bevelled edges and two crescent-shaped openings.
£500 - £700

B03-0305
Spearhead
270mm
Socket with perforations for a fixing rivet.
£200 - £300

B03-0306
Spearhead
210mm
Leaf-shaped blade.
£200 - £300

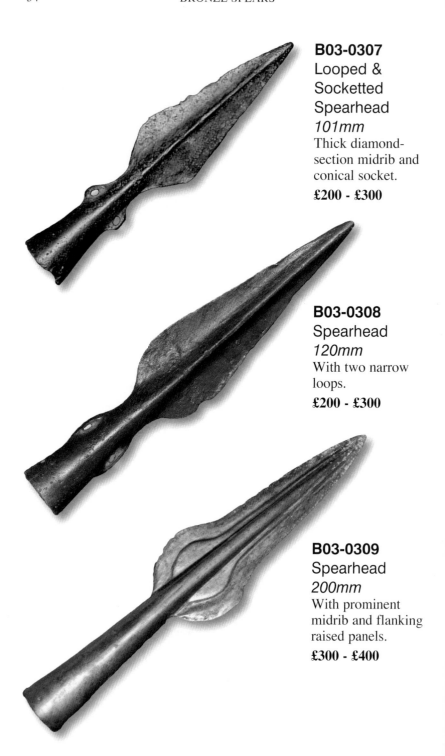

B03-0307
Looped &
Socketted
Spearhead
101mm
Thick diamond-
section midrib and
conical socket.
£200 - £300

B03-0308
Spearhead
120mm
With two narrow
loops.
£200 - £300

B03-0309
Spearhead
200mm
With prominent
midrib and flanking
raised panels.
£300 - £400

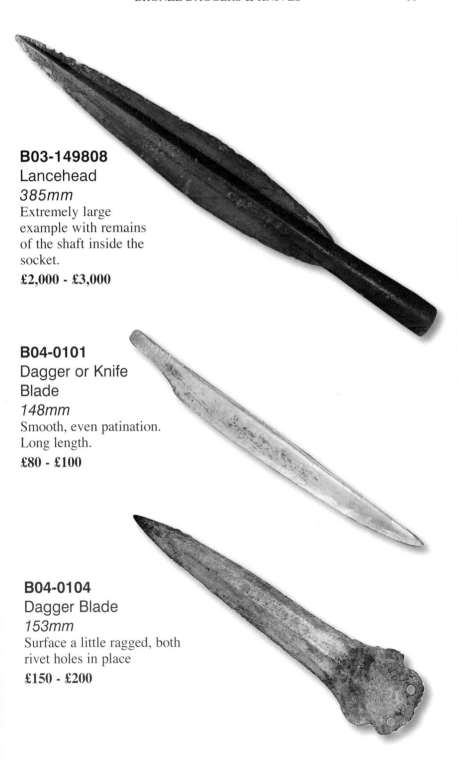

B03-149808
Lancehead
385mm
Extremely large
example with remains
of the shaft inside the
socket.
£2,000 - £3,000

B04-0101
Dagger or Knife
Blade
148mm
Smooth, even patination.
Long length.
£80 - £100

B04-0104
Dagger Blade
153mm
Surface a little ragged, both
rivet holes in place
£150 - £200

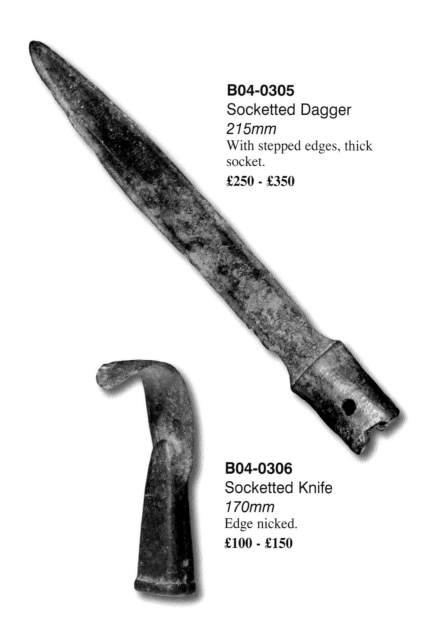

B04-0305
Socketted Dagger
215mm
With stepped edges, thick
socket.
£250 - £350

B04-0306
Socketted Knife
170mm
Edge nicked.
£100 - £150

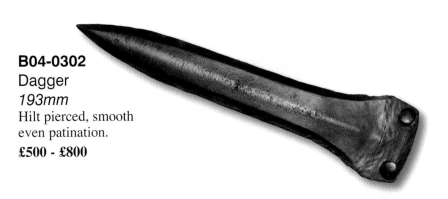

B04-0302
Dagger
193mm
Hilt pierced, smooth
even patination.
£500 - £800

B04-0303
Dagger
84mm
Broad upper end with
holes for attachment
to a wooden hilt.
£100 - £150

B04-0304
Knife
215mm
Slender with curved
upper edge.
£150 - £200

B04-41020
Dirk
235mm
Group I Type.
£800 - £1,000

B04-149809
Dagger Blade
137mm
Complete with two
fixing rivets.
£200 - £300

B04-41008
Sword
4500mm
Ewart Park Type.
£1,500 - £2,000

B04-0301
Sword
675mm
Ewart Park Type with
flanges to the hilt.
From £3,000

B14-0601
Razor
130mm
Surface a little pitted. Sharp
cutting edge.
£300 - £400

B14-0602
Razor
84mm
Decorated. Even green
patination.
£80 - £100

B14-0603
Razor
63mm
Open-work. Bell shape.
Pendant type.
£150 - £200

B99-0905
Razor
90mm
With trefoil head.
£150 - £200

B99-0102
Socketted Gouge
101mm
Even patina. Fragment
broken at the back.
£80 - £100

B99-0103
Socketted Gouge
101mm
Pitted surface. Blade
a little ragged.
£60 - £80

B99-0104
Socketted Gouge
97mm
Very slight pitting.
Ragged blade.
£60 - £80

B99-0105
Socketted Gouge
82mm
Corrosion around
the blade. Attractive
patina.
£60 - £80

B99-0106
Socketted Gouge
82mm
Pleasant example.
Light pitting.
£60 - £80

B99-0201
Tanged Chisel
105mm
Slight damage to the
blade.
£80 - £100

B99-0202
Tanged Chisel
65mm
Smooth, even patina.
Undamaged.
£60 - £80

B99-0203
Chisel
102mm
Slight chip in blade.
£80 - £100

B99-0301
Hammer
75mm
Some tin content.
Scarce item.
£150 - £200

B99-0501
Hoard
Provenanced
and recorded
with a museum.
From £1,000

B99-0502
Hoard
Provenanced.
Mainly broken
objects.
£300 - £400

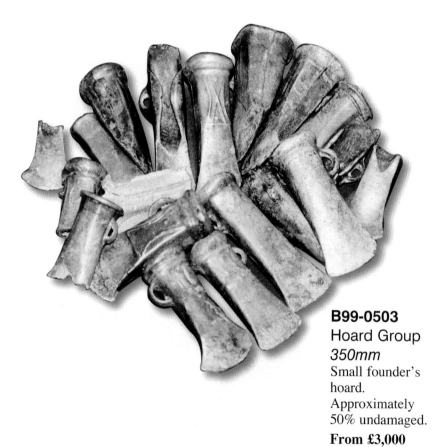

B99-0503
Hoard Group
350mm
Small founder's
hoard.
Approximately
50% undamaged.
From £3,000

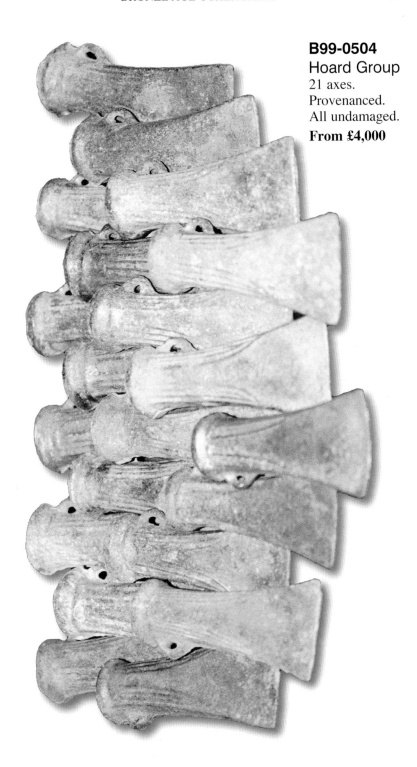

B99-0504
Hoard Group
21 axes.
Provenanced.
All undamaged.
From £4,000

B99-0902
Bracelet
65mm
With hatched and ribbed ornament.
£100 - £150

B99-0903
Gold Ring Money
18mm
Stripes of inlaid silver banding.
From £400

B99-0904
Gold Ring Money
24mm
With crimped ends to form a collar.
£400 - £600

B99-0910
Saw Blade
320mm
With teeth to both edges.
£200 - £300

B99-0701
Dress Fastener (Gold)
Undamaged. Plain with flared terminals. Solid construction.

Lower limit £30,000 (Price substantially higher for decorated example)

B99-0801
Bracelet (Gold)
Undamaged. Plain, solid construction.

Lower limit £4,000 (Price substantially higher for decorated example)

B99-167529
Miniature Anvil
93mm
The Shalford Bronze
Age goldsmith's anvil.
£800 - £1,000

B99-178319
Cup-and-Ring Block
640mm
Red sandstone block with
central circular 'cup'
within four concentric
pecked rings.
From £10,000

B99-92290
Double-looped
Razor.
79mm
£200 - £300

B99-0906
Awl
32mm
One pointed end and one
flat. Fine patination.
£10 - £15

B99-0907
Awl
44mm
Square section, point to
each end.
£10 - £15

B99-0908
Chisel
115mm
With sturdy socket and
flat blade.
£100 - £150

B99-0909
Gouge
63mm
Scooped upper surface
and flat cutting edge.
£80 - £100

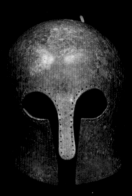

THE CELTIC IRON AGE

The discovery of iron marked a turning-point for the production of edged tools and weapons. The efficiency of iron blades on axes, knives, chisels, swords and spears was remarkably greater than that of their bronze predecessors, and the edges remained keen for longer. The tools were not cast but hammered out from billets of smelted iron, and in the process modifications could be made to the shape and proportions, so that no two items were exactly the same. The iron tools were harder and lasted longer, and iron itself was fairly abundant in the landscape.

Knowledge of iron-smelting and forging reached Britain around 500 BC. The peoples of Iron Age Britain are often referred to as 'Celts', although no ancient sources used the term for inhabitants of these islands. The inhabitants of Britain never regarded themselves as a single people, and their attitudes to disposal of the dead show strong regional tendencies: cremation in most areas but alongside inhumation and in a few regions oddities such as crouched burials, or burials in large square graves within a disassembled chariot.

New types of artefact, found across Central and Northern Europe, came into use in Britain but the old bronze-casting and gold-working techniques were not forgotten. Bronze came to be regarded as a valuable and decorative metal, but was discontinued for the making of tools. Alongside bronze decoration, a taste developed for enamelling – the application of molten coloured glass to prepared cells to create glossy, colourful surface effects. It is surely no coincidence that the earliest British coinage appears towards the end of the Iron Age, as trade links with the Continent became better organised.

The various phases of developing artistic design known from Iron Age artefacts allow a fairly close dating of them to be made - for the first time in British history, a date range of a century or so can be applied to certain objects.

Since the very end of the Iron Age corresponds to Britain's first contact with a literate European culture – the Roman Empire – there are records of individual tribes and persons, some of which have passed into folklore: the Trinovantes and Cantiaci tribes, and the splendidly named leaders Boudica (Boadicea), Prasutagus, Caratacus and Verica. Contact with Rome spelt the end for the independence of most of lowland Britain, and the Iron Age is conventionally understood to finish in 43 AD when Claudius staged his military invasion.

Many Iron Age 'Celtic' items are desired by collectors, and there is enough of an active market in them for dealers to specialise in artefact types (e.g. coins or brooches). Chariot fittings, armrings, torcs, helmets, swords, drinking vessels – all are represented in the finds from Iron Age Britain.

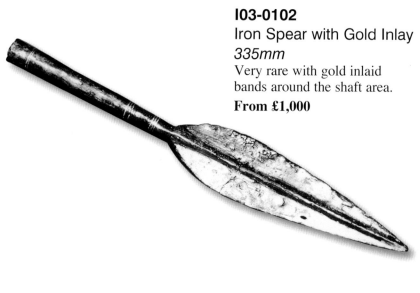

I03-0102
Iron Spear with Gold Inlay
335mm
Very rare with gold inlaid
bands around the shaft area.
From £1,000

I04-168418
Dagger Pommel
46mm
With two bull or boar
heads.
£400 - £600

I04-0101
Sword Pommel
56mm
From a sword, decorated
with punched dot patterns.
£300 - £400

I04-134162
Sword
840mm
Iron sword within its iron
scabbard with fittings.
£5,000 - £7,000

I04-0105
Sword With Scabbard
775mm
Sword still in its original scabbard. Slight damage to the scabbard.
From £1,000

I04-0106
Sword Handle Decoration
22mm
Fully enamelled. Very vivid colours.
£150 - £200

I04-0201
Dagger Pommel
20mm
Cells of orange and white enamel. Ragged surface. Small.
£120 - £180

I04-156369
Dagger Pommel
24mm
'Moustache' type with incised lines.
£150 -£200

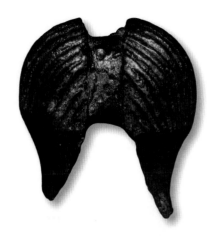

I04-0203
Dagger Pommel
22mm
Moulded triskele design with three pellets.
£100 - £150

I04-0301
Knife Handle
45mm
Crested head. Surface a little ragged.
£150 - £200

I04-43406
Dagger Pommel
57mm
'Moustache' type with incised lines.
£100 - £150

I04-81042
Scabbard Chape
57mm
Scaphoid form.
£100 - £150

I04-0401
Enamelled Dagger Ferrule
20mm
Vivid red and yellow enamel.
£100 - £150

I04-0501
Scabbard Chape
45mm
From the bottom of a sword scabbard with fixing hole.
£100 - £150

I04-0502
Scabbard Mount
51mm
Three domed bosses
with flanking pierced
lugs.
£100 - £150

I04-0503
Sword and Fittings
670mm
Narrow iron blade with square-
section tang. Bronze scabbard
mouth and chape with repoussé
detail. Repaired.
From £4,000

I04-0504
Bronze
Scabbard Chape
42mm
Crescent-shaped
with slight lip
to the upper
edges.
£60 - £80

I06-0101
Bronze Pin Terminal
23mm
Raised curved lines
and protruding bosses.
Remnants of the iron pin.
£100 - £150

I07-0101
Dragonesque Brooch
45mm
Fine, animated Celtic style.
With pin.
£200 - £300

I07-0102
Dragonesque Brooch
40mm
Traces of enamel. Even
patina. With pin.
£300 - £400

I07-0103
Dragonesque Brooch
50mm
Traces of enamel. Unusual
style. With pin.
£300 - £400

I07-0104
Dragonesque Brooch
48mm
Enamelled. With pin.
£600 - £800

I07-0105
Dragonesque Brooch
Enamelled
54mm
Pin intact. Good, even patina.
Most of the enamel intact.
Large size.
£1,000 - £1,500

I07-0106
Dragonesque Brooch
61mm
Orange, blue and yellow enamel.
Pin missing. Large size.
£600 - £800

I07-0107
Dragonesque Brooch
47mm
Even green patination.
Rectangular, enamelled cells.
Complete with pin.
£400 - £600

I07-0108
Dragonesque Brooch
58mm
Turned up snout. Red, yellow
and green enamel cells. No pin.
£200 - £300

I07-0109
Dragonesque Brooch
54mm
Unusual style. Triangular enamel cells. Pin missing.
£200 - £300

I07-0110
Dragonesque Brooch
51mm
Celtic 'eye' design in the central body area. Nice, even green patina. Pin missing.
£200 - £300

I07-177525
Dragonesque Brooch
43mm
Chequerboard and other geometric enamelled cells.
£200 - £300

I07-71813
Dragonesque Brooch
67mm
Median enamel-filled hatched panel and flanking scrolls.
From £1,500

I07-90664
Dragonesque Brooch
72mm
East Brigantian type with S-curved body.
£1,000 - £1,500

I07-106108
Dragonesque Brooch
48mm
Enamel detailing in cells
to the body and finials,
grid pattern to the central
section.
£500 - £800

I07-0202
Brooch (La Tène II)
39mm
One piece, with globular
decoration. Rare.
£40 - £60

I07-0203
Brooch (La Tène)
35mm
Complete, undamaged. Even
patina.
£30 - £40

I07-0205
Brooch (La Tène III)
57mm
Complete. Even green
patination.
£40 - £60

I07-0401
Annular Brooch
31mm
Early Iron Age. Even patina.
£80 - £100

I07-0402
Brooch
70mm
Late Iron Age style. Iron pin
(missing).
£40 - £60

I07-0501
Brooch
48mm
Rare early brooch
with original pin.
£150 - £200

I07-0502
Dragonesque Brooch
59mm
La Tène style scrolled panels
to the body and finials.
£400 - £600

I07-0503
Dragonesque Brooch
34mm
Unusual Z-shaped profile.
Reserved comma-leaf designs
and red enamel fill.
£100 - £150

I07-0504
Dragonesque Brooch
60mm
Incised ring-and-dot to head
and tail and three on the body,
red enamel in the rings.
£300 - £400

I07-0505
Dragonesque Brooch
39mm
With red enamel to the eyes, red
and blue to the central roundel
and flanking panels.
£120 - £180

I07-0506
Gold La Tène I Brooch
33mm
With integral spring,
segmented bow and
recurved foot.
From £800

I07-0507
Dragonesque Brooch
62mm
Three red coral(?) beads to
the body.
£100 - £150

I07-0508
Dragonesque Brooch
45mm
Five cells, three with red
enamel infill.
£200 - £300

I07-0509
Dragonesque Brooch
46mm
Panels of champ-levé
enamel to the body and
head. Collar to the neck
where the pin was attached.
£100 - £150

I08-0201
Stylus Pendant
35mm
Bronze bird with
suspension loop. (Birds
feature prominently in
Celtic mythology.) Rare.
£150 - £200

I08-0302
Pendant
26mm
Punched-point detailing, red
enamel roundel to the upper
corners.
£80 - £100

I08-0303
Triskele Pendant
25mm
Three radiating fronds motif. Rare.
£80 - £100

I09-0101
Belt Mount
22mm
Enamel inlay.
£60 - £80

I09-0102
Belt Mount
27mm
La Tène 'eye' looped belt
decoration with enamel.
Ragged surface.
£50 - £70

I09-0103
Belt Mount
35mm
Celtic 'eye' form. With
enamel.
£80 - £100

I09-0104
Belt Mount
48mm
Double Celtic 'eye' type.
£40 - £60

I09-142905
Mount
45mm
Bull's head type.
£80 - £100

I09-0105
Belt Slider Mount
39mm
Red enamel. Ragged surface.
£50 - £70

I09-0106
Belt Mount
36mm
Red enamel circle design.
Superb green patination.
£400 - £600

I09-155239
Mount
37mm
'Bound captive' type, from a
military triumph monument.
£150 - £200

I09-71806
Belt Mount
39mm
La Tène ornament.
From £3,000

I09-0203
Celtic Deity Mount
40mm
Bearded bust in a cloak. Hood
over the hairstyle.
£120 - £180

I09-90675
Enamelled Mount
89mm
£3,000 - £4,000

I09-0205
Mount
45mm
Typical Celtic style.
£100 - £150

I09-0206
Mount
50mm
Head in the centre. Four
panels of enamel and four
saltires of enamel. Rare.
£600 - £800

I09-0303
Staff Top Mount
65mm
Hallstatt style. Triple-horned animal. Scarce.

£300 - £400

I09-0305
Bull's Head Mount
32mm
European Iron Age. Well modelled. Surface pitted.

£200 - £300

I09-0307
Bull's Head Mount
50mm
Typical Celtic style. Hollow along the neck. Broken.

£80 - £100

I09-0308
Enamelled Mount
36mm
Spectacle type. Two fixing
spikes on reverse. Fully
enamelled.
£120 - £180

I09-0309
Hanging Bowl Mount
39mm
Crude style. A little damage to
one of the horns. Even patina.
£100 - £150

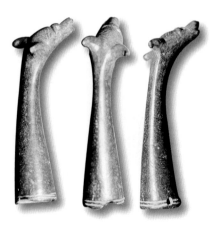

I09-0310
Staff Top Mount
58mm
Wolf-like animal with
elongated neck. Smooth, even
patination.
£400 - £600

I09 142903
Bowl Mount
50mm
Foreparts of a boar with extended forelegs.
£300 - £400

I09-0202
Mount
38mm
Typical Celtic style. Traces of silvering.
£60 - £80

I09-0313
Hanging Bowl Mount
62mm
Crude style of bull with two horns.
£60 - £80

I09-0314
Bird Mount
48mm
Incised line decoration to indicate the wings. Dotted decoration for the feathers. Surface pitted.
£100 - £150

I09-142383
Mask Mount
70mm
Bronze mask with ridged
hair.
£1,000 - £1,500

I09-0316
Mount
45mm
Stylised male bust.
Surface a little ragged.
£120 - £180

I09-0401
Triskele Mount
35mm
Typical Celtic style.
Surface a little ragged.
£60 - £80

I09-0402
Mount
23mm
Two fixing studs on the rear.
Even patina.
£40 - £60

I09-0209
Enamelled Mount
55mm
Ribbed borders surrounding
cells for red and blue
champ-levé enamel.
£150 - £200

I09-0210
Mount
23mm
D-shaped plate with La Tène Style
comma-shaped flanges and a central
recess.
£60 - £80

I09-163969
Staff Terminal
44mm
The Ashwellthorpe
Celtic Staff Terminal.
£3,000 - £4,000

I09-176146
Enamelled
terminal
33mm
Disc of La Tène
comma-leaf motif.
£200 - £300

I09-176160
Janus-Head Terminal
23mm
Addorsed human heads.
£200 - £300

I09-90678
Strap Junction
45mm
£600 - £800

I09-0211
Enamelled Mount
27mm
Round fields of red
enamel in a La Tène
Style motif.
£80 - £100

I09-0215
Enamelled Mount
32mm
Grid of champ-levé enamel in red and
yellow.
£150 - £200

I10-0101
Gold Snake Ring
21mm
Coiled snake. Tail end
broken.
From £800

I11-0101
Rider Warrior
82mm
From a horse-and-rider group. Crested
helmet, cloak and cavalry tunic. Large size.
£600 - £800

I11-0102
Rider Warrior
62mm
From a horse-and-rider group.
Crested helmet. Even patina.

£300 - £400

I11-0103
Rider Warrior
52mm
From a horse-and-rider group.
Crested helmet.
Pronounced phallus.

£200 - £300

I11-0104
Rider Warrior
48mm
From a horse-and-rider group.
Crested helmet.
One leg broken.

£150 - £200

I11-0105
River Goddess Votive Figurine
35mm
Reclining female. Three dimensional. Rare.
£100 - £150

I11-0106
River Goddess Votive Figurine
30mm
Reclining female. Three dimensional. Good detail and patination.
£120 - £180

I11-0107
Rider Warrior
66mm
Cloak flying out behind. Holding a ceremonial staff. Rare.
£300 - £400

I11-0111
Silver Boar Figurine
37mm
Foreparts of a boar with
piercing behind the tusks.
£300 - £400

I11-0109
Captive Figure
43mm
Surface a little ragged, but a
very rare example.
£150 - £200

I11-0110
Horse and Rider
Figurine
83mm
Two-part casting. The horse
with knops to the mane; the
rider with flowing cloak and
crested helmet.
From £10,000

I11-0112
Boar Figurine
49mm
Hollow-cast with incised fur texture.
£300 - £400

I11-0113
Silver-Gilt Boar Figurine
52mm including stand
Foreparts of a boar possibly from a bowl mount.
£800 - £1,200

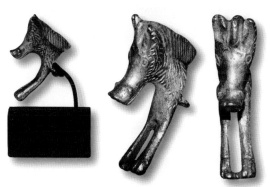

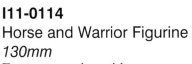

I11-0114
Horse and Warrior Figurine
130mm
Four-part casting with separate spear and base. Minor damage to the base.
From £1,000

I11-151636
Ballyarton Stone Head
460mm
Carved stone head from
County Derry, Northern
Ireland.
£20,000 - £30,000

I11-174911
Boar Statuette
65mm
The Faversham Celtic Boar
Statuette.
£1,500 - £2,000

I11-142906
Boar Statuette
55mm
Fur texture to the flanks and
bristle ridge to the spine.
£800 - £1,000

I09-0306
Bull's Head Mount
45mm
Typical Celtic style. Solid
construction. Surface a little
ragged.
£120 - £180

I09-0312
Bull's Head
45mm
Large, curly horns. Even green
patination. Undamaged.
£100 - £150

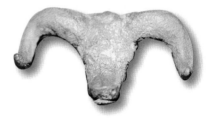

I09-0213
Boar Mount
82mm
Recesses for eyes,
curved back with
bristle detailing to the
upper edge. Ferrous
stain to the underside.
£60 - £80

I13-0101
Clothes Fastener
48mm
Rectangular head with strips of enamel. Surface flaking.
£40 - £60

I13-0102
Clothes Fastener
25mm
Enamelled, rough surface and pitted.
£30 - £40

I13-0103
Clothes Fastener
38mm
Concentric rings with enamel. Some pitting.
£30 - £40

I13-0201
Clothes Fastener
36mm
Square head and devolved Celtic design.
£30 - £40

I13-0202
Clothes Fastener
24mm
Toggle fastener. Ragged surface.
£20 - £30

I13-0203
Clothes Fastener
45mm
Button-and-loop fastener, 'eye' shape.
£30 - £40

I13-0209
Clothes Fastener
30mm
Toggle type. Surface a little pitted.
£40 - £60

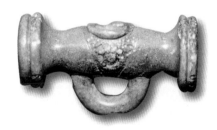

I13-0210
Clothes Fastener
28mm
Toggle type. Surface a little pitted.
£50 - £80

I13-0204
Clothes Fastener
42mm
Button-and-loop fastener.
Domed front and triangular
back loop.
£60 - £80

I13-0205
Clothes Fastener
32mm
Button-and-loop fastener.
Rectangular plate. Raised
dome in the centre. Smooth
even patina.
£40 - £60

I13-0206
Clothes Fastener
55mm
Button-and-loop fastener. Two
raised buttons. One of 'eye'
design.
£60 - £80

I13-0207
Clothes Fastener
27mm
Toggle type. Pitted surface.
£30 - £40

I13-0212
Eye Fastener
37mm
Central domed boss with ring of
white enamel.
£20 - £30

I13-0213
Enamelled Toggle
Fastener
29mm
Four cells of champ-levé enamel
separated by curved arms.
£40 - £60

I13-0214
Toggle Fastener
39mm
Rectangular plate with punched
triangular cells for enamel.
£40 - £60

I14-0101
Woad Grinding
Set
82mm
Both with
suspension loops.
Excellent
patina.
£300 - £400

I14-0102
Woad Grinding
Set
70mm
Both with
suspension loops.
£300 - £400

I14-0104
Woad Grinding Set
45mm
Both parts with
suspension loops. Even
patina.
£150 - £200

I14-71807
Cosmetic Grinder Set
57mm / 75mm
Looped mortar
and grinder set
with ribbing to the
outer face.
£600 - £800

I14-0107
Woad or Cosmetic Grinder Set
95mm
Bull's head type. One horn
missing. Surface a little
uneven.
£300 - £400

I14-0302
Woad or Cosmetic Grinder
70mm
Duck-like shaped base
element of a grinding set, with
suspension loop.
£100 - £150

I14-0201
Woad or Cosmetic Grinder
55mm
Pendant pestle from a grinding set. Even patina.
£40 - £60

I14-0202
Woad or Cosmetic Grinder
49mm
Pendant pestle from a grinding set. Even patina.
£40 - £60

I14-0203
Woad or Cosmetic Grinder
60mm
Pendant boomerang-shaped pestle from a grinding set.
£50 - £80

I14-0301
Woad or Cosmetic Grinder
85mm
Boat-shaped base element of a grinding set, with suspension loop.
£80 - £100

I14-0303
Woad or Cosmetic Grinder
50mm
Banana-shaped base element of a grinding set, with suspension loop.
£80 - £100

I14-0304
Woad or Cosmetic Grinder
88mm
Boat-shaped base element of a grinding set, with suspension loop. Incised decoration. Very large. Excellent patina.
£100 - £150

I14-0305
Woad or Cosmetic Grinder
49mm
Phallus-like base element of a grinding set, with suspension loop. Smooth, even patina.
£80 - £100

I14-0307
Woad or Cosmetic Grinder
63mm
Surface a little ragged. Complete.
£60 - £80

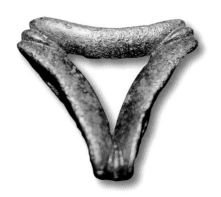

I14-0308
Woad or Cosmetic Grinder
35mm
Unusual triple type.
£60 - £80

I14-0401
Woad or Cosmetic Grinder
78mm
Bull's head. Large size. Excellent patina. Undamaged.
£400 - £600

I14-177521
Woad or Cosmetic Grinder
70mm
Bull-head finial.
£300 - £400

I14-0403
Woad or Cosmetic Grinder
64mm
Recurved duck-head finial,
recessed eyes.
£60 - £80

I14-0404
Woad or Cosmetic Grinder
49mm
Thick loop and La Tène comma
motif. Inner face smooth.
£50 - £70

I14-0405
Woad or Cosmetic Grinder
50mm
Swan's head type. Loop to rear. Rare.
£120 - £180

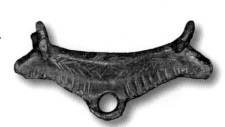

I14-0406
Woad or Cosmetic Grinder
64mm
Thick walls with vertical ribs,
animal-head terminals.
£300 - £400

I14-0407
Woad or Cosmetic
Grinder
83mm
Pierced lug to the underside,
ribbed cone terminals.
£120 - £180

I14-0501
Mirror
300mm
Elaborately decorated.
Some damage. Very
rare.

From £40,000

I14-0601
Razor
75mm
Looped handle.
Even patina.
£80 - £100

I14-0602
Razor
115mm
Decoration along
the handle. Loop on
the end. Surface
ragged.
£100 - £150

I15-0101
Terret Ring
80mm
Enamelled. Undamaged.
Very large.
From £6,000

I15-0102
Terret Ring
75mm
Most enamel missing.
Flaky surfaces.
From £2,500

I15-0103
Terret Ring
65mm
Three enamelled 'eyes'
around the perimeter. Slotted
junction bar.
£300 - £400

I15-0104
Terret Ring
60mm
Undamaged. Some decoration.
£100 - £150

I15-0105
Terret Ring
60mm
Three decorative knops. Complete. Undamaged with an even patina.
£150 - £200

I15-0106
Terret Ring
50mm
Decorated, surface a little pitted.
£100 - £150

I15-0107
Terret Ring
60mm
Plain 'torque' shape. Ragged surface.
£40 - £60

I15-0108
Terret Ring
70mm
Three moulded projections.
Shape a little distorted.
£30 - £40

I15 144685
Terret Ring
39mm
Raised triskele with enamel
pellets.
£1,000 - £1,500

I15-142356
Terret Ring
65mm
Cloisonné enamel panels.
£500 - £700

I15-0111
Terret Ring
58mm
Ring on flared mounting base.
£100 - £150

I15-0112
Terret Ring
60mm
Ring on flared mounting
base. Sharp detail.
£100 - £150

I15-0113
Terret Ring
55mm
Unusual style. Nice, even
patination.
£100 - £150

I15-0114
Terret Ring
48mm
Undamaged. Some decoration.
£80 - £120

I15-95394
Terret Ring
64mm
Running scrolls in red
enamel to both faces.
From £3,000

I15-0116
Terret Ring
70mm
Six moulded projections. Torc
shape. Even patination. Large.
£150 - £200

I15-0117
Terret Ring
55mm
Three enamelled panels around
the perimeter. Torc shape.
Surface pitted.
£200 - £300

I15-0118
Terret Ring
68mm
Decorated, lipped type. Torc style. Even green patination.
£150 - £200

I15-149983
Bridle Cheek Piece
58mm
Enamelled ornament.
£180 - £240

I15-0201
Horse Cheek Piece
102mm
Enamelled, dragonesque shape. Very rare.
From £4,000

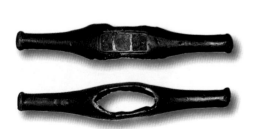

I15-0202
Horse Cheek Piece
90mm
A little ragged. Three panels of enamel. Rare.
£300 - £400

I15-0203
Horse Cheek Piece Toggle
45mm
Zig-zag pattern with enamel. Rare.
£500 - £800

I15-0204
Cheek Piece
29mm
Plain, undecorated. Slight pitting to the surface.
£100 - £150

I15-0205
Bridle Bit Terminal
44mm dia
Openwork disjointed horse design. Superb patination. Rare.
£500 - £800

I15-0206
Bridle Bit Terminal
44mm dia
Three dragon heads design. Rare.
£500 - £800

I15-0301
Strap Junction
50mm
Double 'eye' motif framed
by two panels of inlaid
enamel. Even patina. Enamel
substantially intact.
From £2,000

I15-95251
Strap Junction
47mm
Finely preserved red and
yellow enamel.
£400 - £600

I15-0303
Strap Junction
45mm
Two joined rings with
mounting bars.
£80 - £100

I15-0304
Strap Junction
40mm
Two opposed crescents with
mounting bars.
£120 - £180

I15-0305
Strap Junction
45mm
Two opposed crescents with
mounting bars.
£150 - £200

I15-0306
Strap Junction
50mm
Two loops divided by a
central body with light, incised
decoration. Even patina.
£60 - £80

I15-0307
Strap Junction
75mm
Three ring (lower ring broken)
stylised bull's head. Rare.
£150 - £200 (Broken)
£400 - £600 (Intact)

I15-0308
Strap Junction
30mm
Double boss with moulded disjointed horse design on the surfaces. Rare.
£100 - £150

I15-0309
Harness Strap Junction
57mm
Three dimensional horse's head. Smooth, even green patination.
£150 - £200

I15-0310
Strap Junction
40mm
Bulbous-eyed frog. Even patination. Rare.
£100 - £150

I15-0312
Belt Mount
30mm
Ring with central S-curved bar, at each end a lobed elliptical panel.
£30 - £40

I15-0313
Strap Junction
58mm
Probably from a chariot, with red and blue enamel in three cells.
£200 - £300

I15-103507
Bridle Mount
79mm
Two slider bars to the reverse, incised La Tène style decoration with concentric rings, red enamel cells with stylised faces.
From £30,000

I15-0314
Belt Slider
46mm
Figure of
8-shaped
plate, boss
to the centre
of each loop,
staple to the
reverse.
£30 - £40

I15-66409
Triskele Mount
24mm
Gusset and loop to the
reverse.
£60 - £80

I15-0316
Enamelled Belt Mount
37mm
Fan-shaped cells filled with
red enamel.
£150 - £200

I15-0501
Harness Decoration
38mm
Horse's head. Two copper rivets. Even patina.
£80 - £100

I15-0502
Harness Mount
57mm
Repoussé scrolls and central roundel with polychrome enamel fill.
£600 - £800

I15-0503
Spur
40mm
U-shaped plate with bulb terminals, and large conical bulb with hatched upper surface.
£80 - £100

I15-0504
Enamelled Harness Toggle
102mm
Bridle cheek piece toggle with a rectangle of twelve chequered enamelled cells.

£600 - £800

I15-0505
Enamelled Harness Toggle
90mm
Petal-shaped and square inset cells with red and yellow enamel infill.

£200 - £300

I15-0506
Harness Mount
47mm
Triskele profile with four round recesses filled with red enamel and each with two blue-enamelled pellets.

£400 - £600

I15-0507
Enamelled Cheek Piece
26mm
With La Tène scroll and trumpet
motifs filled with red enamel.
£150 - £200

I15-0508
Enamelled Bridle Mount
67mm
Ornamented with reserved La Tène
scrolls against red enamel fields.
From £5,000

I99-0101
Linch Pin From Chariot Wheel
125mm
Inlaid with enamel.
£600 - £800 (restored)
From £2,000 (unrestored)

I99-0301
Hanging Bowl Mount
36mm
Scrolled bands and two
circular holes; three
attachment holes and small
ledge to the reverse.

£200 - £300

I99-0401
Staff Finial
49mm
Hollow cylindrical neck
and stern male head with
C-shaped horns; eyes
black glass inserts.

£300 - £400

I99-92272
Tankard Handle
130mm

£3,000 - £4,000

I99-0102
Linch Pin From Chariot
150mm
Broken in the centre.
£200 - £300

I15-144867
Terret Mount
37mm
'The Mashbury' terret mount
with enamelled cells.
£1,800 - £2,400

I99-147631
Bell with Maker's Mark
200mm
Stamped panel with maker's
name 'BODVIC[..]'.
£1,000 - £1,500

ROMAN BRITAIN

Britain's first known contact with Rome took place in 55 BC when Julius Caesar led a small expeditionary force across the Channel to intervene in a local war in support of a British leader favoured by the Roman authorities. No invasion took place at that time, and it was not until 43 AD that the Emperor Claudius decided to add Britannia to the list of Roman provinces. Conquest of the island proceeded quickly, despite revolts and massacres, and the main districts of Roman Britain were established by the end of the century. The power of the native priesthood was crushed and the sanctuary on Anglesey razed. Aspects of Roman life took root in southern Britain among the wealthy landowners, and villa estates became a feature of the British landscape.

The Roman authorities at first used British client kings to administer the province, but eventually re-organised the territory into provinciae. The northern part of the island was not ruled directly, although Rome did interfere in tribal affairs through sponsorship; south of the boundary – first the Antonine Wall, and later Hadrian's Wall – lowland Britain was organised into a northern military zone and a southern civil zone. Roman domination of the island lasted nominally till about 410 AD, but the Empire was losing its grip on northern Europe from the middle of the 4th century.

The Roman presence was felt in various ways, not least in architecture. British building tradition favoured round houses, workshops and stores made mainly from wood and thatch; the Romans introduced fired clay tiles and slabs, ashlar stone walls and facings, paved and cobbled roads. Military structures made from stone and concrete were raised, many so durable that they were still in use a thousand years later.

Roman objects are distinctive and unlike their Iron Age predecessors. Many are of types found across the Empire, while others are more restricted in distribution: Roman Britain was a frontier province and shares a range of features with other border areas such as the Rhineland and the Balkans. Many object classes make their first appearance in British archaeology in the Roman period: surgical instruments, locks and keys, gaming pieces, glass vessels, dice, many cosmetic tools, belt buckles, dress pins, cooking equipment and tableware, writing materials and other equipment.

Roman items are very collectible, be they delicate glass bottles or heavy bronze chariot fittings, decorative furniture mounts or hefty weapons. The market for goods from this expansive empire is international.

R04-0101
Knife Handle with Dog
55mm
Running dog. Even, dark patina.
£150 - £200

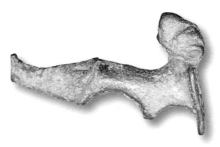

R04-0102
Knife Handle with Panther
60mm
Scarcer type depicting a panther.
£80 - £100

R04-0103
Folding Knife with Hare & Hound
65mm
Smooth, even patina. Most of the blade remaining.
£100 - £150

R04-0104
Folding Knife with Hare & Hound
69mm
Complete with most of the iron blade remaining.
£120 - £180

R04-152770
Folding Knife
62mm
Bone handle carved to show two dogs mating.
£400 - £600

R04-0106
Knife Handle
90mm
Two wrestlers. Superb
patina and rare type.
£600 - £800

R04-0107
Knife Handle
70mm
Smooth, even patina.
Unusual style.
£80 - £100

R04-0108
Knife Handle
55mm
Surface a little ragged.
Shows signs of wear.
£60 - £80

R04-0109
Knife Handle
78mm
Red and blue enamel
cells. Known type.
£100 - £150

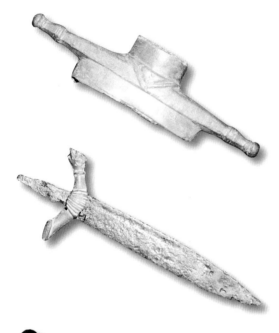

R04-0110
Knife Handle with Hand
60mm
Even patination. Traces of tinning on the surface. Rare type.
£150 - £200

R04-0111
Sword Crossguard
110mm
Complete. Smooth, even patination.
£150 - £200

R04-0113
Knife
115mm
Bronze phallic crossguard with iron blade.
£400 - £600

R04-167716
Dagger
350mm
Pugio in iron scabbard, mineralised wood to the grip.
£2,000 - £3,000

R04-138850
Dagger
345mm
Iron, 'Kunzing' Type
with scabbard in iron
sheath.
From £5,000

R04-134860
Dagger in
Scabbard
290mm overall
Pugio type.
From £3,000

R04-0204
Sword Pommel
50mm
Eagle's head with light green
patina. Decorated with incised
lines. Undamaged.
£200 - £300

R04-0205
Dagger Pommel
43mm
Good detail. Eagle with a
seed in its beak.
£180 - £240

R04-0206
Knife Pommel with
Cupid
40mm
Cupid picking a thorn from
his foot. Even patination.
£200 - £300

R04-0207
Knife or Dagger
Pommel with Phallic
40mm
Hand at one end, phallus at
the other.
£40 - £60

R04-0501
Scabbard Chape
62mm
Large with smooth, even green patination, damaged.
£80 - £100

R04-0502
Scabbard Chape
70mm
Large sword scabbard chape. Good even patination.
£150 - £200

R04-0503
Pommel
68mm
Bound captives type, issuing from a cylinder with foliate edge.
£600 - £800

R04-0504
Knife
100mm
A bust of Hercules
with lion-skin
mantle over his
head, the paws tied
beneath his chin.
£250 - £350

R04-0505
Knife with Duck
Handle
120mm
Single-edged knife
with triangular
iron blade.
£200 - £300

R04-0506
Folding Knife
68mm
A hound chasing a
hare on a baseline,
segmented baluster
below.
£100 - £150

R04-0507
Knife Handle
66mm
'Dog chasing a Hare'
type, openwork.
£60 - £80

R04-0508
Leopard
Folding Knife
71mm
A knife-handle of a
lioness' head with gaping
mouth.
£80 - £100

R04-0509
Knife Handle
58mm
A knife pommel of a standing
figure on a socle base representing
Aequitas, the personification of
justice.
£80 - £100

R04-0510
Enamelled Pommel
36mm
Tutulus type with
enamelled rosette to the
upper and lower faces.
£300 - £400

R04-0511
Knife Pommel
38mm
Male bust in a Gallic-
type H helmet.
£60 - £80

R04-0512
Sword Pommel
40mm
Hollow-cast pommel
with a bust of the
Emperor Hadrian.
£200 - £300

R04-0513
Dagger Pommel
39mm
With discoid base and
collar, two addorsed
panthers' heads.
£200 - £300

R04-0514
Knife Handle
71mm
Formed as a military
galley; ferrous remains
inside.
£100 - £150

R05-0101
Helmet Handle
101mm
Carrying-handle for a military helmet
in the form of the mask of Oceanus
gripped in the jaws of two dolphins.
£150 - £200

R04-176073
Dagger Blade
165mm
Iron blade for a pugio.
£600 - £800

R04-131491
Sword
810mm
Spatha type cavalry
sword.
£1,500 - £2,000

R04-115842
Sword Blade
830mm
Gladius type.
£1,000 - £1,500

R05-141068
Sports Helmet
260mm
Cavalry helmet
representing an
Amazon warrior.
From £50,000

R05-168755
Military Helmet
280mm
Imperial Gallic Type
with embossed skull.
£30,000 - £40,000

R05-168756
Military Helmet
210mm
Montefortino type
with crest knob.
£6,000 - £8,000

R05-144723
Sports Helmet
270mm
Pfrondorf Type
cavalry helmet.
From £30,000

R03-162856
Military Dart
153mm
'Plumbata' type with
lead bulb on iron
shank.
£200 - £300

R05-153449
Hand Finial
225mm
The top of a military
standard.
£2,000 - £3,000

R05-152971
Military Tile
185mm
Stamped 'LEXFR'
(Tenth legion of the
Strait).
£800 - £1,000

R15-133087
Phalera
83mm
Mask of Medusa type.
£600 - £800

R09-134110
Mount
41mm
Inscribed with 'LEG IV'.
£200 - £300

R05-169971
Military Phalera
80mm
Openwork ornament and incised rings.
£200 - £300

R05 149279
Armour Fragments
15-110mm
Scales from a lorica squamata
body armour.
£200 - £300

R05-163549
Shield Boss
175mm
Flange and conical
centre.
£500 - £800

R05-157432
Leg Armour
500mm
Greave and attached
knee-guard.
£1,500 - £2,000

R05-167256
Military Pendant
33mm
Eagle with wings
spread in a wreath.
£300 - £400

R05-139706
Military Phalera
60mm
Sol Invictus with
radiate crown above
horse-heads.
£1,500 - £2,000

R05-160191
Military Diploma
130mm
Diploma tablet with
dense text, issued by
Emperor Antoninus
Pius.
£6,000 - £8,000

R05-134028
Insignia Mount
92mm
Special duty military
service 'Beneficiarius'
insignia.
£200 - £300

R06-0101
Pin
100mm
Decorated terminal.
Smooth, even surface.
£20 - £30

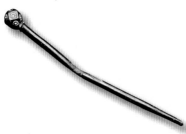

R06-0102
Pin
83mm
Ring-and-dot decorated
hexagonal head.
Surface flaking in places.
£20 - £30

R06-0103
Pin
70mm
Hexagonal head. Smooth,
even patination.
£20 - £30

R06-0104
Pin
115mm
Bird terminal. Decoration
below. Smooth patination.
£60 - £80

R07-166122
Bow Brooch
47mm
Equal-arm type with openwork.
£120 - £180

R07-166121
Bow Brooch
48mm
P-shaped brooch with split bow.
£40 - £60

R07-130876
Bow Brooch
60mm
Iron P-shaped brooch, inlaid silver plate.
£40 - £60

R07-135084
Bow Brooch
44mm
Aucissa type, stylised wolf-head footplate, ball finial.
£120 - £180

R07-0105
Bow Brooch
45mm
Pin intact. Even patina.
£20 - £30

R07-0106
Bow Brooch
45mm
Pin intact. Even patina.
£20 - £30

R07-0107
Bow & Fantail Brooch
38mm
Unusual style. Pin intact. Even
patina.
£60 - £80

R07-0108
Aesica Brooch
48mm
Pin missing. Inlaid panels of
red enamel. Even patina.
£30 - £40

R07-171699
Bow Brooch
99mm
P-shaped type, hatching
and other ornament.
£100 - £150

R07-0121
Bow Brooch
50mm
Smooth patina. No pin.
£5 - £10

R07-175893
Gold Crossbow Brooch
Terminal
26mm
£200 - £300

R07-175766
Brooch with Silver Inlay
29mm
With portrait of Victory.
£300 - £400

R07-0112
Winged Bow Brooch
35mm
Red and blue enamel.
Complete with pin.
£80 - £100

R07-0113
Bow & Fantail Brooch
40mm
Red inlaid enamel. Complete
with pin.
£60 - £80

R07-0109
Knee Brooch
35mm
Complete and undamaged
knee brooch. Light
decoration to edge of
head. Heavily gilded.
£80 - £100

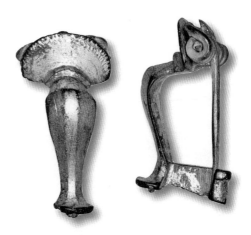

R07-0115
Bow Brooch
30mm
Unusual moulded type.
Smooth, even patination.
No pin.
£40 - £60

R07-0116
Bow Brooch
38mm
Surface a little ragged. No pin.
£30 - £40

R07-0119
Silver Bow Brooch
66mm
Unusual type. With pin.
£80 - £100

R07-0125
Bow Brooch
58mm
Red and blue enamelled cells.
Complete. Even surfaces.
£120 - £180

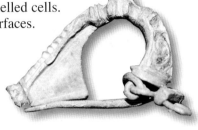

R07-0126
Bow Brooch
63mm
Blue enamelled cells. With pin.
£40 - £60

R07-0127
Bow Brooch
51mm
Trumpet type. Smooth, even
patination. With pin.
£20 - £30

R07-0122
Trumpet Brooch
45mm
Unusual zoomorphic type.
Good, even surface, with
pin.
£40 - £60

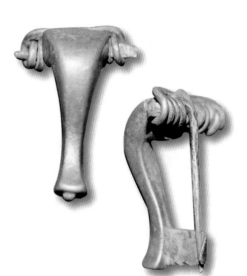

R07-0123
Silver Knee Brooch
40mm
Plain type. Complete.
£80 - £100

R07-155129
Gold Plate Brooch
47mm
Inset sardonyx cabochon
with bust of Apollo.
£8,000 - £10,000

R07-57523
Plate Brooch
50mm
Gryphon type, enamel
detailing.
£500 - £800

R07-0223
Plate Brooch
48mm
Fully enamelled. Lozenge
shape. With pin.
£100 - £150

R07-0222
Plate Brooch
34mm
Star shape with blue and
white enamel. Rough surface.
With pin.
£50 - £80

R07-0128
Trumpet Brooch
Enamelled
66mm
Blue and yellow enamelled
cells. With pin.
£60 - £80

R07-169260
Plate Brooch
35mm
Peacock type with flared
tail.
£100 - £150

R07-175870
Plate Brooch
47mm
Dolphin type with sphere
in the mouth.
£500 - £800

R07-0201
Plate Brooch
30mm
Pin missing. Lunette
shape with inlaid panels
of red and green enamel.
£150 - £200

R07-0202
Chatelaine Plate Brooch
115mm
Chatelaine brooch complete
with the implements attached.
Richly decorated in blue and
yellow enamel. Pin intact.
Rare.

From £1,000

R07-0203
Chatelaine Plate Brooch
50mm
Umbonate type with five
rounded lugs. Yellow and
brown enamel. Pin intact.

£200 - £300

R07-0204
Axe Plate Brooch
30mm
Decorated with blue and
brown enamel. Faint traces of
silvering. Pin intact.

£80 - £100

R07-0205
Sandal Plate Brooch
42mm
Pin and catchplate intact. Blue and yellow enamel. Slight damage.
£120 - £180

R07-0206
Sandal Plate Brooch
42mm
Pin and catchplate intact. Red, blue and yellow enamel. Slightly damaged.
£80 - £100

R07-0207
Sandal Plate Brooch
40mm
Pin intact. Most enamel remaining.
£100 - £150

R07-0208
Dolphin Plate Brooch
30mm
Pin intact. Circular central plate with two dolphins either side.
£60 - £80

R07-0209
Plate Brooch
42mm
Pin intact. Unusual style.
Red and blue enamel.
£80 - £100

R07-0210
Plate Brooch
45mm
Alternating blue and white
enamelled cells. Smooth, even
patination. With pin.
£200 - £300

R07-0211
Plate Brooch
32mm
Alternating red and blue
enamelled cells. With pin.
£200 - £300

R07-0212
Axe Plate Brooch
30mm
Traces of red enamel. With pin.
£100 - £150

R07 54716
Plate Brooch
38mm
£80 - £100

R07 122165
Plate Brooch
23mm
Wheel type with enamelled detailing.
£300 - £400

R07-0216
Plate Brooch
35mm
Surface a little uneven. With pin.
£20 - £30

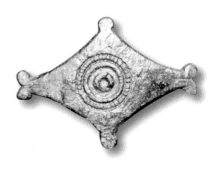

R07-0217
Lozenge Plate Brooch
39mm
Even patination. Green glass stone set in the centre. With pin.
£60 - £80

R07-0218
Equal-Ended Plate Brooch
55mm
Traces of blue enamel. Surface a little patchy.
With pin.
£40 - £60

R07-0219
Plate Brooch
40mm
Orange, white and blue
enamelled cells. With pin.
£100 - £150

R07-0220
Plate Brooch
44mm
Blue and orange enamel.
Surface a little ragged.
With pin.
£50 - £80

R07-122697
Plate Brooch
54mm
Elaborate enamel ornament,
domed profile.
£800 - £1,000

R07-122968
Plate Brooch
Enamel ornament, central stud.
£400 - £600

R07-133854
Plate Brooch
42mm
Champ levé enamel ornament.
£200 - £300

R07-160818
Plate Brooch
30mm
Owl type with white-yellow
enamel panels.
£400 - £600

R07-163944
Plate Brooch
33mm
Labrys type.
£80 - £100

R07-166170
Plate Brooch
34mm
Chevron motifs with
blue and red enamel.
£60 - £80

R07-166144
Plate Brooch
57mm
Millefiori panel inset
with stud.
£300 - £400

R07-163889
Plate Brooch
29mm
Owl type with red enamel
panels.
£400 - £600

R07-0306
Umbonate Brooch with
Glass Spiral
30mm
Gilded and set with a colourful
stone. With pin.
£300 - £400

R07-0301
Umbonate Brooch
35mm
Pin intact. Inlaid with red and
yellow enamel.
£40 - £60

R07-0308
Umbonate Brooch
32mm
Enamelled. Spoked wheel
design. With pin.
£80 - £100

R07-0309
Umbonate Brooch
39mm
Enamelled. With pin.
£60 - £80

R07-0401
Crossbow Brooch
73mm
Pin intact. Dark green even
patina with much gilding
remaining.
£80 - £100

R07-0402
Crossbow Brooch
85mm
Three onion knops.
Decorative lower section.
Pin missing.
£40 - £60

R07-166226
Crossbow
Brooch
85mm
Three knops on the
headplate.
£40 - £60

R07-0404
Silver Crossbow Brooch
72mm
Complete and undamaged.
With pin.
£400 - £600

R07-0405
Crossbow Brooch
75mm
Good, even patination.
With pin.
£60 - £80

R07-0501
Silvered Fish Brooch
41mm
Plate brooch, silvered with
enamel inlay in the eyes. Pin
intact. Rare.
£60 - £80

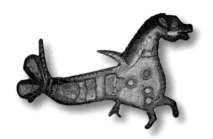

R07-0502
Hippocampus Brooch
50mm
Pin intact. White and orange enamel mainly intact. Head is three dimensional. Rare.
£600 - £800

R07-0503
Hippocampus Brooch
31mm
Pin intact. Blue enamel. Even patina. Rare.
£800 - £1,000

R07-0504
Plate Brooch
30mm
Pin and catchplate intact. Fantastic animal with a rear-facing, crested head. Some blue enamel remaining. Rare.
£150 - £200

R07-0505
Lion Brooch
42mm
Leaping lion. Pin and catchplate intact. Whole surface tinned. Rare type and large.
£300 - £400

R07-0506
Lion Brooch
42mm
Pin intact. Chunky three dimensional lion in a lying position. Traces of silvering. Rare.
£200 - £300

R07-0507
Running Dog Brooch
40mm
Pin intact. Long single cell for enamel (now lost). Undamaged example.
£150 - £200

R07-0508
Running Dog Brooch
35mm
Pin and catchplate intact. Central area for enamel (now lost). Light green patina.
£150 - £120

R07-0509
Plate Brooch
37mm
Pin intact. Head and neck three dimensional. Tinning on the upper surface and red enamel circles on the wings. Rare type.
£150 - £200

R07-0510
Bird Brooch
40mm
Pin missing. Bird in flight. Cells for enamel on wings and tail. Even patina.
£40 - £60

R07-0511
Duck Brooch
38mm
Pin intact. Most enamel remaining. Patina a little patchy.
£120 - £180

R07-0512
Chicken Brooch
36mm
Pin intact. Inlaid with panels of red and blue enamel.
£150 - £200

R07-0513
Eagle & Hare Brooch
34mm
Pin missing. Eagle tearing at a hare. Good condition.
£180 - £240

R07-0514
Hare & Young Brooch
22mm
Pin missing. Decorated with two inlaid enamel hares (only traces of enamel remain).
£60 - £80

R07-0515
Hare Brooch
35mm
Pin intact. Scarce variety with turned up nose.
£80 - £100

R07-0516
Horse & Rider Brooch
40mm
Unusual style. Surfaces a little ragged. Rare.
£150 - £200

R07-0517
Horse & Rider Brooch
28mm
Pin intact. Blue and red enamel.
£80 - £100

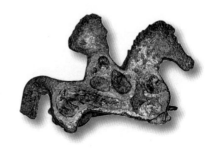

R07-0518
Horse Brooch
50mm
Pin and catchplate intact. Fully enamelled. Rare type.
£600 - £800

R07-0519
Fly Brooch
30mm
Fly or insect brooch. Blue and red enamel intact. Pin intact.
£90 - £100

R07-0520
Fly Brooch
35mm
Enamel intact. Pin in place. Complete example.
£80 - £100

R07-0541
Boar Brooch
40mm
Red and blue enamelled cells. Turned up snout and curly tail. No pin.
£200 - £300

R07-0522
Hare Brooch
30mm
Some enamel remaining
around the eye. With pin.
£100 - £150

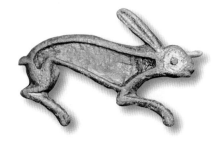

R07-0523
Hare Brooch
22mm
Silver inlay along the body.
With pin.
£80 - £100

R07-0533
Horse & Rider Brooch
33mm
Surface a little ragged. Some
enamel remaining. With pin.
£120 - £180

R07-0534
Horse & Rider Brooch
33mm
Traces of enamel. Surface a
little uneven. With pin.
£150 - £200

R07-0526
Stag Brooch
35mm
Decoration along the body.
With pin.
£80 - £100

R07-0527
Stag Brooch
40mm
Fully enamelled. Ground
line. No pin but scarce type.
£400 - £600

R07-0528
Panther Brooch
45mm
Unusual type with collar
around its neck. Enamel a
little patchy.
£200 - £300

R07-0529
Panther Brooch
44mm
Good light green patination.
No pin.
£200 - £300

R07-0530
Lion Brooch
40mm
Red and blue enamel cells.
Complete with pin.
£200 - £300

R07-0531
Fly Brooch
32mm
Unusual type of fly brooch.
Red and blue enamel. With
pin.
£100 - £150

R07-0545
Frog Brooch
34mm
Surface a little ragged.
Enamelled cells.
Glass beads in eyes. With pin.
£400 - £600

R07-0544
Fish Brooch
43mm
Good detail. Enamelled eye.
Silvered surface.
£150 - £200

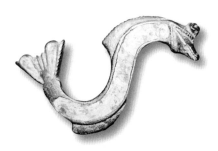

R07-0547
Sea Serpent Brooch
60mm
Eel like sea monster. Enamel
along the body. Scarce type.
No pin.
£400 - £600

R07-0548
Hippocampus Brooch
53mm
Red and blue enamel mainly
intact. Three dimensional head.
No pin.
£600 - £800

R07-0549
Hippocampus Brooch
50mm
Enamelled cells mainly intact.
Smooth, even patination.
No pin.
£600 - £800

R07-0536
Horse & Rider Brooch
30mm
Traces of enamel. Horse has
very large tail. With pin.
£100 - £150

R07-0537
Horse Brooch
35mm
Nice bold example. Surface a
little uneven. With pin.
£400 - £600

R07-0538
Horse Brooch
35mm
Enamelled cells. Ring-and-dot
decoration on the neck and
mane.
£400 - £600

R07-0550
Two-Headed Monster
Brooch
42mm
Most enamel remaining.
Surface a little uneven. No pin.
£300 - £400

R07-0551
Swan Brooch
30mm
Very rare type of brooch in the
form of a swan. Red and blue
enamel. No pin.
£200 - £300

R07-0552
Peacock Brooch
32mm
Complete with pin. Surface a
little pitted.
£150 - £200

R07-0553
Peacock Brooch
30mm
No pin and surface heavily
pitted.
£120 - £180

R07-0554

Duck Brooch

32mm

Complete with pin. Patina a little patchy. Single colour enamel.

£80 - £100

R07-0555

Duck Brooch

31mm

Complete with pin. Beak broken. Surface a little ragged.

£80 - £100

R07-0556

Bird Brooch

40mm

Bird in flight. Pin missing. Enamelled cells.

£80 - £100

R07-0557

Bird Brooch

30mm

Plain type. Incised line decoration. With pin.

£40 - £60

R07-164357
Disc Brooch
46mm
Gilt with inset gemstones.
£100 - £150

R07-147144
Disc Brooch
45mm
Umbonate type with
enamel in the cells.
£100 - £150

R07-166146
Disc Brooch
30mm
Enamel ornament, loop
for a securing chain.
£120 - £180

R07-171707
Pincer Brooch
143mm
£60 - £80

R07-157443
Plate Brooch
46mm
Silver-gilt, crayfish type.
£2,000 - £3,000

R07-163981
Wheel Brooch
26mm
Gilded, punched ornament.
£60 - £80

R07-166169
Rosette Brooch
45mm
With sprung pin.
£60 - £80

R07-0559
Bird Brooch
28mm
Surface a little ragged.
Pin missing.
£20 - £30

R07-0613
Disc Brooch
34mm
Six-pointed star design
within a circle. With pin.
£120 - £180

R07-0601
Disc Brooch
31mm
Pin intact. With red
enamel and inlaid with
panels of millefiori style
yellow enamel.
£60 - £80

R07-0602
Disc Brooch
33mm
Pin intact. Remains of blue
enamel. Unusual style.
£80 - £100

R07-0603
Disc Brooch
36mm
Undamaged with pin intact.
Inlaid with rings of yellow
enamel and one band of blue
and red millefiori style
decoration.
£200 - £300

R07-0604
Disc brooch
39mm
Large size. Fully enamelled.
With pin.
£300 - £400

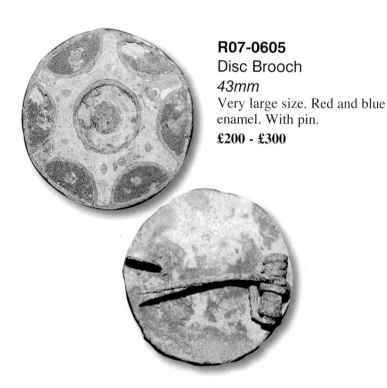

R07-0605
Disc Brooch
43mm
Very large size. Red and blue enamel. With pin.
£200 - £300

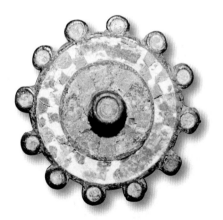

R07-0608
Disc Brooc
39mm
Large size. Enamel damaged in places. With pin.
£150 - £200

R07-0610
Disc Brooch
30mm
Enamel a little fuzzy. With pin.
£60 - £80

R07-0611
Disc Brooch
23mm
Surface a little ragged. With pin.
£40 - £60

R07-0612
Disc Brooch
27mm
Surface a little rough. Stone missing from centre. With pin.
£80 - £100

R07-0701
Penannular Brooch
30mm
Surface a little pitted. Pin
intact. Torque shape.
£10 - £20

R07-0702
Penannular Brooch
22mm
Smooth, even patina. Pin
intact. Incised decoration.
Small size.
£10 - £20

R07-0703
Penannular Brooch
25mm
Silver. Small break at the
end of the pin.
£40 - £60

R07-0704
Horse Brooch
34mm
A horse with enamelled pellets
to the trunk and hip, ring-and-
dot to the neck.
£150 - £200

R07-0705
Plate Brooch
36mm
An equal-ended plate brooch
with collars to the extensions,
rectangular plaque with
incised saltire.
£40 - £60

R07-0706
Plate Brooch
34mm
A lozengiform plate brooch
with knop finials above and
below, central cruciform bar.
£20 - £30

R07-0707
Hippocampus Brooch
36mm
A hippocampus advancing with
enamel pellets and block to the
body.
£80 - £100

R07-0708
Fly Brooch
31mm
An insect with flared wings,
the face segmented with yellow
and blue enamel panels.
£60 - £80

R07-0709
Eros Brooch
30mm
Eros, winged and seated on the
back of a dolphin; punched eye
and scale detail to the dolphin,
feather detail to Eros' wing.
£60 - £80

R07-0710
Enamelled Brooch
33mm
Two plaques, each with a stud to
the centre, and a V-shaped panel
supporting a male mask (possibly
the god Cernunnos), with crescent
above the head; red enamel to the
plaques and crescent.
£60 - £80

R07-0711
Cicada Brooch
84mm
With D-shaped headplate
and lateral eyes, triangular
body and two triangular
wings; incised geometric
detail to the body and head.
£60 - £80

R07-0712
Enamelled Plate Brooch
57mm

With raised centre and terminals,
with radiating red and blue
enamel cells in the outer band and
contrasting colours to the inner band,
dolphin modelled in the round with
enamelled pellets to the tail.

£200 - £300

R07-0713
Enamelled Brooch with Dolphin
51mm

Enamelled disc brooch with central
dolphin figure.

From £1,500

R07-0714
Enamelled Plate Brooch
43mm

With crescent plaque and open
centre, openwork comma-shaped
panels each with a median beast-
head finial; the main plaque
subdivided into enamelled champ-
levé cells with reserved comma-leaf
panels.

£80 - £100

R07-0716
Lion Brooch
40mm
Enamelled pellets in green and orange to the head and body.
£150 - £200

R07-0717
Duck Brooch
40mm
Orange and green enamelled cells with silver borders.
£150 - £200

R07-0718
Fish Brooch
36mm
Engraved with scale detail. Pin to the reverse.
£60 - £80

R07-0721
Hare Brooch
23mm
Surface showing some original tinning. Pin-lugs and catchplate present but pin lost.
£60 - £80

R07-0719
Bow Brooch
63mm
'Anchor' type brooch with knop finials,
coiled spring to the reverse.
£20 - £30

R07-0720
Bow Brooch
13mm
T-shaped brooch with red enamel
fill to the body.
£30 - £40

R07-0722
Plate Brooch
16mm
Four intersecting openwork circles
with a vesica at the centre, amber
discs at the junctions.
£80 - £100

R07-0726
Gold Crossbow Brooch
42mm
With inscription 'VTERE
FELIX' (use this with good
fortune).
From £2,000

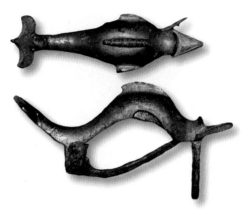

R07-0723
Dolphin Brooch
51mm
Bow formed as the dolphin's body. Large catch plate and hinge pin. Complete with pin and most of the original silvering.
£100 - £150

R07-0724
Peacock Brooch
29mm
The tail is decorated with circles of niello inlay, with niello lines to the wings and neck.
£120 - £180

R07-0725
Peacock Brooch
46mm
Inlaid enamel triangles to the tail and concentric enamelled rings to the crown.
£100 - £150

R07-0727
Cockerel Brooch
25mm
With red and blue enamelled panels
to the body, blue enamel to the eye.
£100 - £150

R07-0728
Silvered Fish Brooch
42mm
With scale detail, silvered face.
£80 - £100

R07-0729
Peacock Brooch
26mm
With tail displayed, blue and green
enamel pellet to the end of each feather.
£100 - £150

R07-0730
Chatelaine Brooch
91mm
With enamel cellwork, two pierced
lugs and transverse rod with four
cosmetic implements (tweezers, round-
section scoop, brush, nail-cleaner).
£600 - £800

R07-0731
Hippocampus Enamelled Brooch
39mm
Sea monster with red and pale blue enamel cells.
£80 - £100

R07-0732
Enamelled Disc Brooch
20mm
Green enamelled field with orange quatrefoil.
£100 - £150

R07-0733
Plate Brooch
34mm
Equal-ended type with silvering to the body.
£20 - £30

R07-0734
Plate Brooch
34mm
Cross type with scrolled ends, central stud cast separately.
£30 - £40

R07-0735
Gilt Plate Brooch
29mm
Urn-and-Dolphins type. Pin
lost.
£80 - £100

R07-0736
Bow Brooch
34mm
Trumpet type with silver
roundels and detailing.
£60 - £80

R07-0737
Enamelled Disc Brooch
25mm
Concentric rings and pellets.
Exceptional condition.
£80 - £100

R07-0738
Enamelled Plate Brooch
37mm
Concentric enamel rings and
roundels, with a central glass
knop.
£50 - £80

R07-0739
Plate Brooch
50mm
Triangular cells to the plates
with enamel fill.
£50 - £80

R07-0740
Disc Brooch
52mm
Domed central panel with
ring-and-dot detail, enamel-
filled cells to the arms and
centre.
£150 - £200

R07-0741
Hippocampus Brooch
52mm
Enamelled panel to the
flank with vertical blue
stripes and recesses.
£600 - £800

R07-0742
Axe Brooch
46mm
Double-bladed axe; pin to
the reverse.
£60 - £80

R07-0743
Bull Brooch
33mm
Reclining with legs extended,
the head and shoulders
modelled in the round.
£150 - £200

R07-0744
Tinned Bird Brooch
36mm
A bird with rounded body
and piriform wings, the
head modelled in the round.
£40 - £60

R07-0745
Annular Brooch
38mm
With white enamel inlay to eight
heart-shaped cells surrounding a
central blue ring.
£120 - £180

R07-0746
Frog Brooch
38mm
Two enamelled panels to the
back and black glass eyes.
£300 - £400

R07-0747
Hare Brooch
33mm
Central panel in green enamel with a line of yellow enamel points.
£300 - £400

R07-0748
Enamelled Swan Brooch
34mm
A swan modelled in the round, with arched neck, single perforated eye and panels of alternating red and blue enamel on the back.
£80 - £100

R07-0749
Boar Brooch
31mm
On the flank, a panel of red enamel.
£100 - £150

R07-0750
Enamelled Disc Brooch
27mm
Central knop and radiating panels of enamel.
£150 - £200

R07-0751
Silvered Horse Brooch
28mm
Silvered, with scrolled line
to the chest and flank.
£150 - £200

R07-0752
Bull Brooch
36mm
Reclining bull with
splayed front leg and
tilted head.
£100 - £150

R07-0753
Boar Brooch
36mm
Inset enamel discs along
the body.
£150 - £200

R07-0754
Gilt Brooch
32mm
An umbonate plate brooch with
central raised cell set with a
cabochon garnet; later modified
with four gold studs and a central
disc with gold rim.
£100 - £150

R07-0755
Enamelled Brooch
26mm
A plate brooch, elliptical in plan, with concentric cells, blue and white mosaic glass in a saltire configuration, central cell now empty.
£40 - £60

R07-0756
Millefiori Brooch
20mm
With inset millefiori glass in checkerboard pattern with panels in yellow-green and blue-green combinations, red borders.
£200 - £300

R07-0757
Hippocampus Brooch
27mm
With hemispherical glass eye and enamelled panels on the neck and flank; pin lost.
£80 - £100

R07-0758
Silvered Peacock Brooch
22mm
Peacock with trailing tail; pin and catchplate present.
£100 - £150

R07-0759
Owl Brooch
30mm
Head facing, wings and eyes
forming cells for enamel infill.
£300 - £400

R07-0760
Axe Brooch
30mm
With red and green enamelled panels
to the head and shaft.
£60 - £80

R07-0761
Hippocampus Brooch
38mm
With pellet eye, hatched
mane and scrolled tail.
£80 - £100

R07-0762
Silver Horse Brooch
36mm
A plate brooch in the form of
a galloping horse, champ-levé
enamel panels to the body in
red, yellow and green.
£400 - £600

R07-0763
Crescent Brooch
32mm
A plate brooch of three-limbed crescentic form with bulb finials and enamelled rosette to the centre.
£60 - £80

R07-0764
Bird Brooch
40mm
With dark blue enamel and inset white enamel pellets.
£150 - £200

R07-0765
Silver Knife and Spoon Brooch
84mm
Silver hinged brooch of a lion with folding tools.
£150 - £200

R08-0101
Phallic Pendant
31mm
Typical style. Worn as a
fertility charm.
£40 - £60

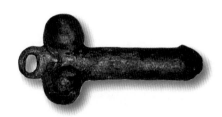

R08-0102
Phallic Pendant
35mm
Phallus pendant of typical
form. Often associated with the
military. Dark patina.
£50 - £80

R08-0103
Phallic Pendant
32mm
Phallic pendant of unusual
form. Even patina.
£40 - £60

R08-0104
Phallic Pendant
31mm
Phallic pendant of usual form.
Even patina.
£40 - £60

R08-0105
Phallic Pendant
35mm
Phallic pendant.
A little pitted on the surface.
Slim style.
£40 - £60

R08-0107
Pendant
40mm
Flat form. Smooth, even patina.
£60 - £80

R08-139715
Phallic Pendant
62mm
Phallus and a hand in the
mano fica gesture.
£100 - £150

R08-0109
Phallic Pendant
40mm
Patina a little uneven. Triple
phallus.
£100 - £150

R08-0110
Phallic Pendant
50mm
Large size. Surface a little
uneven.
£40 - £60

R08-0111
Phallic Pendant
34mm
Basic style. Even patina.
£80 - £100

R08 166862
Phallic Pendant
48mm
£300 - £400

R08-0113
Gold Double Phallus
Pendant
16mm
Ribbed D-shaped loop, one
phallus vertical with testicles
above, second phallus horizontal
with wing to the rear.
From £500

R08-0114
Phallic Military Pendant
62mm
The arms terminating in a
phallus and a hand, with
another phallus placed
centrally.
£80 - £100

R08-0201
Military Pendant
96mm
Disc inlaid with silver sheet,
much remaining.
Pendant portion depicts four
dolphins around a typical
military design.
£300 - £400

R08-0202
Military Pendant
65mm
Inlaid numeral 'V' perhaps
denoting the fifth legion.
£60 - £80

R08-0203
Military Pendant
75mm
Suspension boss with pendant of stylised phallic form. Probably a military belt fitting.
£60 - £80

R08-0301
Votive Axehead
17mm
In the style of a Bronze Age socketed axe. Surface a little ragged.
£20 - £30

R08-0302
Lunar Pendant
22mm
Crescent-shaped pendant. Traces of silver inlay. Surface a little rough.
£30 - £40

R08-0303
Knife Pendant
43mm
Smooth, even green surface. Rare knife pendant.
£80 - £100

R08-0304
Gold Pendant
19mm
Half round stone set in a decorated border.
From £400

R08-0306
Mouse Pendant
40mm
Looped tail, holding
food in its paws.
£100 - £150

R08-143680
Pendant
36mm
Bunch of grapes type.
£80 - £100

R08-157311
Gold Pendant
15mm
Inset cameo panel with
Asklepios and Hygieia.
£8,000 - £10,000

R08-0305
Gold Pendant
62mm
Inset triangular garnet, image of the emperor, TI CAESAR inscription.
From £50,000

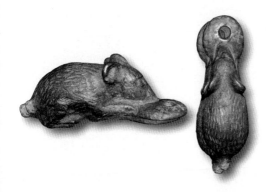

R08-0307
Silver Mouse Pendant
23mm
Shown nibbling on bread, fur finely modelled, the bread pierced to accept an attachment pin.
£200 - £300

R08-0308
Appliqué
32mm
Sol Invictus with radiate crown.
£80 - £100

R09-0101
Mount with Crested Helmet
38mm
Bust in native style. Even patina.
£80 - £100

R09-0102
Mars Mount
44mm
Mars in a Corinthian helmet.
£80 - £100

R09-0104
Mount
32mm
Head with elaborate hair design.
£80 - £100

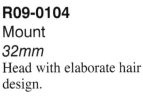

R09-0105
Sol Invictus Mount
37mm
Romano-British bust of Sol Invictus (the sun god). Even patina.
£120 - £180

R09-0107
Sol Invictus Mount
40mm
Classical style. Dark, even patina.
£120 - £180

R09-0108
Cherub Mount
50mm
Hollow back. Lightly moulded features. Probably from an item of furniture.
£100 - £150

R09-0109
Apollo Mount
39mm
Well formed features.
Dark tone.
£100 - £150

R09-0114
Mithras Mount
85mm
Very large. Good detail.
Even patination. Rare.
From £2,500

R09-0115
Mercury Mount
50mm
Head of Mercury.
Good detail. Even
patination.
£600 - £800

R09-0110
Apollo Mount
42mm
Classical style bust of Apollo.
Very fine detail. Rare.
£200 - £300

R09-0111
Mother Goddes Mount
49mm
Bronze mount, probably
representing a mother goddess.
Dark green patina.
£150 - £200

R09-0112
Mount with Military-
Bacchus
37mm
Lunette body with the face of
a bearded deity. Ragged patina.
£100 - £150

R09-0125
Figural Mount
85mm
Probably from a bowl or dish.
Even patination.
£300 - £400

R09-0303
Military Mount
27mm
Native style. Dark patina.
£20 - £30

R09 133085
Mount Set
115mm each
Chariot fittings.
£2,000 - £3,000

R09-0116
Horned God Mount
27mm
Dark patination. Good detail.
£80 - £100

R09-0117
Silver Head Mount
20mm
Horned god in silver.
One horn broken.
£120 - £180

R09-0123
Bust Mount
35mm
Very rough surface.
Detail a little weak.
£40 - £60

R09-0119
Bust Mount
50mm
Rough surface. Dark patina.
Some damage.
£120 - £180

R09-0120
Bust Mount
37mm
Probably from a bowl. Celtic
features.
£80 - £100

R09-0121
Bust of Sol Mount
38mm
Slight scuff across the face.
Good detail.
£120 - £180

R09-152772
Satyr Mount
68mm
Satyr bust, or Silenus.
£600 - £800

R09-166222
Horse Protome
54mm
Forequarters of a horse
emerging from a flat
phalera.
£100 - £150

R09-170145
Door Handle Pair
220mm
Lion mask type, rings held
in the jaws.
£6,000 - £8,000

R09-168465
Disc Mount
36mm
Millefiori ornament.
£3,000 - £4,000

R09-176091
Helmet Mount
20mm
Decorated with central
Chi-Rho Christogram.
£300 - £400

R09-109047
Mount
110mm
Bacchus bust from a
Triclinium couch.
From £1,000

R09-0201
Military Horse Harness Mount
35mm
Two horses' heads back-to-back. Two rectangular fixing loops on the back.
£150 - £200

R09-0202
Horse Mount
37mm
Equestrian mount probably from a bowl.
£40 - £60

R09-0204
Ram's Head Mount
20mm
Ram's head with arched horns. May have been a pin head.
£40 - £60

R09-0206
Lion's Head Mount
54mm
Good detail. Nice, even green
patination.
£150 - £200

R09-0207
Horse's Head Mount
30mm
Patchy surface.
Three dimensional.
£60 - £80

R09-0208
Ram's Head Mount
35mm
Patination a little patchy. Good
detail.
£80 - £100

R09-170476
Furniture Fitting
80mm
Dolphin type with globe in
mouth.
£400 - £600

R09-42206
Furniture Fitting
135mm
Javelin athlete with pillar.
£1,000 - £1,500

R09-155169
Furniture Fitting
92mm
Horse with bridle on a base.
£1,500 - £2,000

R09-162854
Furniture Fitting
54mm
Lion's leg developing to a lily
with putto above, clutching
two bunches of grapes.
£600 - £800

R09-160764
Epigraphic Mount
15mm
Silver-gilt, 'ROMA' in frame.
£300 - £400

R09-130453
Mount
64mm
Male bust of a god.
£150 - £200

R09-0302
Mount
23mm
Circular mount, most enamel
remaining.
£60 - £80

R09-0301
Mount
26mm
Circular floral design with red,
green and yellow enamel.
£60 - £80

R09-0304
Mount
25mm
Hexagonal shape.
Most enamel remaining.
£40 - £60

R09-0401
Owl Mount
40mm
Mounted on a solid circular base, the owl has two cylindrical legs. Examples of owls found in Britain are very rare. Usually associated with the goddess Minerva.
£300 - £400

R09-0404
Sleeping Dog Mount
35mm
Sleeping dog with a collar around the neck. Integral suspension on the dog's back. Perhaps from a hanging bowl or similar. Even patina.
£150 - £200

R09-0402
Baby Turtle Mount
21mm
Traces of silvering and enamel in the eyes.
£30 - £40

R09-0405(a)
Sphinx Mount
30mm
Sphinx (without beard). Fair
detail. Surface a little pitted.
Rare from this country.
£150 - £200

R09-0406
Military Harness Mount
45mm
Typical military style. Good
surface and patina.
£40 - £60

R09-0407
Phallic Mount
30mm
Two fixing lugs underneath.
Undamaged. Even patina.
£50 - £80

R09-0408
Phallic Mount
73mm
Complete and undamaged.
Good, even green
patination. Rare.
£300 - £400

R09-0409
**Military Mount with
Vine Leaves**
71mm dia
Mounting stud on rear.
Small piece of blue enamel
showing, remainder
missing. Good, even
patina.
£300 - £400

R09-0410
Cheekpiece Mount
72mm
Smooth, even surface. Large
size. Good patina.
£150 - £200

R09-0411
Boar Mount
47mm
Very rough surface. Silvered
boar.
£100 - £150

R09-0416
Eagle Mount
50mm
Incised line decoration on the
body.
£80 - £100

R09-0413
Sleeping Dog Mount
38mm
Even green patination.
£50 - £80

R09-0414
Eagle Mount
52mm
Good detail. Surface a little
uneven.
£100 - £150

R09-0415
Eagle Mount
50mm
Crude style. Even patination.
£120 - £180

R09-112214
Winged Phallic Mount
43mm
With unusual detail. Beautiful
patination
£2,000 - £3,000

R09-109468
Phallic Mount
54mm
Used to ward off bad luck.
£1,000 - £1,500

R09-0418
Phallic Mount
38mm
Good detail. Loop on the back.
£100 - £150

R09-0419
Phallic Mount
34mm
Most enamel remaining.
Good size.
£120 - £180

R09-147451
Flying Phallic Mount
113mm
Silver element from a
tintinnabulum.
£6,000 - £8,000

R09-0421
Gladiator Mount
42mm
Murmillo type with large fish-
crested helmet.
£300 - £400

R09-0422
Faun Mount
31mm
Hollow faun head on a D-shaped
plaque.
£120 - £180

R09-0423
Cupid Mount
52mm
Finely detailed facial features.
£50 - £80

R09-0424
Silver Mount
36mm
With opposed lion-head terminal, central silver roundel with a scene of a horse and a winged figure.
£120 - £180

R09-0425
Swivel Mount
26mm
From an oil flask, with round-section ribbed body and thick loop.
£40 - £60

R09-0426
Lioness Mount
65mm
Lioness moving forward on a flat plate, one foot resting on a human head.
£200 - £300

R09-0427
Fish Mount
81mm
A fish with head raised, weight supported on the pectoral fins, mouth open.
£80 - £100

R09-0428
Bacchus Mount
26mm
Bacchus with beard and bald head; hollow to the reverse.
£60 - £80

R09-0429
Boar Mount
31mm
Field of blue enamel with red and yellow roundels, band of punched annulets across the neck.
£100 - £150

R09-0430
Phalera Plaque
82mm
Decorated with the
face of the river-god
Achelous.
£1,500 - £2,000

R09-0431
Dionysus
Appliqué
41mm
A mask of Dionysus
with vine-leaves in
the hair, hollow to the
reverse.
£100 - £150

R09-0432
Silenus Mount
31mm
Silver insert to the
eye.
£80 - £100

R09-0433
Pan Appliqué
45mm
With thick curly hair, curly
beard and goat's ears.
£80 - £100

R09-0434
Dolphin Mount
51mm
With red enamel eye,
white enamel panel to
the flank and three green
enamel roundels.
£60 - £80

R09-0435
Phallic Mount
41mm
Male genitals with
pierced lug above.
£60 - £80

R09-0436
Dionysus Mount
20mm
The bearded head of
Dionysus with wreath to the
brow; stud to the reverse.
£100 - £150

R09-0437
Harness Mount
103mm including stand
A cast hook with rectangular
plates to front and back,
pierced for attachment and
silvered to the front face.
£200 - £300

R09-108110
Millefiori Plaque
35mm
Gold frame enclosing
an octagonal panel.
£1,500 - £2,000

R09-0439
Lion with Severed
Head Mount
50mm
A lion modelled in
the round with both
forepaws on a human
head with thick hair.
£150 - £200

R09-0440
Mercury Mount
57mm
With curled hair, bare-
chested and small wings
to the temples.
£400 - £600

R09-0441
Eagle and Swan
Fitting
135mm
An octagonal tube
with collar to the
mouth, eagle's head
above a quatrefoil
collar; to the front, a
round-section swan's
head and neck.

£600 - £800

R09-0442
Openwork
Roundel
105mm
A cast mount with
three trumpet-whorl
motifs to the interior,
the band with trumpet
detailing.

£200 - £300

R09-0443
Dolphin Mount
105mm
Two dolphins supporting a curved bar.
£100 - £150

R09-0444
Silver Phalera
105mm
Inset coin depicting
Philip I and
Otacilia Severa
with De PIA Mater
Pius Fillius legend.
£1,000 - £1,500

R09-0445
Minerva Mount
75mm
A bust of Minerva with broad
collar and cuirass; helmet
with crest and curved horns;
radiating strokes to the flange;
hollow to the reverse with
square-section mounting peg.
£200 - £300

R09-0446
Actor's Mask Fitting
84mm
Concave cast fitting of a
bearded man in a helmet.
£400 - £600

R09-0447
Mercury Bust Mount
40mm
In winged helmet, with folded
cloak to the shoulders.
£300 - £400

R09-135717
Silvered Plaque
53mm
Impressed standing figure
within a punched wreath
holding a sickle.
£150 - £200

R09-142787
Openwork Roundel
90mm
Band of leaf-and-tendril
motifs.
£300 - £400

R09-158345
Plaque Pair
170-175mm
One with lions and female
figure, the other with snake
and male figure.
£1,000 - £1,500

R10-174323
Gold Ring
26mm
Facing busts of Jupiter as
Serapis and Juno as Isis.
£4,000 - £6,000

R10-57917
Gold Ring
26mm
With beautifully
engraved intaglio.
From £10,000

R10-0102
Gold Ring
24mm
Solid construction (15.25
grams). Bezel depicts clasped
hands. Wearable size. Rare.
From £2,000

R10-117599
Gold Ring
34mm
Inset nicolo gemstone.
£6,000 - £8,000

R10-130685
Gold Ring
21mm
Inscription 'TER / NOC'.
£1,500 - £2,000

R10-144827
Gold Ring
34mm
Inset nicolo gemstone,
eagle and hare.
£6,000 - £8,000

R10-155118
Gold Ring
20mm
Double bezel ring with
pierced-work inscription.
£4,000 - £6,000

R10-160607
Gold Ring
27mm
Inset carved moonstone leaf.
£2,000 - £3,000

R10-155124
Gold Ring
24mm
Set with garnet and sapphire
cabochons.
£6,000 - £8,000

R10-0103
Gold Ring with
Eagle Intaglio
13mm
Orange stone intaglio depicting a
spread eagle. Small size.
£600 - £800

R10-0104
Gold Ring
20mm
Solid construction. Original
intaglio with a crack across the
centre. Wearable size.
From £1,000

R10-0105
Gold Ring with
Garnet Stone
17mm
Unusual style.
Original stone.
Undamaged.
£600 - £800

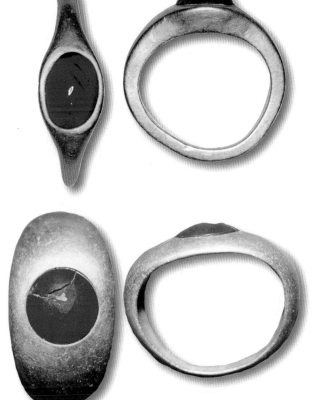

R10-0106
Gold Ring
23mm
Bezel cracked.
Good size
chunky ring.
£600 - £800

R10-0107
Gold Ring
31mm
Decorated band with clasped
hands. Good size. Rare.
From £2,500

R10-0108
Clasped Hands Gold Ring
17mm
Plain band.
Slightly mis-shapen.
£800 - £1,000

R10-0109
Gold Ring
21mm
Perfect in all respects.
Beautiful intaglio. Good
wearable size.
From £2,000

R10-0110
Gold Ring
20mm
Small size.
Openwork band.
Original intaglio.
£600 - £800

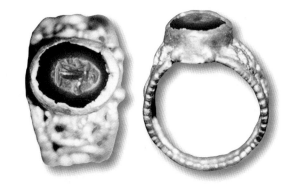

R10-0111
Gold Ring
17mm
Small size.
Original stone set.
£600 - £800

R10-0112
Gold Ring
13mm
Probably a child's ring.
Engraved palm leaf design
on bezel.
£150 - £200

R10-66224
Gold Military Ring
26mm
Inscribed 'Constantino Fidem'
showing allegiance to Emperor
Constantine II.
£6,000 - £8,000

R10-0306
Gold Ring with
Intaglio
23mm
With pale blue intaglio
of a standing deity
holding a sceptre.
From £800

R10-0312
Gold Intaglio Ring
22mm
With inset black stone intaglio depicting a standing helmetted figure with cup in one hand.

From £1,000

R10-0313
Gold Intaglio Ring
21mm
Inset with a black intaglio depicting a standing goddess holding a bowl and amphora.

From £600

R10-0209
Silver Ring
20mm
Traces of gilding. Legionary
eagle on bezel.
£100 - £150

R10-0210
Silver Ring
19mm
Flared shoulders. Light
engraved design on bezel and
on shoulders.
£100 - £150

R10-0202
Silver Ring
15mm
Dark red coloured intaglio
engraved with a female figure.
Small size.
£120 - £180

R10-0211
Silver Ring with Concordia
17mm
Red glass intaglio depicting
Concordia. Wearable size.
£120 - £180

R10-0203
Silver Ring
21mm
Bezel is a silver insert
depicting Mercury. Wearable
size.
£200 - £300

R10-0217
Silver Ring
18mm
Venus engraved on the
intaglio.
£150 - £200

R10-0218
Silver Ring
20mm
Patchy colour.
A little mis-shapen.
£100 - £150

R10-0215
Silver Ring
19mm
Chunky ring. Plain stone.
£120 - £180

R10-0216
Silver Ring
19mm
Crescent moon and stars
engraved on the intaglio
(Hadrian period).
£120 - £180

R10-0219
Silver Ring
18mm
Military shape. Ears of corn
engraved on the intaglio.
£120 - £180

R10-0205
Silver Ring
24mm
Red stone intaglio depicting
Ceres. Good quality
engraving.
£200 - £300

R10-0214
Silver Ring
19mm
Glass intaglio with Venus
engraved.
£150 - £200

R10-0207
Silver Ring
18mm
Red carnelian intaglio
engraved with the figure of
Mars. Wearable size.
£180 - £240

R10-0208
Silver Ring
16mm
Red glass intaglio depicting
Roma or Minerva. Small size.
£150 - £200

R10-0206
Silver Ring
16mm
Chunky but small size with
cornelian intaglio engraved
with the figure of Ceres.
£180 - £240

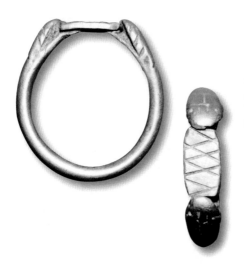

R10-0221
Silver Ring
18mm
Two serpents holding a panel between their mouths.
£100 - £150

R10-0222
Silver Ring
22mm
Wearable ring with inscription.
£120 - £180

R10-0223
Silver Ring
26mm
Chunky and large military
ring. Plain bezel.
£80 - £100

R10-0301
Ring
22mm
Inscription on bezel
'CVTVXCT'. Dark, even
patina. Scarce.
£60 - £80

R10-0302
Intaglio Ring
21mm
Facetted bezel inset with a
blue-green glass intaglio,
engraved with a standing
figure.
£60 - £80

R10-0304
Engraved Ring
19mm
Unusual bronze ring with
engraved bezel.
Good patination.
£60 - £80

R10-0310
'Aelius Titus'
Inscribed Ring
29mm
D-section hoop and
elliptical bezel.
£80 - £100

R10-0311
Gold Ring
20mm
Eight discoid panels, seven with engraved designs including a lyre,
trident, profile bearded head.
From £1,500

R10-170997
Ring with
Gemstone
25mm
Iron ring with inset
nicolo gemstone,
portrait bust.
£1,500 - £2,000

R10-38139
Gilt Ring
22mm
Military eagle intaglio.
£120 - £180

R10-0307
Silver Fede Ring
26mm
Elliptical bezel with
raised central panel,
clasped-hands motif.
£200 - £300

R10-0308
Silver Intaglio Ring
28mm
Intaglio with a female in draped peplos robe with vegetation in one hand and a cornucopia in the other.

£200 - £300

R10-0309
Ring with Deity
22mm
Glass intaglio of a standing figure.

£60 - £80

R10-0401
Jasper Intaglio
27mm
Depicting a bust of
a youthful female
with hair drawn back,
earrings and necklace.
£200 - £300

R10-0501
Gold Earring
23mm
Gold cloison with
conical garnet, four
bulbs set around the
perimeter.
£100 - £150

R10-0502
Gold Earring
16mm
Hexagonal face with
inset blue stone, petal
detailing.
£100 - £150

R10-164815
Gold Earring
33mm
With Medusa cameo
£400 - £600

R10-0601
Gold Bracelet
71mm
With expanding
ends, ribbed collars,
discoid cells with
an amber-coloured
stone.
From £1,000

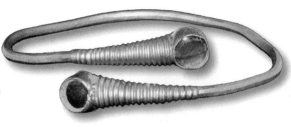

R10-0602
Snake Bracelet
76mm
Military armilla
bracelet, with
snake-head detail
to the terminals.
£60 - £80

R10-0603
Silver Bracelet
61mm
With hinged closure and inset cabochon carnelian.
From £1,500

R11-165086
Asclepius Statuette
55mm
Left hand holding the snake
staff.
£200 - £300

R11-175378
Mars Statuette
126mm
'The Oxshott' Roman Military
Statuette of Mars.
£6,000 - £8,000

R11-164565
Venus Statuette
210mm inc. stand
Goddess standing nude
with right leg bent.
£4,000 - £6,000

R11-165069
Statue Fragment
100mm
Left hand from a statue, with
full open palm.
£1,200 - £1,800

R11-177415
Venus Statuette
230mm incl stand
Venus Pudica of the Medici type.
£20,000 - £30,000

R11-67283
Bound Captive Statuette
53mm
Kneeling nude with hands held
behind his back
£1,000 - £1,500

R11-177410
Priest Statuette with
Patera
140mm
Dressed in a tunic and a
large toga, patera in the
right hand.
£2,000 - £3,000

R11-177512
Apollo Statuette
85mm
Holding a purse in his left
hand.
£800 - £1,000

R11-177413
Head of Child Bacchus
135mm incl stand
Silver inlay to the eyes.
£3,000 - £4,000

R11-175542
Hound Statuette
145mm incl stand
Leaping stance with
open mouth.
£600 - £800

R11-45098
Mercury Statuette
110mm
Seated pose wearing the
winged petasos travellers' hat.
£2,000 - £3,000

R11-69559
Mercury Statuette
120mm incl stand
Wearing a winged petasos and
holding a coin purse.
£1,500 - £2,000

R11-76688
Bust of Hercules
250mm
Holding apples of
Hesperides.
From £20,000

R11-103361
Mount Pair
64-66mm
Theatre masks with silver
inlaid eyes.
£6,000 - £8,000

R11-65008
Luna Statuette
220mm
The godess standing on a globe.
£8,000 - £10,000

R11-103220
Statue Head of Mercury
91mm
With wings and curly hair.
£1,200 - £1,800

R11-100797
Gladiator Statuette
85mm
Murmillo type.
£1,200 - £1,800

R11-109441
Acrobat Statuette
100mm
Finely modelled in active pose.
£4,000 - £6,000

R11-117890
Jupiter Statuette
114mm
With rectangular base.
£12,000 - £18,000

R11 -126976
Hercules Statuette
78mm
With club and lionskin
mantle.
£1,200 - £1,800

R11-127789
Statue Fragment
170mm
Nose, septum, upper and lower lips, chin with trimmed beard and moustache; possibly a statue of Jupiter.

From £10,000

R11-134935
Goddess Statuette
215mm including stand
Figure of the goddess Iphigenia.

£6,000 - £8,000

R11-133689
Statuette
175mm
River god Orontes swimming.
£2,000 - £3,000

R11-133491
Statuette Base
62mm
Socle base for a statuette.
£150 - £200

R11-130395
Charioteer Statuette
64mm
Female wearing a belted
peplos dress and mantle, calf-
length footwear, with hair
gathered in a topknot.
£300 - £400

R11-110358
Mouse Statuette
54mm
Detailed fur, gnawing a nut.
£600 - £800

R11-135688
Bull Statuette
90mm
Advancing pose, on a socle
base.
£800 - £1,000

R11-144702
Asclepius Statuette
120mm
God of medicine holding his
crooked snake-entwined staff.
£2,000 - £3,000

R11-147037
Boxer Figurine
56mm
Bronze figure of a dwarf with
bound hands raised, ready to
attack.
£2,000 - £3,000

R11-141455
Mercury Statuette
96mm
Coin purse in the right hand, mantle to the shoulder, winged hat.

£1,000 - £1,500

R11-144742
Mercury Statuette
98mm
Wreath to the brow and mantle wound round the left arm.

£500 - £700

R11-141835
Faunus Statuette
95mm
Satyr with vine-stick in left
hand and fur mantle to left
shoulder.
£600 - £800

R11-147046
Atlas Statuette
90mm
Nude muscular body, kneeling
with both arms raised.
£800 - £1,000

R11-141675
Miniature Theatrical
Mask
30mm
Braided wig and exaggerated
scooped mouth,
£80 - £100

R11-146706
Ram Statuette
33mm
Advancing pose, detailed
fleece texture.
£200 - £300

R11-151865
Statue Fragment
350mm
Part of the pelvis of an athlete,
god or hero.
£10,000 - £15,000

R11-152745
Venus Statuette
140mm
Partly nude, covered by a
draped cloak.
£3,000 - £4,000

R11-152748
Mercury Statuette
100mm
Holding the caduceus in the
left hand, coin purse in the
right.
£1,500 - £2,000

R11-152755
Priapus Statuette
80mm
Holding a basket of
flowers on his phallus.
£800 - £1,000

R11-152749
Priapus Statuette
90mm
Raising his garment to expose
his phallus.
£800 - £1,000

R11-152434
Miniature Couch
105mm
Model couch for
banqueteer figures.
£600 - £800

R11-158196
Jupiter Statuette
230mm
With silver eyes.
From £20,000

R11-155099
Statue Fragment
280mm
Foot with sandal.
From £50,000

R11-158834
Statue Fragment
390mm
Hand and arm with pointing finger.
From £20,000

R11-161841
Statue Fragment
215mm incl stand
Clenched fist from a statue of a
hero, athlete, etc.
£6,000 - £8,000

R11-163504
Juno Statuette
250mm
Goddess Juno with arms
raised.
£8,000 - £10,000

R11-144818
Bull Statuette
72mm
Stationary pose with head
raised.
£400 - £600

R11-0101
Mars Statuette
85mm
Mars wearing full armour and holding his cloak. Spear and shield missing. Very fine even green patina. Undamaged.
from £1,500

R11-0102
Mercury Statuette
104mm
Superb detail. Feet missing. Good dark matt surface.
£500 - £800

R11-0103
Mercury Statuette
52mm
Mercury holding a caduceus.
Feet missing. Well modelled.
Dark patina.
£100 - £150

R11-0104
Mercury Statuette
58mm
Good detail. Mercury holding
a purse and wearing a winged
cap. Traces of tinning on the
surface.
£120 - £180

R11-0105
Cupid Statuette
70mm
Right leg broken. Good, even
surface.
£200 - £300

R11-0106
Drunken Hercules Statuette
85mm
Hercules holding a drinking vessel in his right hand and a club in his left. A lion's skin draped over his left arm. Good patina and condition.
£500 - £800

R11-0107
Hercules Statuette
75mm
In native Celtic style. Fluid lines to the body. Dark even patina. Right leg broken.
£150 - £200

R11-0108
Venus Statuette
55mm
Even patina. Feet broken away.
£80 - £120

R11-0109
Naked Youth Statuette
102mm
Good detail. Even patina.
Complete and undamaged.

£500 - £800

R11-0110
Female Statuette Holding Purse
92mm
Good even and smooth surface.
Attractive patination.

£500 - £800

R11-0112
Victory Statuette
51mm
Small size. Surface a little uneven.
£80 - £120

R11-0116
Cupid Statuette
70mm
Rare to be holding a torch. One wing missing on back.
£150 - £200

R11-178170
Cupid Statuette
102mm
Holding a bunch of grapes in the right hand.
£500 - £800

R11-0119
Jupiter Statuette
88mm
Good detail. Smooth, even surface. Holding thunderbolt.
£800 - £1,000

R11-0120
Naked Male Statuette
78mm
Rich green patination. Quiver for arrows on his back.
£150 - £200

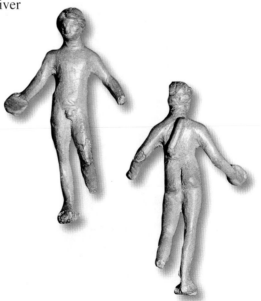

R11-133233
Hippocampus
Statuette
105mm
With curved tail.
£500 - £700

R11-138851
Guardian Statuette
190mm
Bronze 'lar' guardian deity.
£5,000 - £7,000

R11-141317
Fortuna Statuette
130mm
With silver clasps holding the dress.
£1,000 - £1,500

R11-140145
Jupiter Statuette
60mm
Eagle at his feet, muscular, mantle draped across his shoulders.
£300 - £400

R11-0121
Priapus Statue
55mm
Rare statue of Priapus.
£300 - £400

R11-0201
Goat Statuette
42mm
Good detail. Even patina.
One horn missing from top
of head.
£200 - £300

R11-0202
Mouse with Bread
27mm
Patina a little ragged. Small size.
£100 - £150

R11-0203
Eagle Statuette
55mm
Good, even surface.
Has animal at its feet.
£200 - £300

R11-0204
Foot
81mm
Hollow, pierced through the ankle.
£200 - £300

R11-0205
Horse Statuette
57mm
Horse on a pedestal base, head tilted and one foreleg raised, hollow to the underside.

£120 - £180

R11-0206
Victory Figurine
57mm
A winged Victory with neatly dressed hair, wings spread and wreath held at the chest.

£150 - £200

R11-0207
Fortuna Figurine
77mm
Fortuna standing robed and crowned with lamp in the left hand, grasping hem of her dress in her right.

£200 - £300

R11-0208
Hercules Bibax
Figurine
80mm
Hercules reclining, nude,
his weight on his left arm,
a cloth draped from the left
arm over the rump and
right leg; a drinking bowl
held in the right hand.

£400 - £600

R11-0209
Eagle and Bull's
Head Statuette
27mm
An eagle perching
on a bull's severed
head.

£60 - £80

R11-0210
Venus Figurine
150mm
Wearing a loose cloth about the legs, diadem
to the head.

£500 - £800

R11-0211
Athlete Statuette with Silver Bowl
110mm
An athlete standing on a pedestal base, a club or staff in his right hand and lionskin over his left forearm.

£400 - £600

R11-0212
Bound Captive Figurine
46mm
With hands bound at the waist, wearing a belted tunic and pointed cap.

£150 - £200

R11-0213
Military Bust
89mm
With short beard and Corinthian
helmet pushed back on the head,
horse-hair crest above.

£400 - £600

R11-0214
Atlas Statuette
135mm
Atlas with head bowed, hands
braced against the flanks, legs
spread.

£400 - £600

R11-0215
Minerva Bust
76mm
A bust of the goddess
Minerva in a crested helmet
with gorgoneion on the chest;
crest pierced to the rear,
hollow to the reverse.
£200 - £300

R11-0216
Demeter
80mm
Head of Demeter modelled in
the round.
£200 - £300

R11-0217
Mercury Figurine
100mm
In seated pose with right
hand hollow to accept a
money pouch; left foot
absent.

£400 - £600

R11-0218
Mercury Statuette
99mm
Mercury in advancing pose,
nude, two small wings to the
shoulders, bag of coins in the
left hand; the right hand raised,
cast with a hole for insertion
of the caduceus; the right foot
resting on a square-section
plinth.

£300 - £400

R11-135279
Jupiter Statuette
110mm
Poised in the act of
throwing a thunderbolt.
£600 - £800

R11 110299
Statue Hand
240mm
Gripping a small sphere
between fingers.
£4,000 - £6,000

R11-0220
Mercury Figurine
63mm
Cape over the left arm,
winged sandals to the feet.
£150 - £200

R11-0221
Putto Figurine
56mm
Standing on one leg on a ball.
£150 - £200

R11-0222
Lion Fountain Figurine
250mm
Cast hollow with inlet at the tail and
open mouth with outlet aperture.
From £1,500

R11-0223
Female Bust
145mm
Hollow-cast with short-sleeved dress
and shawl.
From £1,000

R11-0224
Hercules Bust
150mm
Wavy hair tied with a fillet and a
lionskin tied around the shoulders.

£600 - £800

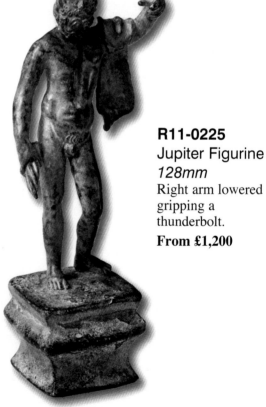

R11-0225
Jupiter Figurine
128mm
Right arm lowered
gripping a
thunderbolt.

From £1,200

R11-0226
Lion Figurine
78mm
Standing with the front
left paw raised.
£200 - £300

R11-0227
Dionysus Statuette
57mm
With neat beard and
wreath in his hair, holding
a jug in his right hand and
cloak in his left.
£150 - £200

R11-0228
Athena Bust
33mm
In Corinthian
helmet with
deep-set eyes,
the hair drawn
back to a knot
behind.
£300 - £400

R11-0229
Capricorn
Figurine
92mm
Horns and tail cast
open.
£500 - £800

R11-0230
Lioness Figurine
35mm
With recurved
tail and snarling
expression.
£150 - £200

R11-0231
Female Head
39mm
The eyes with silver
panels.
£50 - £80

R11-0232
Figurine Fragment
110mm incl stand
Torso of an athletic male with sash.
£400 - £600

R11-0233
Mercury
Figurine
100mm
Mercury with winged petasos cap, bag of gold coins in his right hand and caduceus in his left.
£400 - £600

R11-0234
Putto Figurine
71mm
With the right arm raised
to rest on a ledge; in the
left hand a patera.
£200 - £300

R11-0235
Diana Figurine
166mm
Goddess dressed in a
chiton pinned at the right
shoulder with a disc
brooch.
From £1,000

R11-0236
Eros Statuette
268mm
Supporting a long-stemmed
cornucopia with cinquefoil
mouth.

From £6,000

R11-0237
Gladiator
Statuette
63mm
A retiarius armed
with a net and
trident, and the
galerus neck-guard
at his shoulder.

From £1,500

R11-0238
Eros Figurine
75mm
A naked winged Eros
with staff on his left
arm.

£120 - £180

R11-0239
Foot
80mm
Hollow cast with
strap and sole detail.

£60 - £80

R11-0240
Mythical Beast
65mm
A leocampus with
the foreparts of a lion
and the hindparts of
a fish.

£400 - £600

R11-0241
Eros Figurine
70mm
Winged figure in the action of shooting
an arrow (bow and arrow absent).
£300 - £500

R11-0242
Silver Statuette Fragment
33mm
Slender female arm from a statue
of Venus or similar, with a
miniature gold bracelet.
£150 - £200

R11-0243
Athlete Figurine
108mm incl stand
Roman copy of a Greek original, 'The
Diskobolus of Myra'.
From £800

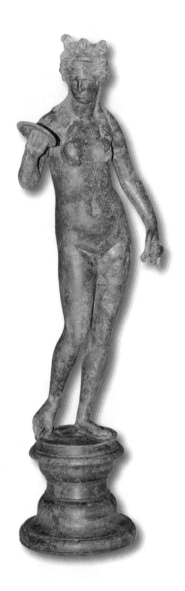

R11-0244
Aphrodite Statuette
272mm

Standing figure of Aphrodite with base, holding and looking into a circular mirror.

From £30,000

R11-167408
Asclepius Statuette
155mm incl stand

Roman god of medicine, Asclepius.

£3,000 - £4,000

R11-134021
Silenus Statuette
113mm
Standing on a pedestal, wearing a
loincloth and holding a wineskin.
£600 - £800

R11-0247
Bacchus Figurine
105mm
A lead-filled
architectural fitting of
the god Bacchus wearing
a fox skin, clusters of
grapes at each shoulder;
square-section mounting
hook to the reverse.

£200 - £300

R12-0201
Buckle with two Dolphins
32mm
Frame in the form of two dolphin heads with a ball held in their mouths. Pin missing.
£80 - £100

R12-0202
Gilded Buckle
34mm
Roman military buckle. Heavily gilded.
£20 - £30

R12-0203
Buckle with Plate
78mm
Enamelled plate. Open-work buckle.
£150 - £200

R12-0204
Buckle with Plate
64mm
Ring-and-dot decoration. Smooth, even patination.
£60 - £80

R12-0205
Military Buckle with Plate
45mm
Ring-and-dot decoration. Surface a little patchy.
£40 - £60

R12-0206
Military Buckle with Plate
101mm
A four-part hinged buckle set of a rectangular plaque with crescent detail, La Tène style void to the rear and central rectangular void with chamfered sides.
£80 - £100

R12-0301
Amphora Type Strap End
53mm
Incised decoration with securing rivets intact.
£40 - £60

R12-0302
Inscribed Strap End
38mm
One face inscribed in capitals 'ABEFDRX/XSNRFF/MII' followed by a chevron and arrowhead.
£100 - £150

R12-136479
Enamelled Buckle
71mm
Remains of enamel on
the plate.
£80 - £100

R12-176136
Military Buckle
with Plate
60mm
Two bands of silver-
inlaid punched
ornament.
£400 - £600

R12-130588
Buckle Plate
61mm
Mask of Medusa on the
plate.
£100 - £150

R12-130593
Buckle with Plate
88mm
Military type with
integral plate.
£80 - £100

R12-0401
Military Belt Fitting
133mm long
Disc with attachment plates.
Even patina.
£150 - £200

R12-0402
Strap Connector
67mm
A plaque with openwork
designs, outer quadrants
surrounding an inner roundel
with scrolled vegetation.
£120 - £180

R12-0403
Millefiori Belt Mount
48mm
Military belt mount with
scrolled ends and rivets to
the reverse; two plaques of
mosaic polychrome glass to
the face.
£300 - £400

R12-0404
Military Strap Junction
90mm
With openwork centre and
raised borders, three pieced
rectangular lugs to the outer
edge; openwork motif of three
phalloi around the central boss.
£150 - £200

R13-141060
Strap Junction
95mm
Legionary eagle clasping
a bull.
£600 - £800

R13-0101
Clothes Fastener
30mm
Decorative and brightly
enamelled, most of which
remains.
£120 - £180

R13-0102
Enamelled Clasp
27mm
Enamelled panels and
T-shaped pegs to the
rear of two arms.
£80 - £100

R14-144595
Cosmetic
Tweezers
66mm
Attached to a
mounting ring.
£30 - £40

R14-0201
Razor with Iron Blade
120mm
Ring-and-dot decoration. Most
of the iron blade remaining.
Rare.
£300 - £400

R14-133498
Hanging Pyxis
230mm
Ribbed sidewall,
trumpet-shaped mouth,
lateral loops with chains
securing a hook and lid.
£400 - £600

R14-133698
Lidded Pyxis
65mm
Silver-gilt with images of Roman gods.
From £10,000

R14-133924
Pyxis Lid
40mm
Band of running tendril ornament.
£400 - £600

R15-139969
Prick Spur
90mm
Applied silver pellets in two rows.
£300 - £400

R15-146304
Bacchus Chariot Fitting
185mm incl stand
With vine-leaf wreath to the hair.
£1,500 - £2,000

R15-144826
Chariot Fitting
71mm
Bronze bull.
£400 - £600

R15-157277
Harness Mount
63mm
Military type, openwork
volute scroll design.
£200 - £300

Roman Bronze Chariot Fitting
Dionysian Satyr - 2-3rd Cent A.D.
From Lower Moesia

R15-166143
Chariot Fitting
160mm incl stand
Bronze bust of a Dionysian
satyr.
£800 - £1,000

R15-134738
Horse Harness Mount
43mm
Openwork text
LEGXVAPOLLINARIS:'
(15th Legion of Apollo).
£300 - £400

R15-52293
Chariot Fitting
94mm
Winged mask of Venus,
gilded surface.
£800 - £,1000

R15 133086
Mount Pair
145mm each
Bronze chariot mounts of
hunting dogs.
£1,500 - £2,000

R15-0103
Chariot Fitting
125mm
A bust of Apollo with
long curled hair and
round eyes, chain and
pendant to the chest,
D-shaped scroll to
the lower edge and
suspension loop to the
rear of the neck.
From £600

R16-0101
Seal Box
32mm
Traces of enamel. Does not
open.
£60 - £80

R16-0102
Seal Box
27mm
Most of the enamel remaining.
Does not open.
£60 - £80

R16-0103
Seal Box
45mm
Damaged on the base. Traces
of enamel. Does not open.
£80 - £100

R16-0104
Seal Box
33mm
Enamel inlay on the
lid. In working order.
Even patina.
£80 - £100

R16-0105
Seal Box
31mm
Enamel inlay on the
lid. Does not open.
Even patina.
£80 - £100

R16-166118
Seal Box
46mm
Leaf-shaped type with
heart-shaped cell.
£60 - £80

R16-0107
Seal Box

32mm

Enamel inlay on the lid which
does not open. Patina a little
uneven.

£60 - £80

R16-0205
Phallic Seal Box

36mm

With knop finial and hinged lid, three holes to
the underside; the face with inset chevron and
ring of mosaic glass, high-relief stylised phallus
to the centre.

£40 - £60

R16-0109
Seal Box

27mm

Beast looking rearwards on the
lid which does not open.

£80 - £100

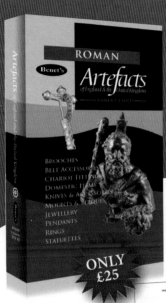
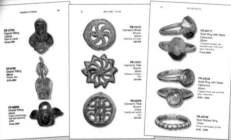

R16-0203
Seal Box with Millefiori
29mm
Concentric rings of millefiori glass and
turquoise pellet to the centre.
£80 - £100

R16-0204
Seal Box
59mm
With hinged loop and a panel
of champ-levé red and blue
enamel.
£50 - £80

R16-0206
Seal Box
32mm
Phallus to the lid.
£80 - £100

R16-0110
Silver Seal Box
37mm
Very rare seal
box in silver with
military insignia.
From £500

R16-0201
Seal Box Lid
30mm
In Celtic style. Lid is
missing its base. Most
enamel present.
£40 - £60

R16-0202
Seal Box Lid
20mm
Celtic style.
Lid missing its
base. Most enamel
remaining.
£60 - £80

R17-144680
Padlock
39mm
Hinged cover
with ram-head.
£400 - £600

R17-0101
Ring Key
19mm
Hollow shank
and offset
wards.
£30 - £40

R17-0102
Ring Key
18mm
Combined finger ring
and key.
£30 - £40

R17-0104
Ring Key
24mm
Combined finger ring and key.
£30 - £40

R17-0105
Ring Key
28mm
Combined finger ring and key.
Even patina.
£40 - £60

R17-0106
Ring Key
35mm
Combined finger ring and key.
Detailed wards with linear
decoration. Good example.
£40 - £60

R17-0107
Ring Key
34mm
Round body with offset wards
of ten pins. Even patina.
Unusual example.
£40 - £60

R17-0108
Ring Key
31mm
Combined finger ring and key.
Fairly plain. Even patina.
£30 - £40

R17-0109
Ring Key
38mm
Offset wards. Perfect and
undamaged.
Outstanding patina.
£80 - £100

R17-0110
Keys
longest 58mm
Group of three keys illustrating the three main varieties. All in good condition.
From £25 each

R17-0201
Keys
longest 90mm
Group of four latch lifter keys made of iron.
From £20 each

R17-0202
Key with Shank
44mm
Typical shank and offset wards. Even patina.
£60 - £80

R17-0203
Key with Shank
44mm
Hexagonal shank. Sharp detail. Even green patina.
£60 - £80

R17-0204
Key With Shank
41mm
Typical shank and offset
wards. Even patina.
£40 - £60

R17-0205
Key With Shank
65mm
Big chunky handle, with light
green decoration. Even green
patina.
£50 - £80

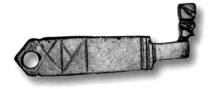

R17-0206
Key With Shank
64mm
Long, solid handle decorated
with simple incised decoration.
Even patina. Perfect condition.
£50 - £80

R17-0207
Key with Lunette Top
34mm
Fine detail. Even patina.
£100 - £150

R17-0208
Key
40mm
Typical form with offset
wards. Surface a little ragged.
£20 - £30

R17-0209
Key
75mm
Pelta shape handle. Very
unusual style for a bronze key.
Rare.
£80 - £100

R17-0210
Key
73mm
Typical form but unusual in
having a bronze rather than an
iron shank.
£80 - £100

R17-0211
Key
30mm
Even patina. Unusual style.
£30 - £40

R17-0212
Key
57mm
Decorated.
Smooth, even patination.
£80 - £100

R17-0213
Key
83mm
Large and chunky. Patina
flaking in places.
£60 - £80

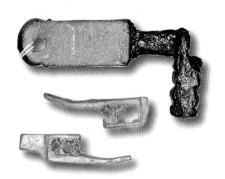

R17-0301
Key & Lock Group
85mm (key)
Key has bronze handle and
iron shank. Iron in good
condition and stable. Two
bronze lock bolts.
£80 - £100

R17-162881
Door Key
110mm
Bronze handle formed as a
lion devouring a calf.
£1,000 - £1,500

R17-0401
Key Handle
75mm
Bronze handle with part of
iron shank remaining.
Typical form.
£30 - £40

R17-0402
Key Handle
70mm
Bronze handle with fraction
of iron shank remaining.
£30 - £40

R17-0403
Lion & Celt Key
Handle
120mm
Patina a little patchy.
Good detail. Rare.
From £500

R17-177526
Lion Key Handle
85mm
Bronze bow from a key
with lion and acanthus
leaf column.
£600 - £800

R17-0405
Lion Key Handle
76mm
Crouching lion with
open mouth and bared
teeth, resting on extended
forepaws.
£100 - £150

R17-0406
Key Handle
57mm
With thick transverse
collar, traces of the iron
shank.
£40 - £60

R17-0407
Key
45mm
The bit with six triangular teeth, large bow with incised lines and crosses.

£60 - £80

R17-0408
Ring Key
30mm
Short shank with bits cut into one face.

£30 - £40

R17-0409
Key Handle
90mm
A crouching lion with prey protruding from the mouth.

From £500

R18-0205
Steelyard Weight
60mm
Good detail. With its
suspension chain.
From £800

R18-0206
Steelyard Weight
90mm
Ring-and-dot decoration.
£40 - £60

R18-0203
Steelyard Weight
55mm
Youthful bust with
good detail. Fine
definition of face and
hair.
£200 - £300

R18-0101
Steelyard Set
115mm
Balance arm with
two hooks and two
scale pans. Steelyard
weight missing.
£150 - £200

R18-0104
Steelyard Balance
89mm
Balance arm with one hook.
£80 - £100

R18-0105
Steelyard Balance
320mm
Suspension hook, steelyard
and spherical lead weight.
£200 - £300

R18-0207
Scale Pan
24mm
With stamped 'BANNAF' maker's mark.
£80 - £100

R18-0208
Steelyard Weight
47mm
Bust of Emperor Vespasian in skull-cap; loop absent.
From £800

R18-0209
Steeelyard Weight
45mm
'Bound captive' type with iron mounting peg to the reverse.
From £800

R18-133091
Weight
60mm
Mason's plumb bob.
£300 - £400

R19-0101
Stylus Pendant
51mm
Pendant with stylus point,
inlaid with dots of red enamel.
Rare.
£100 - £150

R19-0103
Stylus Pendant
58mm
Good detail. Tip broken off.
£80 - £120

R19-0201
Stylus with Eraser
155mm
Two heads set at each end.
Scarce in bronze. Large.
£60 - £80

R19-0202
Stylus with Eraser
114mm
Good condition. Iron
stable.
£40 - £60

R19-0203
Stylus
118mm
Inlaid bronze
decoration. Iron is
substantially corrosion
free.
£80 - £100

R19-0204
Silver Stylus
101mm
Decorated all along its
length. Rare in silver.
£200 - £300

R19-0205
Stylus with Eraser
130mm
Pointed writing tip and
trapezoidal erasing end.
£40 - £60

R19-0206
Stylus with Eraser
120mm
With one tapered tip,
round-section stem
and erasing end.
£60 - £80

R19-46579
Silver Stylus with
Cross and Ligular
120mm
Angled scraper and
chain connectors.
£200 - £300

R19-131038
Plaque Pair
128mm / 150mm
Frieze depicting two
chariots.
£500 - £700

R19-132779
Military Diploma
Fragment
21mm
Text to both faces.
£80 - £100

R19-121258
Military Plaque
40mm
Inscribed for
Domitius Primus.
£200 - £300

R19-134353
Plaque
280mm
Inscription with a Greek dedication to Good Fortune for the preservation of the emperors Septimius Severus and his son Caracalla.
£6,000 - £8,000

R19-129986
Diploma Fragment
71mm x 67mm
Sheet bronze diploma fragment issued by the Emperor Severus Alexander.
£1,000 - £1,500

R19-134016
Military Plaque
79mm
Inscribed for Lucius Vibius.
£400 - £600

R20-0101
Bell
54mm
Typical Roman shape.
Remains of the iron clapper.
Even colour.
£30 - £40

R20-0102
Bell
52mm
Remains of the iron clapper.
Patina a little ragged.
£30 - £40

R20-0103
Bell
54mm
Remains of the iron clapper.
Patina a little patchy.
£30 - £40

R20-0104
Bell
60mm
Good even patina. Remains of
the iron clapper.
£40 - £60

R20-0201
Bell
50mm
Bronze openwork bell.
Triangular cut-out shapes.
£50 - £80

R21-0101
Spoon
200mm
'Rat's tail' handle, flat
spatula-like bowl.
Even patina.
£60 - £80

R21-40218
Patera
345mm
Ram's head handle.
£2,000 - £3,000

R21-142761
Wine Strainer
220mm
Handle with fawn-head finial.
£300 - £400

R21-0201
Silver Spoon
146mm
Classical style. Light facetted
decoration at the shoulders.
Perfect condition.
£300 - £400

R21-0202
Silver Spoon
132mm
Rare silver spoon with
inscription in the bowl. Slight
damage.
From £500

R21-0301
Skillet
214mm
Complete and undamaged.
From £600

R21-131046
Silver Wine Strainer
218mm
With traces of gilding.
£1,500 - £2,000

R21-0302
Patera Handle
138mm
Very strong detail.
Ram's head. Smooth,
even patination.
£400 - £600

R21-0303
Silver Cup
100mm
With ring suspender;
military type.
£300 - £400

R21-0304
Patera Handle
109mm
Ram's head type,
horns to the sides.
£50 - £80

R21-0305
Oil Lamp
120mm
Volute scroll nozzle, loop
handle and crescentic rear
plaque.
£200 - £300

R21-0306
Silver Swan-Necked Spoon
200mm
Spike handle and scrolled openwork junction.
£200 - £300

R21-0307
Jug Handle
114mm
Bacchus-mask type with arms extending along the rim of the jug.
£120 - £180

R21-133365
Situla
190mm
Handle with central
Herculean knot,
terminals with scrolls
and open attachment
loops.
£1,500 - £2,000

R21-133507
Dish Fragment
163mm
Gladiator scene with
lion.
£150 - £200

R21-133509
Dish Fragment
95mm
Hercules with a
boar slung over his
shoulders.
£150 - £200

R21-133506
Dish Fragment
155mm
Combat scene.
£150 - £200

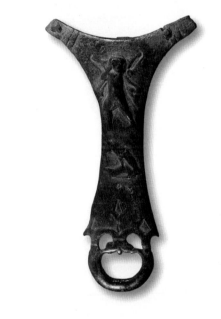

R21-144840
Patera Handle
147mm
Nude winged figure
above a perching bird.
£100 - £150

R21-166149
Vessel Handle
105mm
With CIPIPOLI
maker's stamp.
£60 - £80

R21-163380
Jug with Mask
260mm
Handle with Juno holding a goose to her chest and a facing putto mask.
From £10,000

R21-162316
Bowl Fragment
120mm
Image of brick hearth with flames.
£100 - £150

R21-166297
Amphora Handle
155mm
Stamped 'HISPSAENI' followed by a laurel leaf; used to transport olive oil.
£60 - £80

R21-158360
Jug
140mm
Oinochoe type.
£1,000 - £1,500

R21-170993
Samian Ware
Beaker
165mm
Hunting scene with
hound and hare,
restored.
£4,000 - £6,000

R21-0308
Vessel Handle
120mm
Two lozengiform plates with hooks below, curved handle with slots.
£60 - £80

R21-0309
Military Vessel
320mm
A cast cooking pan with a deep bowl and flat-section handle.
£200 - £300

R21-0310
Patera Handle
120mm
A hollow-cast handle with flared inner end, ribbed shaft and ram-head finial.
£50 - £80

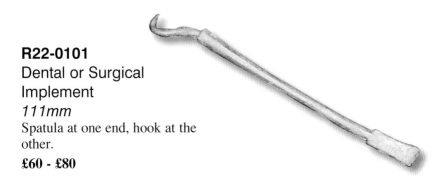

R22-0101
Dental or Surgical
Implement
111mm
Spatula at one end, hook at the
other.

£60 - £80

R22 153450
Medical Situla
145mm
Arched handle

£400 - £600

R22-0105
Medical Implement
159mm
Smooth, even surface.
Undamaged.
£60 - £80

R22-0106
Forceps *135mm*
Very rare forceps with
an inscription.
From £500

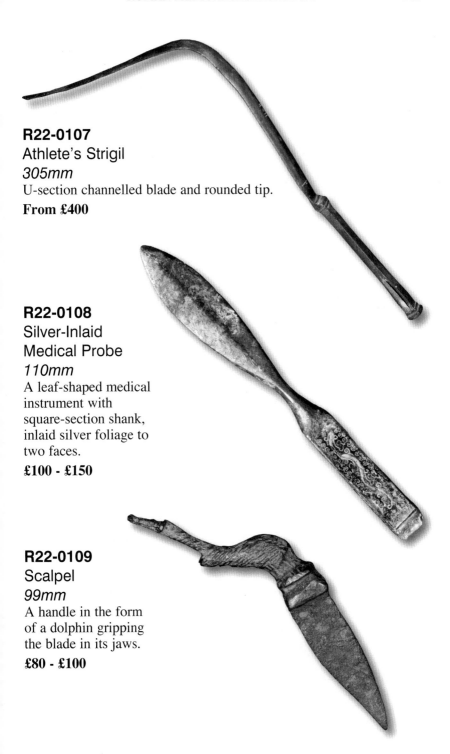

R22-0107
Athlete's Strigil
305mm
U-section channelled blade and rounded tip.
From £400

R22-0108
Silver-Inlaid
Medical Probe
110mm
A leaf-shaped medical
instrument with
square-section shank,
inlaid silver foliage to
two faces.
£100 - £150

R22-0109
Scalpel
99mm
A handle in the form
of a dolphin gripping
the blade in its jaws.
£80 - £100

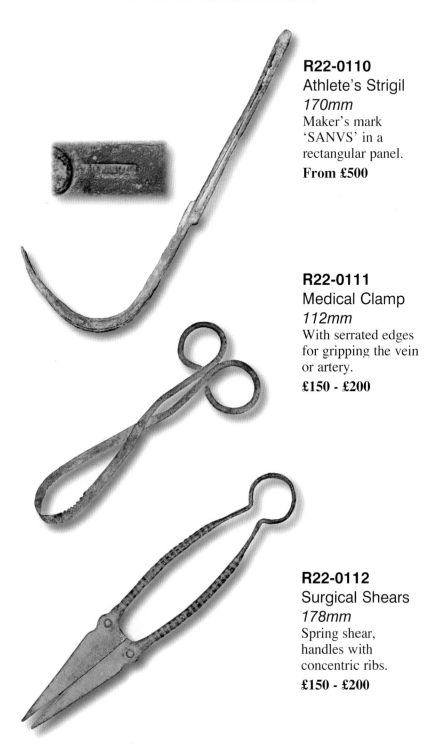

R22-0110
Athlete's Strigil
170mm
Maker's mark
'SANVS' in a
rectangular panel.
From £500

R22-0111
Medical Clamp
112mm
With serrated edges
for gripping the vein
or artery.
£150 - £200

R22-0112
Surgical Shears
178mm
Spring shear,
handles with
concentric ribs.
£150 - £200

R23-38970
Knuckle Bone Gaming Pieces
27mm - 30mm
Legionary for use in the game of knuckle bones.

£150 - £200

R23-0102
Gaming Piece
22mm
A reclining female with hands on her hips, head tilted, legs drawn up to reveal oversized genitals.

£150 - £200

R23-0103
Dice
14mm
Punched dots to each face.

£40 - £60

R24-0101
Diploma Fragment
35mm
With listing of witnesses in four lines, IVLIAN ONMISS POST
-]ASIV[. And on the other face an inscription in six lines [ ]
TIISDIVA / [ ]QVAST OST / INCVLIAS / O[ ]QIVLI ILISNVMI /
.F.CORNEL. Rare.
£150 - £200

R24-0102
Lead Curse Tablet
30mm
Folded lead plate with a curse written on
it, edges folded over.
From £50

R25-0102
Votive Axe
31mm
Decoration on the blade. Good patina.
£40 - £60

R25-0103
Votive Axe
27mm
Socketted style. Patina a little patchy.
£40 - £60

R25-0104
Votive Dagger
32mm
Even patina. Rare.
From £80

R25-0105
Votive Axe
43mm
Typical style. A little
nibbled on the blade.
£40 - £60

R25-0109
Votive Axe
33mm
Decorated. Simple style.
£40 - £60

R25-0107
Votive Axe
35mm
Decorated. Even
patination.
£50 - £80

R25-0108
Votive Axe
37mm
Surface a little rough.
Large size.
£40 - £60

R99-0201
Lifesize Thumb
115mm
Life-size bronze thumb.
Good detail. A little pitting
on the surface. Probably
from a life-size statue.
From £300

R99-0301
Mirror Back with Pan
60mm dia
Silver mirror depicting Pan
embracing a wood nymph.
Good detail.
From £2,000

R99-0401
Casket Leg with Lion's
Head & Paw
72mm
Good detail. Dark even patina.
£80 - £100

R99-0402
Casket Leg
55mm
Good detail. Winged
eagle's claw.
£40 - £60

R99-0501
Fragment
with Inscription
70mm
Piece of bronze bar with
inscription.
£40 - £60

R24-75781
Lead Curse Tablet
26mm
With four lines of
cursive script, one line
to reverse.
£400 - £600

R99-0701
Enamelled Stud
19mm
With enamel-filled
keystone cells.
£50 - £80

R99-0801
Lead Coffin Plate
800mm
With ropework lines in diamonds and triangles
with a row of small urns along the top border.
£300 - £400

R99-0802
Lead Casket
Plate
385mm
End panel from
a funerary
casket, depicting
the exterior of a
temple.
£300 - £400

R24-141291
Incense Shovel
255mm
Batillum with raised edges.
£400 - £600

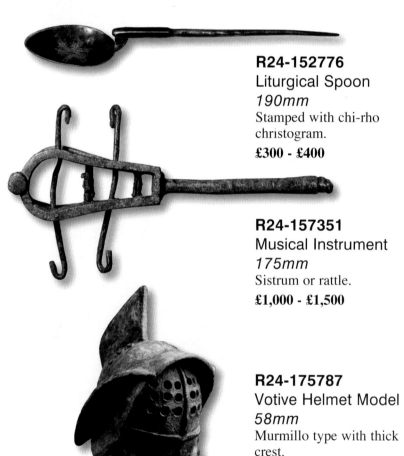

R24-152776
Liturgical Spoon
190mm
Stamped with chi-rho
christogram.
£300 - £400

R24-157351
Musical Instrument
175mm
Sistrum or rattle.
£1,000 - £1,500

R24-175787
Votive Helmet Model
58mm
Murmillo type with thick
crest.
£5,000 - £8,000

R24-162896
Votive Plaque
95mm
Bust of the goddess
Cybele.
£1,500 - £2,000

R24-40319
Votive Altar
28mm
With enamel detailing.
£300 - £400

R24-141326
Minerva Plaque
115mm
Repoussé image of
Minerva in profile wearing
a crested helmet and
draped garment, leaping
lion below.
£150 - £200

R24-144679
Venus Head Mount
68mm
Hair tied at the brow with
a spray of leaves.
£600 - £800

R24-152771
Bust Mount
53mm
Bust of the god Asclepius.
£300 - £400

R99-175764
Decorative Chain
560mm
Some links inlaid with
plaited gold wire.
£600 - £800

R99-132800
Appliqué Die
81mm
Bust of Pan type.
£600 - £800

R99-169265
Candelabrum
1300mm
Stand with floral finial,
female theatre masks.
£6,000 - £8,000

R99-178186
Strigil and
Balsamarium
30mm – 225mm
Bronze toilet set for an
athlete.
£500 - £800

R99-64758
Military Diploma
Section
150mm
Text to both faces, fixing
hole to one corner.
£1,000 - £1,500

R99-134649
Oil Lamp
180mm
Panther-shaped handle.
£600 - £800

R99-130863
Oil Lamp
155mm
Bust of the satyr Silenus.
£2,000 - £3,000

R99-164688
Stamp
59mm
£400 - £600

R99-164689
Stamp
51mm
£400 - £600

R99-164690
Stamp
46mm
£400 - £600

R99-0901
Lead Coin Forger's Mould Group
33-40mm
A group of casting moulds for denarius
coins and blanks.
£60 - £80

R99-1001
Military Purse
110mm
A hollow-cast bronze mount with
ribbed outer surface, punched
ornament; lugs for attachment to a belt.
From £1,000

THE ANGLO-SAXON PERIOD

The end of Roman Britain was caused by a variety of factors including a severe economic downturn, successive plagues, revolts and disturbances. With Roman power gone, the coast of Britain was at the mercy of a number of neighbouring peoples: Picts to the north of the Wall, Hiberni from Ireland and Germanic peoples from across the North Sea. Germanic incursions into the Empire were well under way by the 3rd century AD, and culminated in the eventual collapse of the Empire with the sacking of Rome by the Goths in 410 AD. Most of these warriors had already seen service as mercenaries and auxiliaries in the Roman army, and were familiar with its weaknesses.

The groups which attacked Britain included the Angles, Saxons, Jutes and Frisians, all from parts of the coastland stretching from Jutland to the mouth of the Rhine. They brought new technologies with them, new ways of building houses and managing livestock, new shipbuilding traditions, new social organisations and a new language – English. The 5th and 6th centuries saw the establishment of small-scale communities and the rise of warlords who overran their neighbours – British or Anglo-Saxon – and combined small communities into wider territories. By the early 7th century, a Christian mission arrived in Kent (in 597 AD, the very year that St. Columba, the Irish missionary, died on Iona) and began the work of conversion; the tale is recorded in a later document by the Northumbrian monk, Bede. Anglo-Saxon society developed from its Germanic Iron Age warlord-and-retainers roots into a relatively stable group of kingdoms, each with a kingly family and central stronghold.

The 7th century was thus a period of immense change. The church brought the institutions associated with Christianity and a reverence for the book (the Bible) as well as a widespread use of literacy. The Anglo-Saxons previously used an alphabet called 'runic' which was not suitable for large-scale record-keeping. Coinage was introduced – no coins had been struck in Britain since the mid-4th century – in order to facilitate tax-gathering and the exchange of wealth; some coins have runic legends and some have Roman, or a mix of the two. Access to literacy allowed accurate and detailed record keeping, and thus taxation came to replace tribute-taking as the principal source of royal wealth. Tribute was imposed on leaders by their overlords – supra-regional kings such as Penda of Mercia in the Midlands or Redwald of East Anglia, the most likely candidate for the Sutton Hoo ship-burial. The Anglo-Saxons met a challenge in the later wave of Scandinavian migrants – the Vikings – but the Anglo-Saxon character of England was not radically altered until the 11th century, the Mediaeval period.

The wealth of the Anglo-Saxon kingdoms was often immense, and they regularly used gold to demonstrate this. Items of gold are not uncommon in Anglo-Saxon contexts, and bronze castings were often gilded using a highly dangerous technique involving mercury. Garnets and other stones were used to adorn weapons and jewellery, and finely made glass items. Grave-goods expressed wealth and generosity – a statement by the mourners intended to impress their peers, no doubt – and the graves of women are usually better stocked than those of men (according to the range of materials that survive).

Many kinds of Anglo-Saxon items are collected, including swords and their fittings, spearheads, shield fittings, buckles and fasteners, glass and amber beads, hairpins and wrist-clasps, brooches and pendants. Greenlight publish a series of books by Brett Hammond on the identification of these objects:

British Artefacts vol.1 - Early Anglo-Saxon,
British Artefacts vol.2 - Middle Saxon & Viking,
British Artefacts vol.3 - Late Saxon, Late Viking & Norman.

All available from www.greenlightpublishing.co.uk

A03-0302
Spearhead
366mm
Herringbone pattern to
the blade and notched
socket mouth.
£100 - £150

A04-149133
Gold Sword Fitting
18mm
Sword 'pyramid' with inset
garnets.
From £10,000

A03-0301
Spearhead Mount
18mm
Gilded, raised running animal,
extensions to the lower edge.
£150 - £200

A05-0103
Iron Shield Boss
170mm
Four rivet holes.
One rivet remaining.
Unusual spike in the
centre. Good state of
preservation.
£300 - £400

A05-0101
Iron Shield Boss
120mm
Three rivets
remaining. Slight
break on one
edge. Good state
of preservation.
£150 - £200

A04-0102
Pommel Cap
45mm
Pommel cap from a sword handle. One fixing eye broken.
£60 - £80

A04-0103
Iron Sword
835mm
In good state of preservation. Rare and complete.
From £800

A04-176319
Inscribed Pommel
17mm
Pommel or bolster inscribed 'EA :'; 'DPIN', 'EME', 'EEIT' (Edwin made me).
£4,000 - £6,000

A04-0202
Knife Pommel
15mm
Gilding intact. Face in the centre.
£300 - £400

A04-123531
Sword Pommel
39mm
Silver-gilt with insignia.
£3,000 - £4,000

A04-0301
Sword Pommel
55mm
Surface a little ragged.
Patina patchy.
£200 - £300

A04-0302
Sword Pommel
60mm
Even patina. Smooth
surface.
£200 - £300

A04-0303
Silver Inlaid
Pommel
100mm
Very large and heavy.
Intricate silver inlay
with niello.
Very rare.
From £6,000

A04-0304
Sword Pommel
Cap
22mm
Four leaf-shaped
panels, animals and
foliage.
£150 - £200

A04-0305
Dagger Chape
66mm
Extension bar, rider
and eagle motifs to
the triangular faces.
£120 - £180

A04-0306
Sword Pommel
27mm
A late style of
pommel with
seven lobes, in fine
condition.
£200 - £300

A04-0308
Sheath Mount
38mm
Extension bar, dense
foliage detail to the
rectangular faces.
£50 - £80

A05 60995
Shield Mount
40mm
Gilded bird design.
£500 - £800

A05 94686
Shield Mount
51mm
Gilded cross design.
£800 - £1,000

A06-0101
Silver Pin
58mm
Some of the gilding
remaining. Undamaged.
£150 - £200

A06-121764
Dress Pin
29mm diameter
Gilt, one of a set of three
pins.
£400 - £600

A06-148639
Dress Pin
66mm
Silver-gilt with glass eyes.
£600 - £800

A06-0104
Pin Head Silver
18mm
Three birds' heads holding
a ball. Most gilding
remaining.
£400 - £600

A06-0201
Pin
60mm
Ring-and-dot decoration on the
hexagonal head. Even patina.
£20 - £30

A06 90511
Runic Dress Pin
33mm
Seriffed runes with female
name 'Cnoþheru'.
From £10,000

A06-0303
Gilt Pin Head
93mm
Chip-carved
beasts and
punched dots.
From £1,000

A06-0304
Silver Pin-Connector
61mm
Two circular terminals
and central beast with
interlaced legs, neck and
tail; twisted wire hoop.
From £1,000

A06-0305
Gilt-Bronze Pin
Head
42mm
Drilled for use as a
pendant.
£150 - £200

A06-0306
Silver Pin Terminal
8mm
Beast-head with white
and blue glass eyes.
£300 - £400

A07-0101
Cruciform Brooch
138mm
Long brooch. Square head plate with decoration along the edges. Even patina.
£300 - £400

A07-0102
Cruciform Brooch
125mm
Long brooch. Complete and undamaged. Even patina.
£400 - £600

A07-0103
Cruciform Brooch
112mm
Long brooch. Surface a little pitted. Even patina.
£150 - £200

A07-0104
Bow Brooch
60mm
Cruciform style. Good,
even patina.
£80 - £100

A07-0105
Bow Brooch
75mm
Complete and
undamaged. Even patina.
£100 - £150

A07-0106
Cruciform Brooch
120mm
50% gilding remaining.
Broken in places.
£200 - £300

A07-0107
Cruciform Brooch
Fragment
35mm
Part of a cruciform brooch
showing a face. 50% gilding
remaining. Slight damage.
£50 - £80

A07-0108
Cruciform Brooch
30mm
Face in the centre. 50% of the
gilding remaining.
£100 - £150

A07-170301
Great Square-Headed
Brooch
120mm
Gilt bronze, great square-head
type.
From £2,000

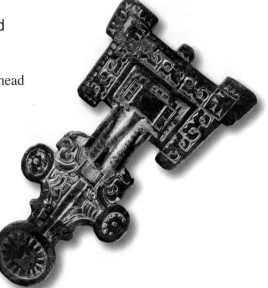

A07-0110
Cruciform Brooch
155mm
Complete with 90% of
the gilding remaining.
From £2,000

A07-0111
Cruciform Brooch
141mm
Small break at the foot.
Patina a little patchy.
£250 - £300

A07-177789
Great Square-
Headed Brooch
115mm
Gilt-bronze square-
headed brooch with
applied silver plaques.
From £2,000

A07-0113
Bow Brooch
102mm
Complete. Colour a
little uneven in places.
£100 - £150

A07-0114
Bow Brooch
121mm
Complete. Traces of iron on
the surface.
£200 - £300

A07 175684
Plate Brooch
44mm
Lozengiform type with hooked
catch.
£400 - £600

A07-0116
Bow Brooch
78mm
Surface a little rough. Signs of
pitting.
£50 - £80

A07-0117
Bow Brooch Pair
75mm
Matching pair with even,
smooth surface.
£300 - £400

A07-0118
Bow Brooch Pair
74mm
Matching pair. Surface a little uneven.
£200 - £300

A07-0119
Bow Brooch
75mm
Complete. Slight bend near the base of the foot.
£60 - £80

A07-0120
Bow Brooch
68mm
Patina patchy in places.
£80 - £100

A07-0121
Bow Brooch
69mm
Decorated over most of the surfaces.
£80 - £100

A07-129897
Bow Brooch
425mm
Square-headed type.
£150 - £200

A07-129868
Bow Brooch
43mm
Small square-headed type,
gilded.
£150 - £200

A07-0201
Bow Brooch
82mm
Small long brooch with
a square top plate. Some
corrosion on the surface.
£60 - £80

A07-155303
Great Square-Headed
Brooch
140mm
Gilt, great square-headed type.
From £8,000

A07-0203
Square-Headed Brooch
145mm
Complete and undamaged.
Gilding missing. Even patina.
From £2,000

A07-0204
Square-Headed Brooch
120mm
Over 75% of gilding
remaining. Well detailed.
Surface a little rough in places.
From £4,000

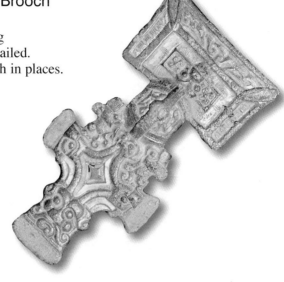

A07-157211
Plate Brooch
60mm
Gilt, lozenge type.
£300 - £400

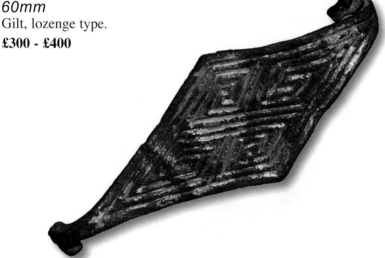

A07-0402
Interlaced Disc Brooch
28mm
Patina a little patchy. Pin missing.
£100 - £150

A07-132692
Disc Brooch
45mm
Band of cable ornament.
£500 - £700

A07-0208
Radiate-Headed Brooch
58mm
Smooth surface. Even patina. Highly decorated. Museum documented.
£60 - £80

A07-0301
Equal-Armed Brooch,
75mm
One half of an equal-arm brooch. Much gilding remaining. Broken at one end. Large size.
£200 - £300

A07-0403
Disc Brooch
34mm
Stones missing from recesses.
At least 50% gilding remains.
£200 - £300

A07-143077
Disc Brooch
35mm
Saucer type with central
cross.
£150 - £200

A07-0304
Equal-Armed Brooch
60mm
Complete with its pin
still in situ.
£60 - £80

A07-0305
S-Shaped Brooch
27mm
Double-headed with
garnets set in the eyes.
Rare.
£400 - £600

A07-0406
Disc Brooch
28mm
Beast looking back. Ring-and-dot decoration.
£100 - £150

A07-0407
Disc Brooch
28mm
Beast looking back. Patina patchy.
£100 - £150

A07-0408
Disc Brooch
30mm
Beast looking back. Sharp
detail. Even patina.
£150 - £200

A07-0409
Interlaced Brooch
29mm
Even patina. Sharp detail.
interlace design.
£150 - £200

A07-0410
Interlaced Brooch
29mm
Patina a little patchy. Weak detail.
£120 - £180

A07-0411
Plate Brooch
28mm
Smooth, even patina. Unusual type.
£120 - £180

A09-132693
Button Brooch
18mm
Button type with stylised
mask.
£200 - £300

A07-0413
Plate Brooch
50mm
Open-work design of a cross.
Surface a little uneven.
£300 - £400

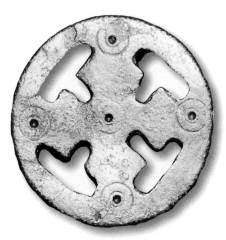

A07-0414
Disc Brooch
31mm
Fully gilded. Silvered around
the perimeter and in the centre.
Complete and undamaged.
£800 - £1,000

A07-129892
Button Brooch
16mm
Button type with male face.
£200 - £300

A07-0416
Gold Composite Brooch
32mm
Gold and silver with garnets.
Inlaid intricate design. Very
rare.
From £12,000

A07-0501
Button Brooch
21mm
Face in the centre is of typical
style. Much of the gilding
remains.
£150 - £200

A07-0502
Button Brooch
18mm
Face in the centre is of typical
style. Nearly all of the gilding
remains.
£180 - £240

A07-0503
Saucer Brooch
38mm
Gilt with most of the gilding
remaining. A little 'nibbled'
around the edge.
£300 - £400

A07-0504
Saucer Brooch
36mm
Gilt with scroll
decoration. A little 'nibbled'
around the edge.
One of a pair (see A07-0506).
£400 - £600

A07-0505
Saucer Brooch
27mm
Gilding virtually intact.
Remains of iron pin on reverse.
Decorated with
geometric patterns.
£800 - £1,000

A07-0506
Saucer Brooch
35mm
One of a pair (see A07-0504).
Edge a little ragged.
£300 - £400

A07-134844
Saucer Brooch
38mm
Five running scrolls ornament.
£300 - £400

A07-0508
Saucer Brooch
25mm
Sun-like face in the centre.
Most gilding remaining.
£500 - £700

A07-0509
Button Brooch
15mm
Face in the centre. Virtually
all gilding remaining.
£100 - £150

A07-0601
Annular Brooch
45mm
Edges a little ragged. Ring and
dot decoration. Bronze. Large
size.
£30 - £40

A07-0801
Lead Nummular Brooch
24mm
Plate brooch imitating a coin
obverse. Rare.
£200 - £300

A07-154004
Annular Brooch
45mm
Bronze with gilt decorative
band.
£600 - £800

A07-0803
Axe-Shaped Brooch
38mm
Unusual brooch, possibly an
adaptation of a larger item.
Border of interlace design.
Bronze fixing pin intact.
£400 - £600

A07-0804
Lead Nummular Brooch
38mm
Aethelred II style portrait. A
little damage. Rare.
£200 - £300

A07-134845
Brooch Die
47mm
Bronze patrix die to create
blanks for saucer brooches.
£600 - £800

A07-0806
Bird Brooch
30mm
Smooth surface and even
patina. Scarce type.
£150 - £200

A07-0807
Cruciform Brooch
140mm
Chip-carved ornament,
'florid cruciform' type.
From £3,000

A07-0808
Saucer Brooch
35mm
Pierced for re-use as a
pendant.
£600 - £800

A07-0809
Cruciform Brooch
131mm
Gilded with swastika in
centre of headplate.
From £2,000

A07-0810
Bow Brooch
94mm
With horse-head terminal and three
knops to the headplate.
£60 - £80

A07-0811
Cruciform Brooch
181mm
A large example with
sheet-silver panels.
From £2,000

A07-0812
Square-Headed Brooch
129mm
Florid type with human mask
on the footplate.
From £2,500

A07-0813
Bow Brooch
63mm
A small example lacking the knops, with flared footplate.

£30 - £40

A07-0814
Radiate Brooch
103mm
With seven knops on the headplate, each with an inset garnet.

£500 - £800

A07-0815
Square-Headed Brooch
39mm
A small example with birds' heads and a bull's head on the footplate.

£200 - £300

A07-0816
Great Square-Headed Brooch
137mm
With interlace bands on the headplate
and middle of the footplate.
From £3,000

A07-0817
Great Square-
Headed Brooch
129mm
Openwork detail
to the headplate,
frieze of animals to
the bow.
From £2,000

A07-0818
Composite Disc Brooch
36mm
Silvered bronze backplate and
repoussé silver sheet with knotwork
motif.
From £600

A07-0819
Saucer Brooch
40mm
Chip-carved beast and central stud.
From £800

A07-0820
Supporting Arm Brooch
47mm
Geometric decoration and gilt panels.
£300 - £400

A07-0821
Square-Headed Brooch
100mm
Human masks on the sides and bottom of the footplate.
From £2,000

A07-0822
Great Square-Headed Brooch
109mm
With human mask at the bottom of the
footplate, animal heads below the bow.
From £3,000

A07-0823
Button Brooch
17mm
With helmetted
head motif.
£200 - £300

A07-0824
Great Square-Headed Brooch
106mm
Traces of gilding in the chip-carved
ornament.
From £2,000

A07-0825
Bow Brooch
146mm
A large example with horse-head on the footplate.
£300 - £400

A07-0826
Quoit Brooch
43mm
Chip-carved detailing in four panels.
£200 - £300

A07-0827
Ansate Brooch
41mm
Scroll motifs to wings and bow.
£80 - £100

A07-0828
Cruciform Brooch
151mm
Chip-carved faces and
a horse-head to the
footplate.
From £500

A07-0829
Plate Brooch
65mm
With five 'legs'
around a central
roundel.
£600 - £800

A07-0830
Plate Brooch
57mm
'Basketwork' design.
From £1,500

A07-0831
Disc Brooch
27mm
Regardant beast
within a segmented
border; ring-and-dot
detailing.
£120 - £180

A07-0832
Disc Brooch
24mm
Champ-levé design
with enamel fill.
£150 - £200

A07-0833
Brooch Terminal
Fragment
42mm
Footplate terminal
with mask.
£60 - £80

A07-0834
Silvered Disc Brooch
59mm
Ring-and-dot detail and
punched dots forming a cross.
£100 - £150

A07-0835
Saucer Brooch
58mm
Florid cross to the centre,
chip-carved design.
From £1,500

A07-0836
Face Brooch
25mm
Disc brooch with facing
mask, similar to early
sceatta designs.
£80 - £100

A07-163440
Great Square-
Headed Brooch
134mm
'The Oving' great
square-headed
brooch.
£4,000 - £6,000

A07-159467
Radiate-
Headed Brooch
103mm
'The Melton
Mowbray' radiate-
headed bow
brooch.
£1,200 - £1,800

A07-0839
Cruciform
Brooch
168mm
Facing masks on
the footplate and
headplate.
From £3,000

A07-0840
Saucer Brooch
28mm
Five running spirals and a
central ring.

£400 - £600

A07-0841
Saucer Brooch Pair
47mm
With a deep flange,
chamfered inner ridge
with punched S-shaped
motifs, a band of decoration
surrounding a central boss.

£2,000 - £3,000

A08-0101
Pendant
34mm
Swastika design in the centre.
Suspension loop broken. Most
of the gilding remains. Rare.
£200 - £300

A08-129139
Silver Penny Pendant
21mm
Silver CRVX type penny of
Ethelred II by the moneyer
Eadmund.
£200 - £300

A08-0414
Silver-Gilt Pendant
29mm
Four knotwork panels and
a reserved cross.
£400 - £600

A08-0201
Silver Pendant
22mm
Fully gilded with the letters
LA/AG. Large suspension
loop. Cross design.
£400 - £600

A08-0301
Pendant Hanger
53mm
Four birds' heads with a
central chip-carved design.
Virtually all of the gilding
intact. Rare.
£200 - £300

A08-0302
Pendant Hanger
34mm
In the form of a crouching
animal. Gilded.
£150 - £200

A08-0416
Head Pendant
36mm
Male face with beard, crescent above the head.
£3,000 - £4,000

A08-0417
Pendant with
Tusk
46mm
Tusk preserved
close to the bronze
strip fitting.
£150 - £200

A08-0413
Bell-Shaped Pendant
51mm
'Bell' type with facing
mask.
From £600

A08-0404
Gold Pendant with Garnet
20mm
Dark garnet set in a gold mount. Complete and undamaged.
From £600

A08-0402
Gold Pendant with Shell & Garnet
28mm
Central garnet in a gold mount set on a white shell boss. Scroll filigree ornament. Damaged at lower edge.
From £3,000

A08-0406
Gold Pendant with Garnet
26mm
Set with a flat topped, large deep red garnet.
From £600

A08-0407
Gold Pendant
with Garnet
21mm
Set with a deep red, flat topped
garnet. Pendant complete and
undamaged.
From £1,000

A08-0415
Gold Cross Pendant
28mm
Hollow, formed from
gold wire, cells with
garnet cabochons.
From £6,000

A08-0409
Gold Coin Pendant
17mm
Gold coin formed into a
pendant.
From £1,200

A08-0418
Gold Pendant with
Garnet
13mm
With triangular garnet
insert, loop missing.
£400 - £600

A08-0411
Gold Spacer Pendant
20mm
Spacer from a necklace.
Slightly mis-shapen.
£300 - £400

A08-0412
Bell-Shaped Pendant
16mm
Miniature axehead with billeted
border.
£60 - £80

A08-0419
Gold Pendant with
Garnet
31mm
With garnet insert, ropework
border and cross.
£2,000 - £3,000

A08-0420
Gold Pendant with
Garnet
21mm
With pear-shaped garnet
insert.
£1,000 - £1,500

A08-0421
Gold Pendant with
Garnet
13mm
With triangular garnet
insert.
From £600

A09-0101
Mount with Garnet
23mm
Decorative mount with most of the gilding remaining. Garnet in the centre.

£500 - £800

A09-144870
Hanging Bowl Mount
38mm
Enamel and silver decoration.

£100 - £150

A09-0103
Equal-Armed Mount
57mm
Hatched box design in the centre with faces at each end. 30% gilding remaining.

£150 - £200

A09-0104
Zoomorphic Mount
31mm
Decorative mount. 50% gilding remaining.

£150 - £200

A09 135617
Casket Mount
36mm
Gilt, central cross motif
£200 - £300

A09-0106
Bird Mount
28mm
Most of the gilding remaining.
Complete and undamaged.
£400 - £600

A09-0107
Rectangular Mount
31mm
Zoomorphic moulded panels
and remains of enamel inlays.
No gilding remaining.
£150 - £200

A09-0108
Scabbard Mount
50mm
Gilded and silvered mount.
Probably from a scabbard.
£120 - £180

A09-0109
Pelta-Shaped
Mount
60mm
Most of the gilding
remains. Depicts two
entwined birds or
serpents. Complete and
undamaged.
£500 - £800

A09-0110
Bowl Mount
26mm
Tribrach pattern.
Silvery surfaces with traces of
red enamel.
£100 - £150

A09-0111
Disc Mount
30mm
Bronze mount with engraved
detail of two birds feeding on
branches, all within a border.
£300 - £400

A09-0112
Button Brooch
17mm
Most of the gilding remaining.
Chip-carved face in the centre.
£300 - £400

A09-154200
Casket Mount
34mm
Gilt-bronze, interlace and
animal ornament.
£400 - £600

A09-0114
Disc Mount
29mm
Stone missing from the centre.
Most of the gilding remaining.
A little pitting on the surface.
£500 - £800

A09-0115
Triangular-Shaped Mount
35mm
Fragment from a larger piece.
Edges a little ragged.
£80 - £100

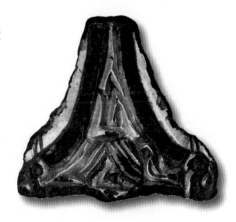

A09-175585
Irish Cross Mount
24mm
Insular style triquetra
knotwork motifs.
£200 - £300

A09-177520
Keystone Mount
32mm
Central polished domed
garnet and keystone garnets
surrounding.
£400 - £600

A09-31227
Applied Disc Brooch Pair
56mm - 60mm
Fragile condition.
£1,500 - £2,000

A09-117200
Mask Mount
35mm
Bearded head with
moustache.
£3,000 - £4,000

A09-129514
Bowl Mount Pair
75mm
Celtic design with the majority
of the enamel remaining.

From £20,000

A09-0120
Bird Mount
35mm
Fully gilded bird with curled beak.
£400 - £600

A09-0124
Disc Mount
39mm
Heavily gilded round mount. Cross separating four panels with foliate design.
£400 - £600

A09-0125
Bell-Shaped Mount
47mm
Heavy bronze bell-shaped mount. Most of the gilding remaining, loop missing.
£500 - £800

A09-136927
Mask Mount
39mm
Inset garnet cloisons in the
eyes, gilded.
£8,000 - £10,000

A09-136514
Mask Mount
21mm
Mask with bird-heads.
£150 - £200

A09-163974
Mask Mount
29mm
'The Nethergate' Anglo-Saxon
masked mount (finial from a
cruciform brooch).
£600 - £800

A09-0122
Square Mount
17mm
Small mount. Surface a little
pitted.
£80 - £100

A09-0131
Scabbard Mount
30mm
Iron with silver inlay and
niello. Rare.
£200 - £300

A09-0132
Disc Mount
44mm
Large chip-carved mount.
Slight damage on one edge.
£500 - £800

A09-154874
Head Mount
24mm
'The Bainton' gilt Woden
head appliqué.
£600 - £800

A09-133853
Rectangular Mount
45mm
Gilded with chip-carving.
£200 - £300

A09-0134
Wolf Mount
30mm
Possibly the top of a pin.
Unusual.
£100 - £150

A09-0136
Face Mount
34mm
Smooth, even green patina.
Good detail. See Sutton Hoo
Mound 17.
£400 - £600

A09-0137
Mount with Rock
Crystal
22mm
Rock crystal set into a
mount. Traces of gilding.
£100 - £150

A09-0138
Enamelled Hanging
Bowl Mount
61mm
Rare mount. Fully
enamelled in the form of a
bird.
£1,500 - £2,000

A09-0201
Silver Pyramid Mount
15mm
Garnet missing from the
top of pyramid. Triangular
recesses are gilded.
Undamaged. Rare.
£400 - £600

A09-0202
Silver Pyramid Mount
10mm
Small size with niello inlay.
£200 - £300

A09-0203
Mount with Silver Inlaid
Panels
60mm
Large mount with a beast's
head at each of the four
corners and with four inlaid
panels.
£1,500 - £2,000

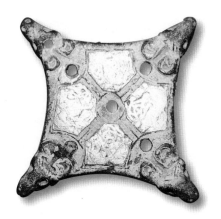

A09-0204
Silver Bird Mount
22mm
Undamaged with niello inlay.
Rare.
From £600

A09-0301
Mount with Cross
26mm
With facing mask and
ravens to the sides.
£400 - £600

A09-0302
Bell-Shaped Mount
36mm
With facing mask and
chip-carved animals.
£1,000 - £1,500

A09-0303
Lozenge-Shaped
Mount
29mm
Chip-carved with
central fylfot.
£200 - £300

A09-0304
Equal-Arm Mount
46mm
T-shaped ends and gilt
centre section with chip-
carved rosette.
£200 - £300

A09-0305
Mount with Garnet
22mm
Garnet insert and chip-
carved panels.
£80 - £100

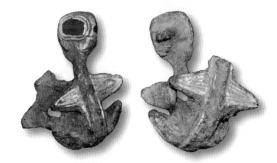

A09-0306
Zoomorphic Mount
34mm
With crouching figure,
chip-carved.
£600 - £800

A09-0307
Floral Mount
28mm
Trefoil motifs, chip-carved.
£150 - £200

A09-0308
Lozenge-Shaped Mount
30mm
Knotwork design with beasts, two pierced corners.
From £2,000

A09-0309
Silver Zoomorphic Mount
28mm
Beast-head with rosette panel.
£800 - £1,000

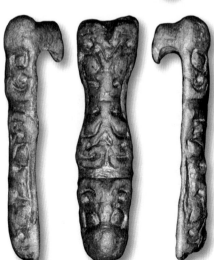

A09-0310
Zoomorphic Mount
60mm
Beast-head with ribbed detailing, pellet eyes.
£200 - £300

A09-0311
Disc Mount
42mm
Knotwork panel,
pierced for re-use.
From £800

A09-0312
Pyramid Mount
13mm
With inset garnet to the top.
£300 - £400

A09-0313
Equal-Arm
Mount
31mm
Chip-carved
beasts in each
rectangle.
£120 - £180

A09-0314
Rectangular Mount
60mm
Knotwork with facing
masks.
£1,000 - £1,500

A09-168710
Scabbard Mount
45mm
Gilt bronze with chip-
carved ornament.
£300 - £400

A09-0316
Silver Mount
21mm
With niello background.
£200 - £300

A09-0317
Masked Mount
77mm
From the tip of a
shield boss, chip-
carved.
£1,000 - £1,500

A09-0318
Bird Mount
36mm
Eagle type.
£1,000 - £1,500

A09-0319
Bird Mount
27mm
Chip-carved confronted
ravens.
£200 - £300

A09-0320
Disc Mount
31mm
Continuous knotwork
band, pierced for re-use
as a pendant.
£100 - £150

A09-0321
Silver Cross Mount
40mm
Cross with a beast on
each arm.

From £3,000

A09-45532
Interlaced Terminal
32mm
From a drinking horn.

£3,000 - £4,000

A09-0323
Disc Mount
44mm
Three panels with beasts
and central disc.

From £3,000

A09-0324
Silver Clad Mount
53mm
Runic text to both faces.
From £800

A09-0325
Sword Mount
24mm
Chip-carved beasts and
billetted bands.
£200 - £300

A09-0326
Disc Mount
31mm
Running knotwork band.
£300 - £400

A09-0327
Silver Book Mount
31mm
Knotwork beasts design
on a niello field.
£200 - £300

A09-0328
Cross Mount
38mm
Four beast-heads and a
central stud.
£300 - £400

A09-0329
Cross Mount
29mm
Quatrefoil with raised
knotwork centre.
£30 - £40

A09-0330
Disc Mount
32mm
Radiating arms and
scrolls with domed rivets.
£60 - £80

A09-0331
Disc Mount
22mm
Raised knotwork with
pellets.
£150 - £200

A09-0332
Bird Head Mount
16mm
Billetted body and curved
neck with beast-head
terminal.
£60 - £80

A09-35809
Bronze Die
76mm
Interlaced design.
£3,000 - £4,000

A09-0334
Shrine Roof Mount
105mm
From the top of a house-shrine; gilded knotwork panels and beast-heads.
From £10,000

A09-0335
Cross Mount
47mm
Tau cross with mask above, knotwork panels.
From £3,000

A09-0336
Triangular Mount
51mm
Chip-carved background and scrolled beast with spiral hip; decorative panel from a later lead weight.
From £2,000

A09-0337
Cross Mount
36mm
Chip-carved running scroll decoration.
£400 - £600

A09-0338
Silver Mount
28mm
Knotwork and plant motifs on a niello field.
£500 - £600

A09-0339
Zoomorphic Mount
25mm
Small tongue-shaped plaque with chip-carved beast.
£60 - £80

A09-0340
Rectangular Mount
27mm
Chip-carved beast motif.
£500 - £800

A09-0341
Pelta-Shaped Mount
33mm
Three-band knotwork motifs, bird-heads at the top.
£400 - £600

A09-0342
Pyramid Mount
14mm
Garnet and blue glass inserts; gridded backing foil exposed.
£120 - £180

A09-0343
Square Mount
34mm
Bands of knotwork and
central cell for a garnet
(absent).
£600 - £800

A09-0344
Silver Disc Mount
36mm
With central garnet and
three beasts.
From £1,500

A09-0345
Rectangular
Mount
25mm
With two square
garnets and chip-
carved beasts.
£800 - £1,000

A10-57899
Gold Ring
20mm
Hound's head motif.
From £10,000

A10-163172
Runic Ring Fragment
18mm
Silver, incised seriffed
runic text.
£1,500 - £2,000

A10-0101
Silver Ring
18mm
Typical form of twisted wire.
Undamaged.
£100 - £150

A10-0346
Silver Ring
11mm
With cross motif, niello-inlaid.
£150 - £200

A12-0101
Strap End
35mm
Interlaced design. Even patina.
£30 - £40

A12-0102
Strap End with Silver
Inlaid Panels
68mm
Large strap end. Panels of
silver inlay. Dark, smooth
patina.
£100 - £150

A12-0103
Strap End
29mm
Decorative design.
£30 - £40

A12-152692
Strap End
46mm
Silver inlaid with beast-head
finial.
£300 - £400

A12-0105
Strap End
38mm
Glass beads in the eyes (one
missing). Unusual fixing lug
on the underside. Even patina.
Silver rivets.
£200 - £300

A12-0106
Strap End
45mm
Banded silver inlay. Even
patina.
£150 - £200

A12-0107
Strap End
34mm
Inlaid panel of niello
decoration.
£50 - £80

A12-0108
Strap End
40mm
Inlaid panels of silver. Dark
patina.
£100 - £150

A12-0109
Strap End
38mm
Inlaid linear detail. Good
patina.
£100 - £150

A12-0110
Strap End
47mm
With silver inlay.
£40 - £60

A12-0111
Strap End
56mm
With traces of silver inlay.
Exaggerated ears. Even, dark
patina.
£100 - £150

A12-0112
Strap End
53mm
With silver panel in the centre
and silver inlay on each head.
Even patina. Rare.
£120 - £180

A12-0113
Strap End
39mm
With two enamel inserts. Dark,
even patina.
£40 - £60

A12-0114
Strap End
51mm
With zigzag decoration. Good
patina.
£30 - £40

A12-0115
Strap End
34mm
With beast design and enamel
inlay.
£40 - £60

A12-0116
Strap End
51mm
With silver inlay showing a
crude face. Even patina.
£40 - £60

A12-0117
Strap End
32mm
With inlaid silver scroll
patterns.
£120 - £180

A12-0118
Zoomorphic Strap End
58mm
Three moulded animal masks.
Even patina.
£60 - £80

A12-0119
Lugged Strap End
40mm
Protruding lug on the
underside. Even patina.
£60 - £80

A12-0120
Strap End
42mm
With an inset panel of gold.
Even green patina.
£120 - £180

A12-0121
Strap End with Runes
45mm
Glass stones in the eyes. Runic
inscription on the
underside. Slight pitting on the
surface. Very rare.
From £800

A12-154965
Strap End
20mm
Gilt, knotwork motif.
£300 - £400

A12-168670
Strap End
74mm
Winchester Style acanthus-
leaf ornament.
£300 - £400

A12-0213
Strap End
41mm
Punched crescents
and narrow beast-head
terminal.
£20 - £30

A12-0214
Strap End
35mm
Beast-head terminal and
beast reserved against
white filled background.
£20 - £30

A12-0215
Strap End
21mm
Small, D-shaped with large rivets,
made from two soldered plates.
£200 - £300

A12-0126
Strap End
38mm
Single rivet. Smooth, even patina.
£30 - £40

A12-0128
Strap End
44mm
Good, smooth patina. Some of the silver inlay damaged.
£200 - £300

A12-0201
Strap End
45mm
Silver with niello inlay. Slight fracture across the centre. Rare.
£800 - £1,000

A12-0202
Silver Strap End
43mm
Silver Trewhiddle style beasts and interlace design. Undamaged. Rare.
From £800

A12-0204
Silver Strap End
46mm
Silver with glass bead eyes.
Good detail. Undamaged.
From £800

A12-0205
Silver Strap End
32mm
Small size with niello inlay.
Complete.
£400 - £600

A12-0206
Silver Strap End
40mm
Average size and complete.
£400 - £600

A12-0207
Silver Strap End
40mm
With full gilding and
undamaged.
£400 - £600

A12-0209
Silver Strap End
43mm
Interlaced beast on a
niello field, two domed
rivets.
£400 - £600

A12-33594
Silver Strap End
36mm
Crude zoomorphic design.
£300 - £400

A12-0210
Strap End
35mm
With notched border and
beast-head terminal.
£180 - £240

A12-0211
Strap End
45mm
Silver appliqué panels.
£40 - £60

A12-0208
Strap End
42mm
Faux beaded-wire beast.
£40 - £60

A12-19776
Silver Strap End
40mm
Trewhiddle design.
£200 - £300

A12-0203
Silver Strap End
Fragment
30mm
Broken. Good detail.
£120 - £180

A12-0212
Strap End
32mm
Knotwork motifs and a
beast-head terminal.
£30 - £40

A12-0301
Buckle with Silver Inlay
70mm
Openwork belt-plate decorated with a silvered centre motif. Complete and undamaged.
£180 - £240

A12-0302
Buckle with Glass Inlay
65mm
Incised decoration on the plate with glass inlay in one of the recesses. Good, even patina.
£80 - £100

A12-0303
Scorpion Buckle
44mm
In the form of a scorpion. Complete and undamaged. Ring and dot decoration. Good, even patina. Rare.
£150 - £200

A12-0308
Buckle with Plate
75mm
Large size. Two fantastic animals in the centre panel. Complete.
£400 - £600

A12-0305
Buckle with Garnets
25mm
Damaged. Surface a little rough. Three flat garnets remaining.
£100 - £150

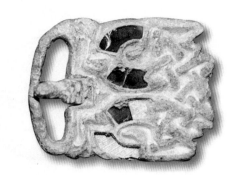

A12-0311
Triangular-Shaped Buckle
92mm
Very large buckle. Patina patchy in places. Two studs remaining.
£100 - £150

A12-0312
Buckle with Plate
50mm
Traces of iron around the pin.
£80 - £100

A12-0401
Buckle with Garnet
38mm
Bowed frame type. Garnet inset into the pin.
£50 - £80

A12-0403
Silver Buckle with Rivets
32mm
Silver buckle with rivets from the plate.
£80 - £100

A12-0501
Buckle Plate
32mm
Strap end plate. Trewhiddle Style beast. Good, even patina.
£150 - £200

A12-0502
Buckle Plate
41mm
A face in the centre. Rough surface.
£150 - £200

A12-0601
Buckle Tongue
25mm
'Shield-on-tongue' type with inset garnet and chequered cells.
£100 - £150

A13-0201
Silver Hooked Tag
45mm
Three panels with a beast in each one. Intricate design.
From £800

A13-0301
Silver Hooked Tag
29mm
D-shaped plate with reserved beast on a niello field.
£500 - £800

A13-134978
Gusset Plate
50mm
Gilded, gusset plate from a wrist-clasp set, slightly concave sides terminating in a stylised beast's head with roundel eyes.
£150 - £200

A13-0303
Wrist Clasp Set
29mm
Pair of two-part clasps
with notched bands.
£100 - £150

A13-0304
Wrist Clasp
40mm
Panel with facing mask
and chip-carved beasts.
£80 - £100

A13-0305
Wrist Clasp Plaque
52mm
Gusset plate from a
wrist-clasp set.
£150 - £200

A13-0306
Wheel Stud
24mm
Chip-carved radiating spokes,
peg to the reverse.
£100 - £150

A13-130199
Wrist Clasp Pair
43mm / 44mm
Row of leaf-shaped panels
to the rear edge with incised
borders.
£60 - £80

A13-139508
Gilt Wrist Clasp
32mm
Pelletted borders on the loops.
£80 - £100

A13-162244
Garment Hook
28mm
Silver, niello field and beast
with interlace.
£800 - £1,000

A14-0101
Tweezers
with Loop
61mm
Patina flaking a little.
£40 - £60

A14-0102
Tweezers
with Loop
80mm
Decorated. Good, even
patina.
£50 - £80

A14-0103
Tweezers
70mm
Decorated. Good,
even patina.
£40 - £60

A15-136526
Horse Harness
Pelta Mount
35mm
Gilt bronze with
Style I motif.
£200 - £300

A15-0301
Harness Mount
39mm
Chip-carved animals,
pierced at each end.
£600 - £800

A15-0302
Harness Mount
33mm
Pelta-shaped with chip-
carved beast.
£150 - £200

A16-0301
Seal Matrix
17mm
Facing intaglio mask with
text MOH and HIA.
From £500

A17-0101
Key
38mm
Large plain disc handle and simple wards. Good, even patina.
£80 - £100

A17-0102
Key
50mm
Suspension loop at top. Even patina.
£120 - £180

A17-0103
Key
42mm
Typical form. Good even patina.
£80 - £120

A17-0104
Lyre Key
62mm
Tuning key for a lyre or similar musical instrument. Decorated on the face. Rare.
£120 - £180

A17-0302
Casket Key
55mm
Elliptical plate
and small loop.
£50 - 80

A17-0303
Key
39mm
Looped bow with ring-
and-dot detailing.
£150 - £200

A17-0301
Key
40mm
With openwork cross.
£80 - £100

A18-0101
Lead Weight
32mm
Gilt-bronze insert.
£150 - £200

A21-134154
Bucket with
Handle
210mm
Incised ornament.
£400 - £600

A21-0101
Decorated Bucket
220mm
Bronze handle, hoops
and strips mounted on
a modern stave-built
reproduction.
From £600

A21-0101
Openwork Bowl
Mount
82mm
With bird-head hook,
central void.

£400 - £600

A21-35825
Bowl Mount
41mm
In the shape of an
enamelled bird.

£300 - £400

A99-0301
Limestone Cross-Shaft
800mm
Re-used section with
re-shaping.
From £4,000

A21-0201
Girdle Hangers
140mm
Pair of girdle hangers, one slightly bent but otherwise complete.
£200 - £300

A21-0202
Girdle Hanger
127mm
Decorated all along its surface.
£80 - £100

THE VIKING PERIOD

The 'Viking period' in Britain officially begins in 793 AD when a group of raiders sacked the monastery of Lindisfarne, off the Northumbrian coast, and shocked the four large Anglo-Saxon kingdoms. Previous minor raids and looting expeditions had focussed on markets and towns – and were a fact of life in mediaeval Europe – but the impunity with which a holy church could be sacked and destroyed indicated that this was a new kind of threat.

The word 'Viking' is rather a job description than an ethnic marker– like 'pirate' or 'highwayman', a Viking could be of any group but the most common intruders in Britain were Danish and Norwegian. Viking activity centred on the North Sea and the Baltic, with occasional forays into France and Spain, or down the great rivers of eastern Europe to Byzantium (modern Istanbul, then a bastion of Christianity).

Through organising large groups of able men and providing them with transport, Viking leaders were able to bring overwhelming force to bear on small communities, and to take whatever plunder they wanted – gold and silver, textiles, skins and slaves being the most favoured. One by one the Anglo-Saxon kingdoms fell, unable to form alliances in time to meet the threat of lightning raids. East Anglia and Northumbria, with their long North Sea coasts, were overrun and settled by farmers in search of new opportunities. Mercia – the heartland of the English Midlands - was toppled. It fell to the kingdom of Wessex in the south to find a way to deal with them. The king who did most to stem the tide of Viking advances was Alfred, an able statesman and ruler who realised that military victories and defeats were always temporary: he managed to come to terms with the chief Viking leader, Guthrum, and eventually struck a deal with him which ceded some territory in the east. From that point onwards, the West Saxons under Alfred's son (Edward) and grandson (Athelstan) undertook to reconquer the Viking-dominated territories; Athelstan became the sole King of England after a hefty defeat of his Irish and Norse foes at the battle of Brunanburh in 937AD. And in time, a Danish warlord was able to outfight the Anglo-Saxon King Edmund and take the throne for himself – Knut Svensson, known to us as King Canute. Knut proved an able and far-sighted king, but short-lived. His successor – Edward the Confessor – was of the old Wessex royal line but had been brought up in Normandy in exile among his mother's people. This royal debt to the Normans later proved disastrous for England.

Identifiable Viking artefacts are not plentiful in Britain, but are much prized. The problem is that very few objects are found which can be said to belong to the 'Vikings' – a lot of their wealth was plundered and therefore is Irish or Mercian or Frankish in character. Distinctive types of sword fittings can be identified, as well as objects with Scandinavian stylistic motifs such as stirrup-mounts. Women's jewellery items, such as tortoise brooches and trefoil brooches, indicate the settlement of Danish brides in England. Many Viking period items are products of a hybrid Anglo-Scandinavian culture. Greenlight publish books by Brett Hammond on the identification of these objects: British Artefacts vol.2 - Middle Saxon & Viking, British Artefacts vol.3 - Late Saxon, Late Viking & Norman.

V01-114435
Axehead
160mm
Silver inlaid
dragons.
£6,000 - £8,000

V03-130257
Impacted
Spearhead
330mm
Point curled under
impact.
£150 - £200

V04-162257
Scabbard Chape
57mm
Openwork Jellinge
style ornament.
£600 - £800

V04-151832
Sword with Silver-Inlaid Hilt
915mm
Viking or Anglo-Scandinavian type, inlaid
chequer pattern.
£8,000 - £10,000

V04-162254
Sword Blade and Chape
220mm
Iron sword-blade fragment
with bronze chape attached.
£1,000 - £1,500

V04-170402
Scabbard Chape
66mm
Borre style decoration and bear
masks.
£600 - £800

V04-176586
Sword Pommel
55mm
Five-lobed type.
£200 - £300

V04-131542
Sword Pommel
75mm incl stand
Applied bands of
silver wire.
£800 - £1,000

V04-129150
Sword Chape
80mm
Ringerike style
design.
£1,500 - £2,000

V04-175186
Sword
915mm
Iron sword with five-lobed pommel.

£6,000 - £8,000

V04-175187
Sword
920mm
Iron sword with five-lobed pommel and boat-shaped quillons.

£6,000 - £8,000

V04-31539
Sword
970mm
Pattern-welded construction.

£6,000 - £8,000

V04-0301
Scabbard Chape
54mm
Interlaced tendrils
and leaves, flared
corners.
£400 - £600

V04-0302
Sword Pommel
57mm
With three lobes,
ring-and-dot motifs.
£800 - £1,000

V04-0303
Silver Sword
Pommel
48mm
With three lobes and
two flanges to the
sides.
£400 - £600

V04-0304
Sword Pommel
58mm
'Brazil nut' type.
£600 - £800

V07-42257
Box Brooch
44mm
Drum-shaped brooch with four raised arms and central knop to the upper face, knotwork bands to the edge.
£8,000 - £10,000

V07-45951
Plate Brooch
36mm
Urnes style.
£3,000 - £4,000

V07-166951
Trefoil Brooch
65mm
Three radiating flanges each with a facing male mask.
£4,000 - £6,000

V07-172065
Disc Brooch
30mm
Gilt, Borre Style ornament.
£400 - £600

V07-100044
Plate Brooch
58mm
Urnes style.
£1,500 - £2,000

V07-0106
Cloisonné Disc
Brooch
28mm
Praying figure in the
centre. Scarce type.
£500 - £800

V07-0108
Disc Brooch
25mm
Beast facing back.
£180 - £240

V07-0109
Enamelled Disc Brooch
28mm
Red enamelled face in the centre.
Rare type.
£150 - £200

V07-0201
Trefoil Brooch
42mm
Incised decoration.
Even patina.
£400 - £600

V07-0202
Trefoil Brooch
48mm
Interlaced design.
Even patina.
From £3,000

V07-0203
Silver Trefoil Brooch
50mm
Interlaced design is quite worn.
Probably three beasts. Traces
of iron on the reverse. Rare in
silver.
From £2,000

V07-0204
Trefoil Brooch
43mm
Interlaced design.
Even patina.
From £2,000

V07-0301
Eagle Brooch
30mm
Light decoration. Pin missing.
Even green patina.
£100 - £150

V07-0302
Silver Bird Brooch
38mm
Pin intact. Most of the gilding
remaining. Very rare.
From £1,500

V07-0303
Zoomorphic Brooch
50mm
Very rare brooch. Rotate
it to see different beasts
depicted. Even patina.
£400 - £600

V07-0102
Cloisonné Disc Brooch
25mm
Cross design in the centre.
All seven lugs remain, five
of which still have their glass
insets. Pin and catchplate
intact. Traces of gilding.
£200 - £300

V07-0305
Bird Brooch
35mm
Dove supporting a cross
on its wing.
£200 - £300

V07-0306
Trefoil Brooch
55mm
Boss to each arm and one in
the centre, knotwork designs.
From £1,000

V07-0307
Cloisonné Disc Brooch
25mm
Champ-levé enamel and seven
small lobes to the rim.
£150 - £200

V07-0308
Cloisonné Brooch
42mm
Champ-levé enamel imitating
garnet cellwork.
£200 - £300

V07-0309
Bird Brooch
39mm
Dove with cross, incised detailing.
£300 - £400

V07-0310
Horseman Brooch
31mm
Horseman facing a standing cloaked figure with a shield.
£400 - £600

V07-0312
Cockerel Brooch
42mm
Detailed plumage and radiating comb to the head.
£300 - £400

V07-160819
Disc Brooch
29mm
Raised Borre Style decoration.
£200 - £300

V07-0103
Cloisonné Disc Brooch
24mm
Cross design in the centre.
No protruding lugs. Traces of
gilding. Pin missing.
£150 - £200

V07-0314
Disc Brooch
36mm
With Borre Style knotwork
motif.
£40 - £60

V08-0101
Figural Pendant
38mm
In the form of a woman
(Valkyrie) holding
a spear and shield.
Undamaged. Rare.
From £1,000

V08 176655
Erotic Pendant
34mm
Embracing couple with
triquetra and coil motifs.
£1,200 - £1,800

V08-0301
Silver Pendant
21mm
Beast-head with niello detail.
£200 - £300

V08-0302
Silver Pendant
29mm
Thor's hammer type.
From £500

V09-0101
Stirrup Mount
46mm
Single central head of a bat-like creature. Even patina.
£100 - £150

V15-146537
Stirrup Mount
56mm
Openwork with beast-heads.
£200 - £300

V15-147129
Stirrup Mount
41mm
Interlaced serpent design with head above the lower edge.
£400 - £600

V09-0104
Stirrup Mount
50mm
Howling beast in the centre.
Surface a little pitted.
£200 - £300

V09-0105
Stirrup Mount
50mm
Howling beast in the centre.
Even patina.
£300 - £400

V15-134988
Stirrup Mount
56mm
Palmette and bear's mask
type.
£200 - £300

V15-136522
Stirrup Mount
54mm
Tendrils and ribs-and-pelvis
motifs.
£400 - £600

V15-176342
Stirrup Mount
56mm
Urnes style knotwork and
beast.
£2,000 - £3,000

V09-0109
Stirrup Mount
43mm
Even patina. Tendrils and ribs-
and-pelvis motifs.
£200 - £300

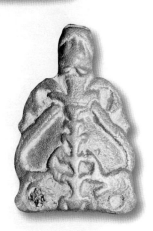

V15-176340
Stirrup Mount
48mm
Entwined tendrils above a
facing zoomorphic mask.
£1,500 - £2,000

V15-176354
Stirrup Mount
39mm
Interlaced serpentine body and
thick rim.
£800 - £1,000

V15-177518
Stirrup Mount
43mm
Trefoil terminal, stylised
bear's head.
£1,500 - £2,000

V15-176349
Stirrup Mount
65mm
Fleur-de-Lys type.
£200 - £300

V15-127556
Stirrup Mount
38mm
Facing mask type.
£400 - £600

V15-131183
Stirrup Mount
49mm
Howling wolf type.
£300 - £400

V15-136523
Stirrup Mount
44mm
Bear's head mask.
£300 - £400

V09-0201
Mount
38mm
Interlace design in the Jellinge style. Dark even patina.
£100 - £150

V09-0202
Zoomorphic Mount
43mm
Two entwined beasts. Traces of silvering. Even patina.
£300 - £400

V09-0203
Book Mount
58mm
Good detail and even patina. Beast with entwined serpent around its body. Very rare.
From £3,000

V09-0204
Zoomorphic Mount
61mm
Two entwined beasts. Surface
a little rough.
£200 - £300

V09 162268
Mask Mount
46mm
Gilt bronze with mask and
scrolls
£4,000 - £6,000

V09-0206
Mount
38mm
Bronze mount with traces of
gilding. Borre style.
£200 - £300

V09-0301
Mount
40mm
Interlaced design.
Probably two serpents.
Even patina.
£120 - £150

V09-0302
Mount
61mm
Openwork with
Ringerike Style beast.
From £600

V09-0303
Mount
45mm
Harness, stirrup or
bridle mount with
notched edges.
£30 - £40

V09-0304
Mount
38mm
Champ-levé enamelled
field with reserved
facing mask.
£400 - £600

V09-0305
Mount
60mm
Openwork plaque with
Ringerike Style beast.
From £1,500

V09-0306
Mount
63mm
Bridle strap junction.
£400 - £600

V09-0307
Staff Finial
50mm
Horse-head design
with hatched detail.
From £1,000

V09-0308
Openwork Mount
26mm
Knotwork beast design.
£300 - £400

V09-0309
Stirrup Mount
55mm
Looped serpent with
head extending beyond
the lower edge.
£300 - £400

V15-133748
Stirrup Mount
52mm
Howling wolf type.
£150 - £200

V09-149969
Mount
57mm
Urnes Style mount with
coiled serpent.
£200 - £300

V09-0312
Stirrup Mount
43mm
Central beast-head motif,
ledge to rear.
£150 - £200

V09-0313
Stirrup Mount
48mm
Mask with
moustache, high
relief.
£400 - £600

V10-0101
Silver Bracelet
67mm
Of typical style.
Complete and
undamaged.
From £600

V10-0201
Ring
20mm
Surface a little ragged.
Traces of gilding.
£100 - £150

V10 171910
Gold Ring
21mm
Glass inlay.
£6,000 - £8,000

V10-0302
Gold Ring
23mm
Stamped with horseshoe
and ring punchmarks.
From £1,000

V10 45990
Gold Bracelet
81mm
From £10,000

V10-0303
Gold Ring
20mm
Punched plate
with ends tied to
the rear.
From £1,000

V10-0304
Gold Ring
27mm
Twisted bars with
twisted wire between
From £1,000

V10-0306
Gold Ring
19mm
With punched pelletted triangles.
From £1,000

V10-0307
Ring
19mm
With ring-and-dot design.
£40 - £60

V10-0308
Gilt Ring
29mm
Classic twisted-rods design.
£150 - £200

V11-0101
Silver Statuette
22mm
Helmetted figure maybe
representing Thor. Left arm
broken at the elbow. Rare.
From £2,000

V12-0101
Strap End
65mm
Good even patina. Ring-and-
dot decoration. Beast with
eight heads.
£300 - £400

V12-0102
Strap End
31mm
Dark patina. Undamaged.
Chip-carved.
£50 - £80

V12-0204
Strap End
50mm
Openwork with
opposed beasts.
£200 - £300

V12-0201
Strap End
56mm
Openwork design.
Complete and
undamaged. Good
even patina.
£120 - £180

V12-0401
Buckle with Plate
90mm
Large buckle. Even
colour. Patina flaking
in places. Rare.
£200 - £300

V12-0402
Belt Buckle
32mm
D-shaped buckle with facing
mask, flat-section tongue.
£50 - £80

V12-141845
Strap Junction
64mm
Female mask to the
centre.
£200 - £300

V15-0301
Harness Pendant
47mm
Formed as two running wolves,
hatched fur detailing.
From £800

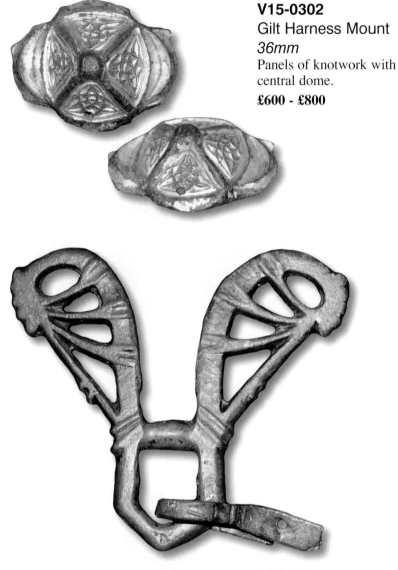

V15-0302
Gilt Harness Mount
36mm
Panels of knotwork with central dome.
£600 - £800

V15-0303
Bridle Mount
90mm
Openwork cheek-piece with loop for the reins.
£300 - £400

V15-0304
Harness Mount
36mm
Cross-shaped plaque with
Ringerike Style ornament.
£50 - £80

V15-0305
Horse Mount
36mm
In the shape of the divine
horse, Sleipnir.
£300 - £400

V16-0101
Comb
46mm
Small comb with suspension
loop, coarse teeth.
£300 - £400

V17-0101
Key
110mm
Suspension loop.
Twisted shank. Even
patina. Rare.
£400 each

V17-0102
Key
55mm
Complete and
undamaged. Good even
patina.
£120 - £180

V17-0103
Key
44mm
Suspension loop. A little
damage. Even patina.
£120 - £180

V17-0104
Key
55mm
Suspension loop.
Complete and
undamaged. Good even
patina.
£120 - £180

V17-75566
Lock & Key Set
165mm
Barrel padlock with ribbed
tubular case.
£200 - £300

V17-0201
Iron Key
156mm
Good state of preservation.
Suspension loop.
Very large. Rare.
£200 - £300

V17-0301
Key
90mm
Spiral of gilded
inlay to the shank.
£400 - £600

V18-35313
Trade Weight Set
14mm - 29mm
Graduated sizes.
£400 - £600

V18-0201
Weight (Bronze Iron Filled)
26mm
Circular with two flat ends. Decoration on both faces. Iron bursting through the bronze. Rare.
£200 - £300

V18-0202
Weight
15mm
Circular with two flat ends.
Decoration on both faces.
£50 - £80

V18-0301
Lead Weight
28mm
Centre contains part of a
gilded chip-carved brooch.
£120 - £180

V18-0302
Lead Weight
29mm
Gilt insert.
£150 - £200

V18-0303
Lead Weight Set
36mm largest
With gilt inserts.
From £2,000

V18-0304
Lead Weight
36mm
With niello and
glass inlays.
£500 - £800

V99-120752
Hacksilver 'Hoard' Group
Chatelaine: 91mm
2.1 kilograms of silver and
ceramics.
£6,000 - £8,000

V99-0301
Firesteel
36mm
Openwork design of a man
and birds on a baseline.
From £500

V99-0401
Horn Terminal
33mm
With beast-head finial and
socket; loop for attachment
of a strap.
£50 - £80

THE MEDIEVAL PERIOD

The 'medieval period' (or Middle Ages) covers broadly the centuries from the Norman invasion in 1066 down to the end of the Tudor dynasty in 1603. The records of this period are comprehensive enough that we can both understand the politics of kings and archbishops and read the private communications of relatively humble merchants and landowners on a scale not possible for any earlier period.

The Norman invasion and the establishment of a French-speaking aristocracy changed permanently the relationship between the upper classes and those on whom they depended to work their lands and process its products. Although the Norman dynasty lasted less than a century, the crown's ties to France and the Holy Roman Empire were far-reaching. England was drawn into religious wars in the Near East (the Crusades) and lengthy and futile wars on the Continent (the Hundred Years' War) which benefitted only a few key families with landholdings on both sides of the Channel. Wars between England, Wales and Scotland occupied a large part of the earlier medieval period, followed by an invasion of Ireland. Rivalries within the English and Welsh aristocracies produced more bloodshed, while the period ended with an age of exploration and empire-building on the far shores of the Atlantic Ocean.

Literacy was a key factor in the medieval period, and despite the insistence on French for official record-keeping and court procedures, English remained the language of the people of England (and Welsh for Wales). Therefore it is not unusual to find both languages represented in inscriptions in this period. Spelling was not fixed until much later, so variation in word-forms reflects local dialects. Aids to teaching, such as hornbooks, played a major part in spreading literacy while ampullae and pilgrim badges show that religious devotion was important.

Another highly visual medieval phenomenon is heraldry – originally a means of instant visual recognition for the battlefield which in time became a sophisticated system to indicate ancestry and affiliation. Using a combination of heraldic information and dating by technique and style, it is sometimes possible to assign an object to a particular family and even an individual. This opens up a broad field for discovery and interpretation of artefacts.

Medieval objects range in quality and rarity, and the majority of them are heavily collected. Heraldic and ecclesiastical items such as horse-harness mounts and seal matrices are among the more obvious collectibles. Weapons such as bullock daggers and hand-guns are also popular. A sudden surge in interest in hawking rings and vervels saw prices leap more than 500% in recent years at TimeLine Auctions. From the Tudor period, even relatively humble items such as dress pins, tags, belt fittings survive in sufficient quantity to form the basis of a comprehensive collection.

M01-0101
Iron Axehead
350mm
Large axe with
maker's marks.
Good state of
preservation.
£150 - £200

M02-0301
Arrowhead
125mm
Iron, 'fire-arrow'
type.
£100 - £150

M02-0101
Iron
Arrowheads
Longest 114mm
Various shapes and
sizes.
From £20 each

M02-0102
Iron Arrowhead
55mm
Barbed and tanged
(swallowtail) arrowhead.
Surface a little uneven.
£80 - £100

M02-0103
Iron Arrowhead
125mm
Barbed and tanged with a very
long socketted tang. Some
decoration. Rare type.
£100 - £150

M04-162201
Sword
610mm
Two-edged iron
blade, hilt and
D-shaped pommel.

£1,000 - £1,500

M04-134165
Sword
1250mm
Two-handed
double-edged type.

From £5,000

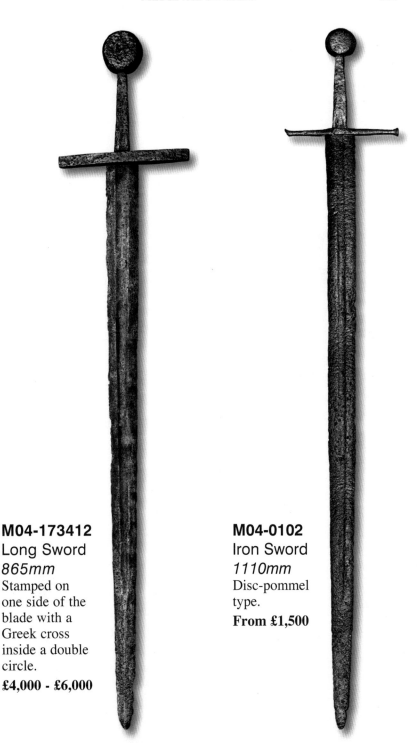

M04-173412
Long Sword
865mm
Stamped on
one side of the
blade with a
Greek cross
inside a double
circle.

£4,000 - £6,000

M04-0102
Iron Sword
1110mm
Disc-pommel
type.
From £1,500

M04-134166
Dagger
480mm
'Main Gauche' parrying
dagger.
£800 - £1,000

M04-0103
Dagger with Bone Handle
365mm
Complete with its handle and
crossguard. Chain mail
piercing blade.
£600 - £800

M04-0104
Dagger with Pommel
470mm
Bronze crossguard and
pommel. Iron blade.
Large size.
£1,000 - £1,500

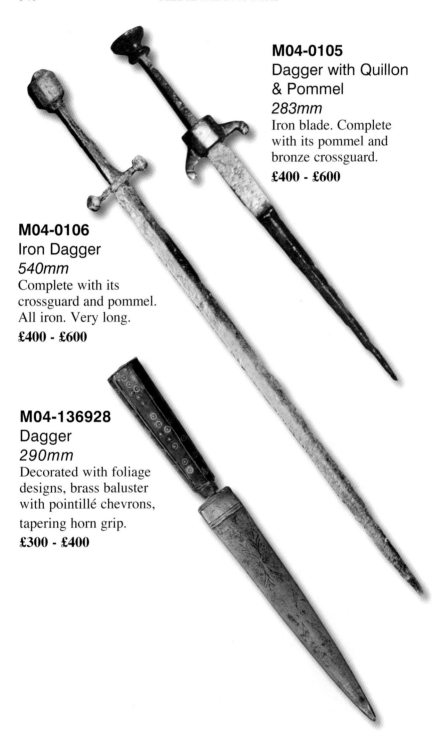

M04-0105
Dagger with Quillon & Pommel
283mm
Iron blade. Complete with its pommel and bronze crossguard.
£400 - £600

M04-0106
Iron Dagger
540mm
Complete with its crossguard and pommel. All iron. Very long.
£400 - £600

M04-136928
Dagger
290mm
Decorated with foliage designs, brass baluster with pointillé chevrons, tapering horn grip.
£300 - £400

M04-0108
Iron Dagger
262mm
Plain simple design.
£200 - £300

M04-134163
Dagger
300mm
Ballock type with
wooden grip.
£500 - £700

M04-162203
Dagger
410mm
Iron with bronze
crossguard.
£400 - £600

M04-0202
Knife Handle
55mm
Bronze, in the form of a dog.
Even patina.
£60 - £80

M04-0201
Knife Handle with
Hooded Figure
65mm
Hooded and cloaked figure.
Even patina. Complete.
£100 - £150

M04-89706
Dagger Hilt Fittings
24mm-39mm
Pommel and guard.
£50 - £80

M04-0301
Eagle's Head Dagger
Pommel
26mm
Sharp detail. Even patina.
£40 - £60

M04-0303
Dagger Pommel
21mm
Bronze dog's head.
Even patina.
£20 - £30

M04-129856
Dagger Pommel
30mm
Annular with four turrets.
£40 - £60

M04-176587
Sword Pommel
54mm
Disc type with raised hub.
£600 - £800

M04-0304
Sword Pommel
58mm
Pommel decorated on both sides. Rare.
£400 - £600

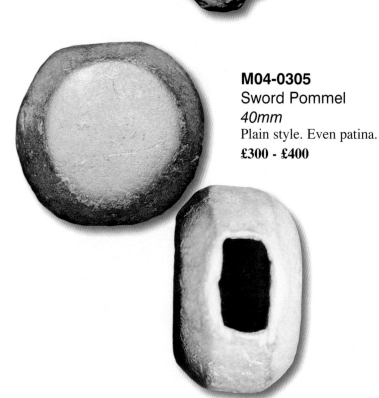

M04-0305
Sword Pommel
40mm
Plain style. Even patina.
£300 - £400

M04-0306
Dagger Pommel
50mm
Traces of blue and white
enamel. Lozenge shape.
£500 - £800

M04-0307
Dagger Pommel
45mm
Engraved design of a crowned
lion. Smooth, even patina.
£500 - £800

M04-0308
Dagger Pommel
40mm
In the form of an expanding
cross with red and blue
enamel. Surface a little uneven.
£150 - £200

M04-117184
Dagger Pommel
29mm
Twisted type.
£50 - £80

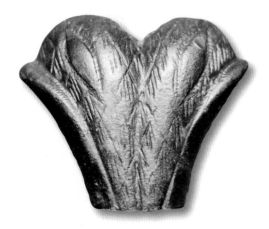

M04-0310
Dagger Pommel
33mm
Resembling two birds'
heads.
Good, even patina.
£100 - £150

M04-0311
Dagger Pommel
35mm
Iron filled. Pellet
decoration.
£60 - £80

M04-0312
Sword
Pommel
34mm
Crusader period type.
£800 - £1,000

M04-0313
Sword Pommel
50mm
Type F (Oakeshott).
£2,000 - £3,000

M04-0314
Dagger Pommel
30mm
With four turrets.
£40 - £60

M04-0315
Dagger Pommel
65mm
Crowned design.
£40 - £60

M04-0316
Sword Pommel
36mm
Openwork type with
enamel.
£1,500 - £2,000

M04-0401
Dagger Quillon
85mm
Light decoration.
Even patina.
Complete.
£80 - £100

M04-0402
Dagger Quillon
60mm
Even patina and complete.
£40 - £60

M04-0403
Dagger Quillon
70mm
Decorated. No patination.
River find.
£40 - £60

M04-0501
Scabbard Chape
55mm
Pierced design. Even patina.
£30 - £40

M04-0502
Gilded Chape
49mm
Gilding intact. Engraved detail
and initials.
£120 - £180

M04-0503
Dagger Chape
50mm
Decorated with cut-out
quatrefoil design.
£15 - £20

M04-0504
Scabbard with Chape
202mm
Decorated leather scabbard
with its chape. Rare.
£150 - £200

M04-116585
Silver Dagger Chape
42mm
Engraved both sides.
£300 - £400

M04-0506
Silver Dagger Chape
35mm
Decorated on each facet. Rare.
£120 - £180

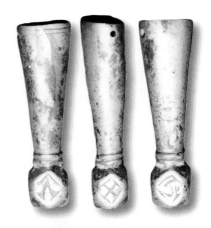

M04-0507
Silver Dagger
Chape
59mm
With punched
decoration.
£100 - £150

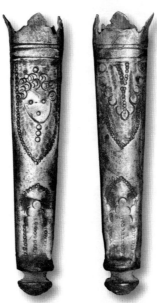

M04-0508
Gold Dagger
Chape
15mm
£800 - £1,200

M04-0509
Belt Chape
28mm
Facing birds motif.
£40 - £60

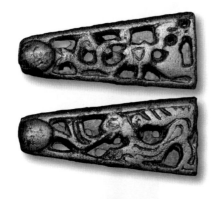

M04-0510
Dagger Chape
42mm
With openwork beast design.
£150 - £200

M05-147869
Great Helm
256mm
Battle damaged and poorly preserved.
From £10,000

M05-0101
Mace Head
45mm
Even patina. Heavy and solid.
Rare.
£200 - £300

M05-0102
Iron Mace Head
278mm
Socketted with fins. Good state of
preservation.
£300 - £400

M05-0201
Crossbow Bolt
Socketted
80mm
Good state of preservation.
£10 - £20

M05-0202
Iron Crossbow Bolt
Tanged
108mm
Good state of preservation.
£10 - £20

M05-0203
Iron Crossbow Bolts
Longest 100mm
From £10 each

M05-0301
Archer's Ring
40mm
Incised decoration.
Even patina. Chunky.
£60 - £80

M05-0302
Archer's Ring
38mm
Even patina.
Thin construction.
£60 - £80

M05 146675
Iron Macehead
66mm
Raised lobes to the
circumference.
£60 - £80

M05-0401
Sword or Dagger
Hanger
60mm
Surface a little ragged.
Zoomorphic.
£30 - £50

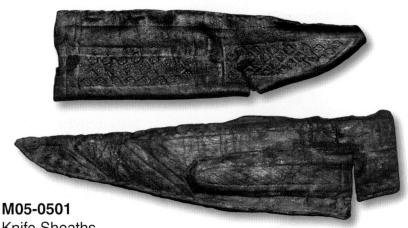

M05-0501
Knife Sheaths
165mm
Leather.
£80 - £100 each

M07-70330
Posy Ring Brooch
21mm
Inscribed 'I am here in place of a lover'.
£600 - £800

M07-85628
Gold Ring Brooch
34mm
Inset with sapphires.
From £10,000

M07-85629
Gold Ring Brooch
22mm
Two opposed four petalled flowers with stalks forming the ring, each set with a sapphire and a garnet.
£3,000 - £4,000

M06-0301
Silver-Gilt Hat Pin
21mm
With religious text.
£600 - £800

M07-0101
Ring Brooch
25mm
Incised lines
decoration.
Complete and
undamaged.
£20 - £30

M07-0107
Ring Brooch with Turrets
21mm
Six turrets. Even patina.
£60 - £80

M07-0103
Ring Brooch with Clasped
Hands
30mm
Smooth even patina. Single
turret. Complete.
£40 - £60

M07-0104
Ring Brooch
18mm
Smooth even patina. Two
beasts eating each other's tails.
Complete. Small size.
£40 - £60

M07-0105
Ring Brooch with Stones
17mm
Six turrets with stones.
Small size.
£80 - £100

M07-0106
Ring Brooch with Turrets
30mm
Eight turrets.
Domino-like decoration.
£80 - £100

M07-0113
Ring Brooch
25mm
Slight traces of gilding.
Surface a little uneven.
With inscription.
£80 - £100

M07-0108
Ring Brooch with Turrets
33mm
Four turrets containing paste.
Smooth even patina.
£30 - £50

M07-0109
Ring Brooch
26mm
Six turrets. Some gilding.
Complete.
£30 - £50

M07-0110
Gilded Ring Brooch
17mm
Four knops on the ring and
one on the pin. Corrosion in
places.
£20 - £30

M07-0112
Ring Brooch
23mm
Six turrets with white paste.
£30 - £50

M07-0201
Silver Ring Brooch
21mm
Plain style. Complete.
£40 - £60

M07-0208
Silver Ring Brooch
22mm
Heart-shaped. Inscribed
on one side. Complete and
undamaged.
£300 - £400

M07-0214
Silver Ring Brooch
16mm
Four beasts' heads. Gilded with
sharp detail. Rare.
£300 - £400

M07-0210
Silver Ring Brooch
32mm
Four knops on the ring
and one on the pin.
Complete.
£150 - £200

M07-0205
Silver Ring Brooch
25mm
Inscription on both sides. Also inscribed all around the edge. Rare.
£800 - £1,000

M07-0206
Silver Ring Brooch
18mm
Inscribed on one side.
Complete and undamaged.
£500 - £800

M07-0207
Silver Ring Brooch
15mm
Inscribed on one side.
Complete and undamaged.
Small size.
£400 - £600

M07-0211
Silver Ring Brooch
23mm
Intricate openwork style. A little
damaged in places.
£300 - £400

M07-0218
Silver Ring Brooch
26mm
Decorated ring. Single
knop on the pin.
£80 - £100

M07-0213
Silver Ring Brooch
20mm
Two birds. Most of the gilding
remaining. Rare.
£300 - £400

M07-0304
Coin Brooch
19mm
Edward I penny.
£150 - £200

M07-0305
Silver Ring Brooch
21mm
Decorated on one side.
£100 - £150

M07-0306
Silver Ring Brooch
20mm
Inscribed and with clasped hands.
£200 - £300

M07-0307
Silver Ring Brooch
23mm
With faux-twist decoration.
£40 - £60

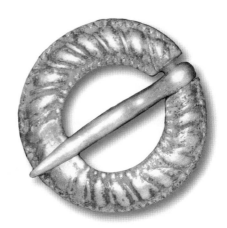

M07-0303
Gold Ring Brooch
17mm
With raised bosses and pellets.
£600 - £800

M07-0309
Silver Ring Brooch
16mm
Inscribed with 'Amor Vincit
Omnia' (Love conquers all).
£200 - £300

M07-0310
Gold Ring Brooch
29mm
With saphires and
rubies.
From £8,000

M07-0302
Silver Ring Brooch
49mm
Penwork with bosses.
£80 - £100

M07-0312
Silver Ring Brooch
19mm
Chain design.
£60 - £80

M07-0313
Ring Brooch
33mm
With inscription.
£50 - £80

M07-0314
Ring Brooch
60mm
With inscription.
£80 - £100

M07-0315
Combat Brooch
27mm
Norman period. Angel
and beast confronted with
human mask between.
£100 - £150

M08-0101
Banneret
22mm
Arms of Sir Thomas
de Pin.
£200 - £300

M08-0102
Banneret
57mm
Arms of John
L'Estrange.
£1,000 - £1,500

M08-0103
Banneret
44mm
White Hart motif.
£400 - £600

M08-0104
Banneret
44mm
Arms of the Applegh
family.
£500 - £800

M15-65479
Banneret
67mm
Arms of the Neville
family.
£200 - £300

M15-65490
Banneret
36mm
Arms of the Duke of
Bourgogne.
£200 - £300

M15-131537
Horse Harness
Banneret
35mm
Bifacial, with heater
shield to one face and
quartered arms to the
other.
£1,200 - £1,800

M15-131527
Horse Harness
Stud
53mm
Red enamelled field
with silvered cross or
saltire.
£600 - £800

M15-131529
Horse Harness
Stud
51mm
Arms of the
Haversage family.
£1,500 - £2,000

M15-131532
Horse Harness
Stud
28mm
Lion rampant type.
£150 - £200

M15-131528
Horse Harness
Mount
43mm
Manticore motif.
£300 - £400

M15-149985
Horse Harness
Mount
38mm
Gilded, arms of the
Beauchamp family.
£800 - £1,000

M15-149957
Horse Harness
Mount
43mm
Gilded, arms
of William of
Harpenden.
£500 - £700

M15-149956
Horse Harness
Mount
30mm
Enamelled field with
Maltese crosses.
£200 - £300

M15-152996
Horse Harness
Mount
31mm
Arms of the Latimer
family.
£200 - £300

M15-160812
Horse Harness
Pendant
43mm
Arms of the Howard
family.
£150 - £200

M15-163822
Horse Harness
Pendant
29mm
Champ-levé
enamelled king seated
on his throne.
£150 - £200

M15-169852
Horse Harness
Banneret
50mm
Arms of Baron Grey
de Rotherfield.
£300 - £400

M15-168104
Horse Harness
Pendant
29mm
Lozenge type, bird of
prey standing left on
a falconer's gloved
hand.
£600 - £800

M15-169047
Horse Harness
Pendant
31mm
Warenne family arms.
£150 - £200

M15-61651
Horse Harness
Pendant
40mm
Castile and Leon.
£400 - £600

M15-61495
Horse Harness Stud
27mm
Chequy pattern, or and
gules.
£200 - £300

M15-60999
Horse Harness
Pendant
45mm
Field in red enamel
divided per pale with three
reserved lions passant
gardant to the left, barry
gules and or with three
torteaux above to the right.
£300 - £400

M08-0105
Banneret
48mm
Patina a little patchy. Most of
the enamel remaining. Scarce.
£400 - £600

M08-0201
Horse Harness Pendant
55mm
With hanger. 50% of the gilding remaining.
£400 - £600

M08-0202
Horse Harness Pendant
With Hanger
55mm
Enamelled griffin on the
hanger. Geometric design on
the pendant. Some gilding.
£150 - £200

M15-65488
Horse Harness
Pendant
40mm
Benhall family arms.
£300 - £400

M15-63269
Horse Harness Mount
71mm
Arms of the Welsh
Prince 'Gruffydd ap
Gwenwynwyn'.
£1,000 - £1,500

M15-67823
Horse Harness
Pendant
42mm
Gilded with red enamel
lattice.
£300 - £400

M15-84379
Horse Harness Inlay
38mm
Beauchamp family arms.
£600 - £800

M15-90644
Horse Harness
Pendant
45mm
Arms of the Prince of
Wales.
£300 - £400

M15-90641
Horse Harness
Pendant
48mm
Arms of the Bardolph
family.
£300 - £400

M15-90508
Horse Harness
Pendant
49mm
Edmund Crouchback, Earl
of Lancaster, Second son
of Henry III.
£600 - £800

M15-90514
Horse Harness
Pendant
45mm
Arms of Aylmar de
Valence.
£150 - £200

M15-112206
Horse Harness
Pendant
44mm
Arms of the Wycliffe
family.
£400 - £600

M15-127561
Horse Harness
Pendant
39mm
Crossed keys type.
£300 - £400

M15-131539
Horse Harness
Pendant
82mm
Two robed maidens in
a landscape with a tree,
foliage to each side and
hatched ground, the
maidens supporting a
heater shield.
£1,000 - £1,500

M15-131530
Horse Harness
Pendant
45mm
Key and sword symbols.
£300 - £400

M15-131538
Horse Harness
Pendant
72mm
Swan between fronds
type.
£1,500 - £2,000

M15-131535
Horse Harness
Pendant
68mm
Arms of Castille.
£400 - £600

M15-131540
Horse Harness
Pendant
66mm
Arms of Castille,
quartered.
£600 - £800

M15-131533
Horse harness
Pendant
61mm
Bifacial pendant with
arcade to one face,
heraldic shield to the
other.
£500 - £700

M15-130971
Horse Harness
Pendant
57mm
Arms of the Paray-le-
Monial family.
£150 - £200

M15-107629
Horse Harness
Pendant
53mm
Blackletter 'a',
surmounted by a crown
for 'Alfonso'.
£400 - £600

M15-139506
Horse Harness
Pendant
50mm
Arms of the Dacre
family.
£600 - £800

M15-136533
Horse Harness
Pendant
16mm
Two lions passant type.
£300 - £400

M15-141017
Horse Harness
Pendant
40mm
Enamelled field,
chevron and fleurs-
de-lys.
£150 - £200

M15-139499
Horse Harness
Pendant
50mm
Hinged suspension lug
and stud.
£150 - £200

M15-140916
Horse Harness
Pendant
40mm
Lozenge type, arms of
the Hotham family.
£150 - £200

M15-139494
Horse Harness
Pendant
36mm
Enamelled and
silvered.
£150 - £200

M15-136567
Horse Harness
Pendant
38mm
Arms of the Clifford
family.
£300 - £400

M15-149955
Horse Harness
Pendant
36mm
Gilded, arms of John
de Warenne, Earl of
Surrey.
£200 - £300

M15-152148
Horse Harness
Pendant
32mm
Five lines of
calligraphic script on
the reverse.
£100 - £150

M15-157214
Horse Harness
Pendant
36mm
'Great helm type
with eye-slits.
£200 - £300

M15-160841
Horse Harness
Pendants
36mm – 79mm
Arms of the de
Thorpe family.
£400 - £600

M15-159077
Horse Harness
Pendant
75mm
Gilded, enamelled
heater shield.
£600 - £800

M08-0203
Horse Harness Pendant
With Hanger
46mm
50% of the gilding remaining.
£150 - £200

M08-0204
Horse Harness Pendant
With Hanger
36mm
Unusual style. Silvered of
which 50% remaining. Hanger
intact. Rare.
£100 - £150

M08-0205
Horse Harness Pendant
With Hanger
70mm
Large size. Much of the
enamel remaining. Silvered
surface.
£300 - £400

M08-0206
Horse Harness Pendant with Hanger
65mm
Dual pendant. Enamel intact.
Rare type.
£200 - £300

M08-0207
Horse Harness Pendant with Hanger
50mm
Pendant with hanger bearing a
monkey-like head. most
gilding remaining.
£80 - £100

M08-0208
Horse Harness Pendant with Hanger
65mm
Unusual pendant with hanger.
Two opposite facing eagles.
Virtually all of the gilding
remains.
£180 - £240

M08-141023
Pendant
28mm
Hunting dog motif.
£100 - £150

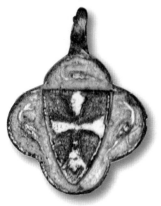

M08-0210
Horse Harness Pendant
29mm
Quatrefoil-shaped silvered
pendant with cross in the
centre and three birds around.
Red enamel surrounds the
cross.
£200 - £300

M08-0211
Horse Harness Pendant
40mm
Quatrefoil-shaped. Most of the
enamel remaining. Owl in the
centre.
£300 - £400

M08-0212
Horse Harness Pendant
43mm
Quatrefoil-shaped. Most of the enamel remaining. Minstrel-like figure in the centre. Rare.
£500 - £800

M08-0213
Horse Harness Pendant
39mm
Some of the enamel remaining. Lozenge-shaped.
£200 - £300

M08-0214
Horse Harness Pendant
28mm
Lozenge-shaped. Most of the enamel remaining. Small size.
£150 - £200

M08-0215
Horse Harness Pendant
35mm
Trefoil-shaped. Traces of
enamel present.
£150 - £200

M08-0216
Horse Harness Pendant
44mm
Trefoil-shaped. Most of the
enamel remaining. Large size.
£300 - £400

M08-0217
Horse Harness Pendant
45mm
Shield-shaped. Colourful
enamel. Crude style lion. Rare.
£150 - £200

M08-0218
Horse Harness Pendant
43mm
Traces of enamel remaining.
Shield-shaped.
£150 - £200

M08-0219
Horse Harness Pendant
39mm
Shield-shaped. Full enamel
present.
£200 - £300

M08-0220
Horse Harness Pendant
35mm
Shield-shaped. Surface a
little ragged. Most enamel
remaining.
£200 - £300

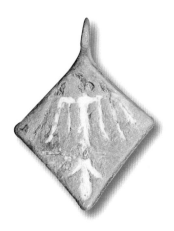

M08-0221
Horse Harness Pendant
44mm
Lozenge-shaped. Most of the
enamel remaining.
£150 - £200

M08-0222
Horse Harness Pendant
38mm
Heavily gilded with full
enamel. Face in the centre.
£200 - £300

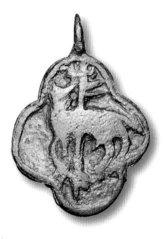

M08-0223
Horse Harness Pendant
46mm
Quatrefoil-shaped. Traces of
enamel. Sacrificial lamb.
£200 - £300

M08-0224
Horse Harness Pendant
43mm
Quatrefoil-shaped. Much of the
enamel remaining. Griffin in
the centre.
£200 - £300

M08-0225
Horse Harness Pendant
42mm
Lozenge-shaped. Enamel
intact. Surface a little ragged.
£150 - £200

M08-0226
Horse Harness Pendant
45mm
Quatrefoil-shaped. Depicting
an archer pursuing a stag.
Enamel missing. Rare.
£150 - £200

M08-0227
Horse Harness Pendant
40mm
Shield-shaped. Much of the
enamel remaining.
£100 - £150

M08-0228
Horse Harness Pendant
48mm
Shield-shaped.
Enamel virtually intact.
£200 - £300

M08-0229
Horse Harness Pendant
49mm
Shield-shaped. Traces of
enamel.
£150 - £200

M08-0230
Horse Harness Pendant
36mm
Castle or priory in the centre.
£200 - £300

M08-0231
Horse Harness Pendant
35mm
Interlaced design.
£50 - £80

M08-0236
Horse Harness Pendant
40mm
Square-shaped. 50% of the
gilding remaining.
£20 - £30

M08-0239
Horse Harness Pendant
47mm
Lozenge-shaped. Enamel
intact. Suspension loop
missing.
£150 - £200

M08-0240
Horse Harness Pendant
30mm
Traces of enamel.
Suspension loop intact.
£200 - £300

M08-0241
Horse Harness Pendant
with Hanger
96mm
Large pendant with its hanger.
Much of the gilding remaining.
£100 - £150

M08-0238
Horse Harness Pendant
65mm
Shield-shaped. Letter 'M' in
the centre. Quatrefoil
decoration around the edge.
Large size.
Suspension loop missing.
£200 - £300

M08-0255
Horse Harness Pendant
42mm
Surface a little rough. Blue
enamel still remains.
£120 - £180

M08-0256
Horse Harness Pendant
46mm
Surface a little rough. Most of the
blue enamel remains.
£120 - £180

M08-0245
Horse Harness Pendant
50mm
With its hanger and most of
its enamel.
£150 - £200

M08-0246
Horse Harness Pendant
62mm
With hanger. White
enamelled owl.
£200 - £300

M08-0247
Horse Harness Pendant
56mm
Heraldic with all enamel and
most gilding remaining.
£200 - £300

M08-0248
Horse Harness Pendant
54mm
With hanger. Lozenge-shaped.
With butterfly.
£150 - £200

M08-0249
Horse Harness Pendant
57mm
With hanger. Traces of gilding.
£300 - £400

M08-0250
Horse Harness Pendant
50mm
Surface rough. With dog.
£150 - £200

M08-0251
Horse Harness Pendant
56mm
With hanger. Most of the enamel remaining.
£200 - £300

M08-0252
Horse Harness Pendant
45mm
With hanger. Full enamel. Arms of William of Harpendene.
£200 - £300

M08-0253
Horse Harness Pendant
60mm
With hanger and butterfly.
£120 - £180

M08-0260
Horse Harness Pendant
42mm
Most enamel remaining. Rare
crossed key and dagger design.
£150 - £200

M08-0258
Horse Harness Pendant
45mm
Surface a little rough. Red and
blue enamel remaining.
£200 - £300

M08-0262
Horse Harness Pendant
64mm
Large, unusual pendant. Three
poppies or flowers in red. Gilding
around.
£200 - £300

M08-0263
Horse Harness Pendant
25mm
Most of the enamel and gilding
remaining. With flowers.
£150 - £200

M08-0264
Horse Harness Pendant
46mm
Surface rough. Blue enamelled
rampant lion.
£120 - £180

M08-0265
Horse Harness Pendant
60mm
Large quatrefoil pendant.
Approximately half of the enamel
and gilding remaining.
£200 - £300

M08-0279
Horse Harness Pendant
59mm
Large pendant heavily gilded with
the letter 'T' in the centre.
£120 - £180

M08-0267
Horse Harness Pendant
44mm
Strong detail. Enamelled dog in a
lying position.
£120 - £180

M08-0268
Horse Harness Pendant
44mm
Virtually all enamel and gilding
present. Rare.
£300 - £400

M08-0269
Horse Harness Pendant
39mm
Surface a little rough.
£150 - £200

M08-0270
Horse Harness Pendant
42mm
Traces of gilding. Enamel
missing. Umfraville family.
£120 - £180

M08-0271
Horse Harness Pendant
43mm
Surface a little rough.
Three crowns.
£100 - £150

M08-0272
Horse Harness Pendant
33mm
Unusual pendant depicting a
hawk, an arm and a ring brooch.
£200 - £300

M08-0273
Horse Harness Pendant
42mm
Raised, gilded cross on a plain
background.
£100 - £150

M08-0274
Horse Harness Pendant
56mm
Large pendant. Traces of gilding.
£20 - £30

M08-0301
Horse Harness
Pendant
45mm
Arms of Henry de
Pembridge.
£200 - 300

M08-0302
Horse Harness
Pendant
44mm
With gilt lion.
£150 - £200

M08-0303
Horse Harness
Pendant
49mm
Royal arms.
£300 - £400

M08-0304
Horse Harness
Pendant
41mm
With blue enamel and
fleur-de-lys.
£120 - £180

M08-0305
Gold Pendant
29mm
'Jesus walking on
the water' motif.
From £5,000

M08-0306
Horse Harness Pendant
42mm
Eagle motif.
£400 - £600

M08-0307
Horse Harness
Pendant
68mm
Regardant lion motif.
£300 - £400

M08-0308
Horse Harness
Pendant
65mm
Arms of the Chamberlayne
family.
£3,000 - £4,000

M08-0309
Horse Harness
Pendant
64mm
Westminster Abbey type.
£2,000 - £3,000

M08-0310
Horse Harness Pendant
27mm
Enamelled quatrefoil motif.
£120 - £180

M08-0311
Horse Harness Pendant
54mm
Religious motif of 'Pelican in her Piety'.
£150 - £200

M08-0312
Heraldic Pendant
23mm
Religious text 'AVE MARIA GRACIE' Hail Mary full of Grace and heater shield.
£300 - £400

M08-0313
Horse Harness
Pendant
66mm
Discoid with notched
border.
£300 - £400

M08-0314
Horse Harness
Pendant
45mm
Arms of the Ballantyne
family.
£200 - £300

M08-0315
Horse Harness
Pendant
44mm
Arms of the Camden
family.
£200 - £300

M08-0316
Horse Harness
Pendant
48mm
Arms of Paray-le-Monial.
£500 - £800

M08-0317
Horse Harness
Pendant
39mm
Arms of the Multon
family.
£300 - £400

M08-0318
Horse Harness Pendant
62mm
Arms of the Howard family;
with hanger.
£1,000 - £1,500

M08-0319
Horse Harness Pendant
34mm
Arms of the 'Pecche' Peachey family.
£200 - £300

M08-0320
Horse Harness Pendant
31mm
With Royal arms, diferenced.
£150 - £200

M08-0321
Horse Harness Pendant
62mm
With hanger, gilded.
£300 - £400

M08-0322
Horse Harness
Pendant
40mm
Double-sided.
£300 - £400

M08-0323
Horse Harness
Pendant
64mm
Arms of the House of
Lancaster.
£200 - £300

M08-0324
Silver Horse Harness
Pendant
30mm
Arms of 'Baron de la Pole'.
From £2,000

M08-0325
Horse Harness
Pendant
48mm
Arms of William de
Valoynes.
£150 - £200

M08-0326
Horse Harness
Pendant
40mm
Arms of the Peverell
family.
£200 - £300

M08-0327
Silver Pendant
23mm
Large amethyst set in a
silver
surround.
£300 - £400

M08-0328
Gold Posy Pendant
20mm
Gold with 'DIEU
PLERRA QANT
MEUIZ SERRA'
inscription.
From £4,000

M09-0102
Horse Harness Mount
27mm
Shield-shaped. Some enamel remaining. Surface a little uneven.
£200 - £300

M09-0103
Heraldic Mount
35mm
Shield-shaped. Some enamel remaining. Traces of gilding.
£150 - £200

M09-0104
Horse Harness Mount
45mm
Trefoil-shaped. Traces of enamel. Large.
£150 - £200

M09-0105
Horse Harness Mount
35mm
Most of the enamel remaining.
£100 - £150

M09-0106
Horse Harness Mount
19rnm
Shield-shaped. Most of the
enamel remaining. Chequered
design. Small.
£120 - £180

M09-0107
Horse Harness Mount
60mm
Most of the enamel remaining.
Good detail of a lady crowning
her knight. Rare.
From £2,000

M09 50507
Limoges Buckle
Mount
42mm
Figure of St Michael.
From £1,000

M09-0109
Horse Harness Mount
45mm
Square-shaped. Most of the
enamel remaining.
£300 - £400

M09-0110
Horse Harness Mount
40mm
Shield-shaped. Most of the
enamel remaining, three lions.
£200 - £300

M09-0111
Horse Harness Mount
with Lion of St Mark
45mm
Traces of red, blue, green and
white enamel and traces of
gilding.
£300 - £400

M09-84381
Horse Harness Armorial
Mount
60mm
Heraldic design of ermine
field and fess with three
scallops.
£400 - £600

M09-0113
Horse Harness Mount
39mm
Unusual depiction of a
crowned winged beast with a
human head.
£300 - £400

M09-116774
Buckle plate
25mm
Enamelled bust of a
nobleman.
£400 - £600

M09-128386
Horse Harness
Mount
63mm
Rampant lion with
enamel fill.
£600 - £800

M09-0116
Horse Harness Mount
46mm
Large heraldic mount. Rampant
lion. Red enamelled background.
£150 - £200

M09-131543
Purse Mount
125mm incl stand
Silvered scallop-shell type.
£80 - £100

M09-0118
Horse Harness Mount
49mm
Three gilded lions.
Red enamelled background,
most remaining.
£200 - £300

M09-0119
Horse Harness Mount
60mm
Large heraldic mount
with gold inlay.
£400 - £600

M09-0120
Horse Harness Mount
23mm
Small gilded stud.
£40 - £60

M09-177511
Stag's Head Mount
59mm
Modelled in the round.
£200 - £300

M09-0122
Buckle Plate
34mm
Cloisonné type inlay.
£80 - £100

M09-0123
Buckle Plate
40mm
Fully gilded. Traces of red
enamel.
£300 - £400

M09-149977
Armorial Mount
60mm
Arms of the Seckford
family.
£400 - £600

M09-0125
Mount
30mm
Most of the enamel
remaining.
£300 - £400

M09-0201
Pyramidial Mount
16mm
Square-shaped. Loop at the
back. Most of the gilding
remaining.
£100 - £150

M09-0202
Mount with Two Beasts
44mm
Two protruding heads. Pierced
for mounting.
£40 - £60

M09-0203
Zoomorphic Mount
35mm
Even patina. Beast with its
tongue sticking out.
£40 - £60

M09-175574
Disc Mount
35mm
'The Eastry' enamelled
limoges mount.
£600 - £800

M09-0205
Beast Mount
65mm
Beast with its foot in its mouth.
Surface a little ragged.
£100 - £150

M09-0206
Rampant Lion Mount
50mm
Openwork design. Good even
patina. Complete. Rare.
£200 - £300

M09 140921
Belt Mount
28mm
Openwork foliage tracery and
seated crowned figure
£100 - £150

M09-0208
Lion Belt Mount
28mm
Openwork design. Small size.
£80 - £100

M09-0209
Lis Mount in Pewter
55mm
Shield-shaped. Lis in the
centre. Openwork design.
£50 - £80

M09-0210
Ecclesiastical Mount
55mm
Design comprising openwork
triangles. Even patina.
£80 - £100

M09-0211
Mount with Inscription
55mm
Lettering on one side.
Floral design on the other.
£150 - £200

M09-0212
Mount with Inscription
85mm
Thin strip with rivets at each end.
£100 - £150

M09-0213
Roundel Mount
62mm
Two figures either side of
an altar with banners above.
Creased down the centre.
From £1,000

M09-0214
Roundel Mount
59mm
Two angels either side of a
shield.
£300 - £400

M09-0215
Roundel Mount
40mm
Crowned key in the centre.
Traces of enamel.
£150 - £200

M09-0216
Ecclesiastical Mount
47mm
Even patina. Design of
openwork triangles.
£80 - £100

M09-0217
Ecclesiastical Mount
62mm
Surface a little rough.
Openwork design.
£80 - £100

M09-0218
Silver Mount
37mm
Decorated with niello inlay.
£50 - £80

M09-0219
Mount
29mm
Most gilding remains.
Depicting winged beast
in a crouched position.
£150 - £200

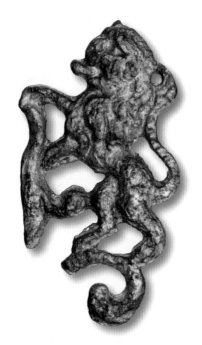

M09-0302
Heraldic Badge
33mm
Rampant lion,
royalist motif.
£80 - £100

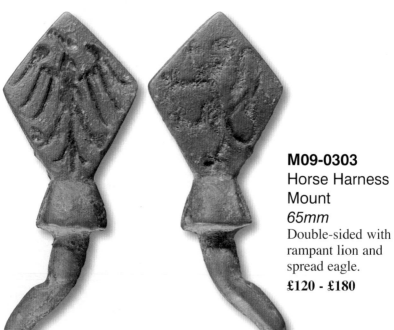

M09-0303
Horse Harness
Mount
65mm
Double-sided with
rampant lion and
spread eagle.
£120 - £180

M09-0304
Mount
19mm
With beast walking
left.
£60-80

M09-0305
Figurine
42mm
Lion couchant
motif.
£500 - £800

M09-0306
Belt Mount
32mm
Swordsman motif.
£300 - £400

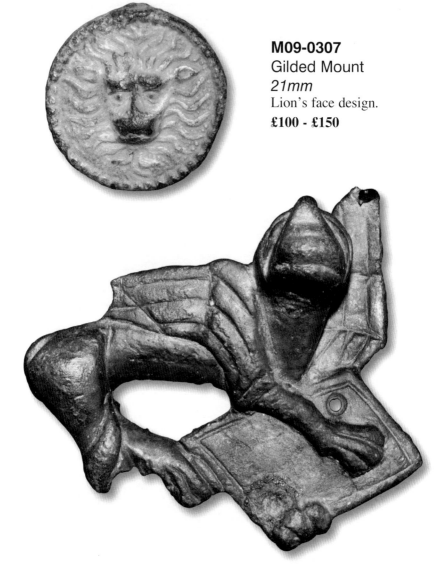

M09-0307
Gilded Mount
21mm
Lion's face design.
£100 - £150

M09-0308
Book Mount
77mm
Lion of St Mark motif.
£600 - £800

M09-0309
Tudor Roundel
40mm
Lion mask motif.
£400 - £600

M09-136516
Heraldic Roundel
46mm
Enamelled field, trefoil
motif.
£400 - £600

M09-0310
Book Mount
18mm
With recumbent beast.
£100 - £150

M09-0312
Book Mount
57mm
Lion of St Mark
motif.
£60 - £80

M09-0313
Tudor Mount
43mm
Cherub motif.
£30 - £40

M09-0314
Gold Stud
35mm
Of hollow sheet
form.
£300 - £400

M09-0315
Mount
47mm
In the style of a
female head.
£100 - £150

M09-0316
Mount
44mm
With figure holding
an apple.
£150 - £200

M09-0317
Book Mount
32mm
Lion couchant motif.
£30 - £40

M09-0318
Norman Gold
Panel
15mm
Fleur-de-lys motif.
£800 - £1,200

M09-0319
Livery Badge
34mm
Plantagenet 'sun,
moon and star'
design.
£20 - £30

M09-0320
Book Mount
51mm
Lady-with-purse motif.
£100 - £150

M09-0321
Book Mount
38mm
Norman period. Bird
with human head,
hatched body.
£150 - £200

M10-0108
Ring with Letter P
22mm
Good even patina. Large size.
£50 - £80

M10-0102
Ring with Crowned T
19mm
Even patina. Small size.
£50 - £80

M10-0103
Ring with Letter P
22mm
A little pitted on the surface.
Large size.
£50 - £80

M10-0104
Ring with Crowned TI
24mm
Good even patina. Unusual. Two
entwined letters. Very large size.
£100 - £150

M10-0105
Ring with Hand and Sword
23mm
Good even patina. Unusual.
Hand and sword on the bezel.
Large size.
£50 - £80

M10-0111
Ring with Letter A
20mm
Surface a little uneven. Simple
style.
£50 - £80

M10-0112
Ring with Letter R
24mm
Good even patina. Sharp detail.
Very large size.
£80 - £120

M10-0107
Ring with Letter I
20mm
Round bezel. Engraved
decoration. Maybe a letter I.
Even patina.
£30 - £50

M10-0114
Ring with Crowned I
21mm
A little mis-shapen. Uneven
surface.
£40 - £60

M10-0115
Ring with Saint
18mm
Unusual figure of a saint
on the bezel. Good smooth
surface with even patina.
£120 - £180

M10-0116
Ring with Letter R
28mm
Even patina.
£100 - £150

M10-0113
Ring with Crowned RI
21mm
Unusual spiral shape band.
Sharp detail. Even patina.
£120 - £180

M10-0118
Ring with
Crowned M
22mm
Surface a little
uneven. Large
size.
£50 - £80

M10-0119
Ring with
Castle
20mm
Smooth surface.
Traces of gilding.
Castle on the
bezel.
£150 - £200

M10-0201
Silver Ring with Lis
22mm
Good silver.
£150 - £200

M10-0202
Silver Ring with Letter M
19mm
Crude style.
£100 - £150

M10-0203
Silver Ring with Letter T
21mm
Good silver.
£100 - £150

M10-0204
Silver Ring with Four
Bezels
19mm
Devices engraved on each of
the four bezels. Good silver.
Small size.

£120 - £180

M10-0205
Silver Iconographic Ring
19mm
Figure of a saint on the bezel.
Spiral design on the band.

£300 - £400

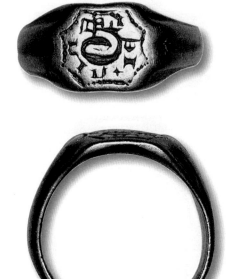

M10-0206
Silver Ring with
Inscription
22mm
Good silver. Wearable
size. Inscription on bezel.
£200 - £300

M10-0207
Silver Ring with
Inscription
22mm
Thin band. 50% of the
gilding remains. Large
size.
£200 - £300

M10-0208
Silver Ring with Inscription
21mm
Most of the gilding remaining.
Decorated band. Sharp detail.
Undamaged. Wearable
size.

£300 - £400

M10-0109
Ring with Letter W
21mm
Surface a little uneven. Crude
style.

£40 - £60

M10-0110
Ring with Letter W
22mm
Surface a little ragged. Simple
style.

£40 - £60

M10-0213
Silver Ring with Inscription
23mm
Unusual style. Much of the gilding remaining. Large size.
£400 - £600

M10-0214
Silver Iconographic Ring
22mm
Two saints on the bezel. Two shields either side. Most of the gilding remaining.
Decorated band. Large size.
£800 - £1,000

M10-0215
Silver Iconographic Ring
19mm
Two saints on the bezel. Flower design on the shank. Some gilding remaining. Small size.
£500 - £800

M10-0219
Silver Ring with Niello
21mm
Decorated band. Niello inlay.
Good condition.
£150 - £200

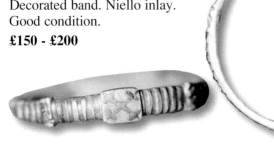

M10-0217
Silver Ring with Bead Bezel
20mm
Unusual style. Ancient bead in
the centre of the bezel. Good
silver.
£150 - £200

M10-0226
Silver Ring
with garnet
19mm
Double inscription on the outside.
Two beasts' heads holding the
bezel. Set with a garnet. Rare
type.
From £1,500

M10-0227
Silver Ring
with Amethyst
19mm
Most gilding remaining.
Bezel a little damaged.
Pretty amethyst setting.
£400 - £600

M10-0228
Silver-Gilt Ring
20mm
Large size. Decorated all
around the band and bezel.
£300 - £400

M10-0229
Silver Ring with Inscription
22mm
Fully gilded. Inscription on the
bezel. Large size.
From £1,000

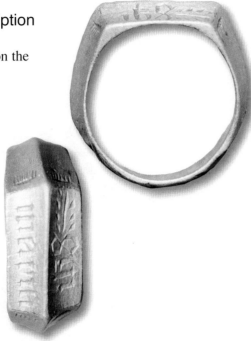

M10-0230
Silver Iconographic Ring
18mm
Saint on the bezel. Flower design
on the shank. Small size.
£600 - £800

M10-0231
Silver Iconographic Ring
20mm
Surface a little ragged. Weak detail.

£300 - £400

M10-0232
Silver Iconographic Ring
18mm
Surface a little worn in places. Two saints engraved.

£400 - £600

M10-0301
Gold Stirrup-Shaped Ring
with Stone
23mm
Large wearable size.
Undamaged. Original perfect
stone.
From £1,000

M10-0302
Gold Stirrup-Shaped
Ring with Turquoise
20mm
Slightly mis-shapen. Small
size. Original perfect stone.
From £1,000

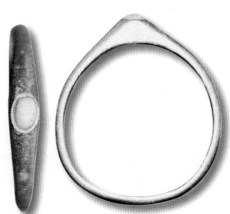

M10-0303
Gold Ring with Garnet
25mm
Large original garnet.
Complete and undamaged.
Wearable size.
From £2,000

M10-52850
Gold Ring
24mm
Inscribed 'I am Loyal'.
From £15,000

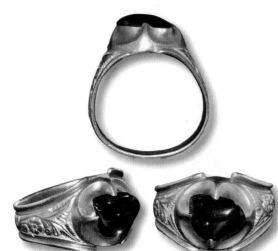

M10-65482
Gold Posy Ring
21mm
Inset sapphire.
From £15,000

M10-65480
Gold Ring
20mm
St Catherine motif.
From £5,000

M10-64974
Gold Ring
21mm
Memento Mori type.
From £8,000

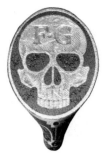

M10-71017
Gold Signet Ring
23mm
Elizabethan type.
From £10,000

M10-66228
Gold Signet Ring
24mm
Elizabethan type, inscribed
'WG'.
From £10,000

M10-70678
Gold Signet Ring
23mm
Elizabethan type, inscribed
'WHA'.
From £10,000

M10-076994
Gold Signet Ring

22mm

Heater shield containing an engrailed saltire and a rose in the upper centre; above the shield a knight's helmet with closed grill, on which rests a torpe.

From £10,000

M10-85206
Gold Signet Ring
23mm
Inscribed, with hound at rest.
From £15,000

M10-94825
Gold Signet Ring
25mm
Crowned I motif.
From £10,000

M10-95240
Armada Gold Ring
25mm
Portrait of Elizabeth I, probably celebrating
victory over the Spanish Armada.
£50,000 - £70,000

M10-112180
Gold Ring
21mm
Inscribed 'b-i-e-n' (well).
From £10,000

M10-127749
Gold Ring
24mm
Inscribed 'en bon an' ('a good year').
From £10,000

M10-114652
Gold Ring
26mm
Inset with very early cut diamond.
From £10,000

M10-131137
Gold Swivel Ring
25mm
Inscribed on one face '+ KNOWE · THY · SELF' and on the other
a heater shield and helmet with arms of the Earls of Macclesfield.
From £10,000

M10-135063
Gold Ring
26mm
Inset diamond to the centre.

£8,000 - £10,000

M10-135064
Gold Ring
25mm
Merchant's signet ring with crossed keys.

£6,000 - £8,000

M10-130246
Gold Ring
24mm
Inset sapphire cabochon.
£800 - £1,000

M10-134285
Gold Memento Mori Ring
20mm
Reserved text in capitals ':: John Enys Esq: Ob: 11 Oct:1802:Æt:31'.
£500 - £700

M10-129043
Signet Ring
22mm
Lion rampant motif.
£400 - £600

M10-135133
Gold Memento Mori Ring
23mm

Traces of white and green enamel on the scrolls; inscription 'MEMENTO MORI' with traces of black enamel.

£1,500 - £2,000

M10-140919
Gold Reliquary Ring
20mm

Inset panel with crystal(?) window and behind a wooden(?) sliver (a saint's relic).

£5,000 - £7,000

M10-139828
Gold Monogram Ring
25mm

Inset with natural pyramidal diamond.

£5,000 - £7,000

M10-166366
Gold Serjeant's Ring
20mm
Inscription 'VIVAT REX ET LEX' : 'Long live the king and the law'.

£3,000 - £4,000

M10-168684
Gold Love Ring
29mm
Scrollwork design and 'AMA' (love) 'DIO' (God).

£10,000 - £15,000

M10-167355
Gold Ring
21mm
'The Fleet' Medieval gold iconographic ring with the Holy Trinity.

£2,000 - £3,000

M10-168697
Gold Ring
28mm
Portrait of Edward de Vere, the 17th Earl of Oxford, with radiate crown of an emperor in the classical style.

From £20,000

M10-172895
Gold Ring
17mm
Bezel featuring an equal-armed cross with pellet in each angle.

£600 - £800

M10-0304
Gold Ring with
Amethyst
15mm
Small size. Unusual style
bezel. Original stone.
£2,000 - £3,000

M10-0305
Gold Ring with
Turquoise
19mm
Stirrup style. Original stone.
Undamaged. Small size.
£1,000 - £1,500

M10-0306
Gold Ring with Rock
Crystal
16mm
Black and white enamel. Very
small size. Rock crystal stone.
£1,500 - £2,000

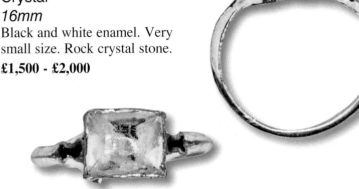

M10-0307
Stirrup-Shaped Gold Ring
21mm
Plain band. Claw style bezel
holding a turquoise stone.
£800 - £1,000

M10-0308
Gold Ring
16mm
Hollow construction. Enamel
missing. Small size.
£800 - £1,000

M10-0309
Gold Ring with Enamel
18mm
Much of the enamel remaining. Inscription on the inside. Rare.
£1,500 - £2,000

M10-0310
Gold Ring with Horse Hoof
22mm
Seal ring. Chevron design on the shank. Undamaged and attributable to a family. Rare.
From £8,000

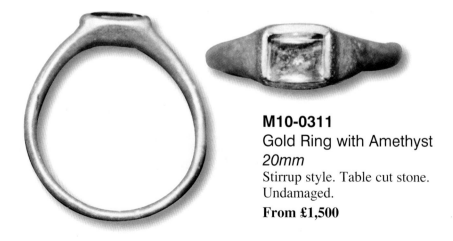

M10-0311
Gold Ring with Amethyst
20mm
Stirrup style. Table cut stone. Undamaged.
From £1,500

M10-0312
Gold Ring with Blue Sapphire
20mm
Facetted bezel and stone.
Undamaged.
From £3,000

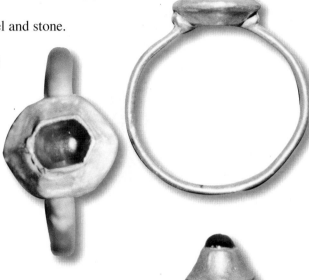

M10-0313
Gold Ring with Black
Sapphire
25mm
Large size. Undamaged. Perfect
in all respects.
From £3,000

M10-0314
Gold Ring with Amethyst
21mm
A little mis-shapen. Uneven
bezel.
£1,500 - £2,000

M10-0315
Gold Ring with Garnet
22mm
Decorated band. Large size. A
little uneven around the stone.
£2,000 - £3,000

M10-0316
Gold Ring with Sapphire
23mm
Large size. A little mis-shapen
around the stone setting.
From £1,500

M10-0317
Gold Ring with Sapphire
19mm
Small ring. Some damage
around the bezel.
From £1,500

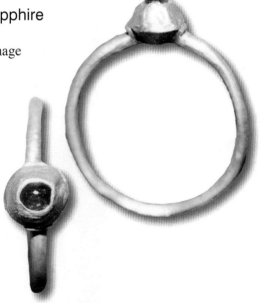

M10-0318
Gold Ring with Garnet
17mm
Small size. Decorated band.
Pretty garnet setting.

£1,500 - £2,000

M10-0319
Gold Ring with Inscription and Blue Sapphire
22mm
Large size. Inscription around the outside of the band.

£2,000 - £3,000

M10-0320
Gold Ring with Emerald
18mm
Thin band. Rectangular bezel set
with an emerald. Stone damaged.
£1,200 - £1,800

M10-0321
Gold Ring with Amethyst
20mm
Traces of black enamel on the
shoulders. Petal design bezel.
£2,000 - £3,000

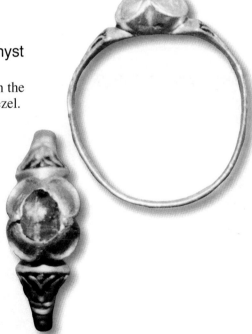

M10-0322
Gold Ring with Amethyst &
Sapphires
18mm
Unusual style. Heart-shaped
amethyst in the bezel. Stones set
from underneath.
From £1,500

M10-0323
Gold Ring with Turquoise
20mm
Large bezel with turquoise setting
surrounded by rock crystals.
£1,500 - £2,000

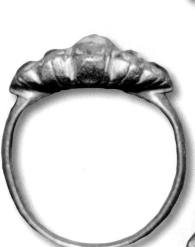

M10-47339
Gold Ring
19mm
Iconographic ring with Corpus
Christi in loincloth with raised
arms, flanked by figures in
three-quarter view.
From £5,000

M10-43830
Gold Ring
26mm
Sapphire cabochon.
From £6,000

M10-66226
Gold Ring
22mm
Tudor, with inset diamond.
From £5,000

M10-0326
Gold Ring with Flower
15mm
Small size. Flower engraved on the bezel. Possibly saffron plant.

£800 - £1,000

M10-0327
Gold Skull Ring
19mm
Thin band. Small bezel of a skull. Black enamel inlaid. Decorated shoulders.

£1,000 - £1,500

M10-89144
Gold Ring
21mm
Royal Fleur-de-lys type.
From £15,000

M10-0329
Gold Ring with Three Saints
20mm
Three saints, each one forming
a separate bezel. Decorated
between each bezel. Perfect and
rare.
From £8,000

M10-68136
Gold Buckle Posy Ring
19mm
Tudor. Inscribed 'HOPE IS MI HOLDE
TILL HAP SHALL HELPE'.
£4,000 - £6,000

M10-149568
Posy Ring
21mm
Silver-gilt, inscribed 'PENCES POVR
MOYE DV' (Think of me, God willing).
£600 - £800

M10-141134
Gold Posy Ring
18mm
Inscribed 'amer et celer'
French for: 'love and
conceal.
£5,000 - £7,000

M10-0333
Gold Posy Ring
21mm
With three bands of text.
From £8,000

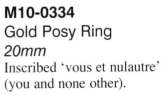

M10-0334
Gold Posy Ring
20mm
Inscribed 'vous et nulautre'
(you and none other).
From £3,000

M10-0335
Gold Ring
18mm
Interlocking hearts motif.
£2,000 - £3,000

M10-0336
Gold and Garnet
Ring
25mm
With large bezel.
From £6,000

M10-0337
Gold Ring
26mm
With inset amethyst
cabochon.
£4,000 - £6,000

M10-0338
Gold Ring
23mm
With inset garnet stone.
£1,000 - £1,500

M10-0339
Gold Ring
20mm
With inset turquoise stone.
£1,000 - £1,500

M10-0340
Gold Ring
26mm
With inset cabochon ruby.
From £2,000

M10-0341
Tudor Signet Ring
23mm
With initials 'BW' in a border.
£60 - £80

M10-0342
Gold Ring
24mm
With cabochon stone and inscription.
From £4,000

M10-0343
Gold Ring
38mm
With tiered bezel and inset cabochon stones.
From £6,000

M10-0344
Gold Ring
19mm
Inscribed PRVDENTIA 'wisdom'.
£1,000 - £1,500

M10-153431
Gold Ring
23mm
Bezel with inset diamond.
£2,000 - £3,000

M10-150055
Gold Ring
25mm
Inset table-cut emerald.
£2,000 - £3,000

M10-0346
Gold Ring
21mm
St Catherine motif.
From £4,000

M10-0347
Gold Finger Ring
21mm
Inscribed.
£5,000 - £8,000

M10-0348
Gold Ring
24mm
Inscribed '+avemaria
.sinelabe origin concep'.
£2,000 - £3,000

M10-0349
Silver Iconographic
Ring
25mm
Winged angels motif.
£400 - £600

M10-0350
Gold Ring
23mm
With inset sapphire.
£3,000 - £4,000

M10-0351
Gold Stirrup Ring
22mm
With inset garnet.
£1,000 - £1,500

M10-0352
Gold Stirrup Ring
29mm
With amethyst cabochon.
From £4,000

M10-157934
Gold Ring
26mm
Inset early cut diamond in
the bezel.
From £6,000

M10-0354
Gold Lock Ring
23mm
'Fidelity in Love'
symbolism of the lock.
From £4,000

M10-0355
Gold Ring
23mm
With inset ruby.
From £3,000

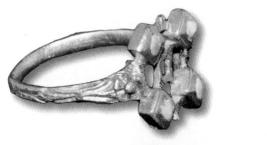

M10-0356
Renaissance Gold
Ring
21mm
With inset turquoise
stone.
£2,000 - £3,000

M10-0357
Gold Ring
19mm
Twisted wreath design.
£800 - £1,000

M10-0358
Ring
25mm
With horned devil motif.
£150 - £200

M10-0359
Gold Ring
16mm
With ruby and
turquoise gemstones
£2,000 - £3,000

M11-0101
Crucifix Figure
57mm
Some gilding remaining.
Letters engraved on each arm.
£150 - £200

M11-0102
Silver Crucifix
50mm
Suspension loops at the top
and bottom. Most of the
gilding remaining.
£300 - £400

M11-0103
Crucifix Figure
75mm
Good detail. Undamaged. Even
patina.
£100 - £150

M11-0104
Figure of a Saint
62mm
Enamel remaining on the face
but missing from the body.
£600 - £800

M11-0105
Figure of a Saint
55mm
Fairly ragged surface. Weak
detail.
£150 - £200

M11-0106
Figure of a Saint
70mm
Weak detail. Surface a little
uneven. Large size.
£400 - £600

M11-0107
Figure of a Saint
58mm
Gilding and enamel all intact.
Glass eyes in place.
From £1,000

M11-0108
Figure of a Saint
62mm
Gilding and enamel all intact.
Glass eyes in place.
From £1,200

M11-0109
Crowned Head
38mm
Traces of gilding. Clear detail.
£150 - £200

M11-177523
Crowned Figure
89mm
'The Chaldon' crowned
female figure.
£3,000 - £4,000

M11-0305
Figural Mount
30mm
Mary Magdalene religious
motif.
£400 - £600

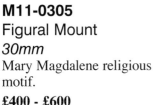

M11-178179
Dog Terminal
65mm
Sitting dog with gaping
mouth, possibly a priest's
laver.
£1,000 - £1,500

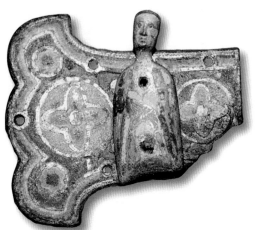

M11-0113
Arm From Cross
with Figure of Saint
85mm
Virtually full enamel
and gilding. Figure
probably represents St
John. Very rare.
From £4,000

M11-0301
Norman Crucifix
Figure
110mm
Typical early crown
clothing.
£2,000 - £3,000

M11-0302
Crucifixion Mount
23mm
Gilt with some damage
£150 - £200

M11-0303
Limoges Plaque
57mm
Religious motif of the
Lion of St Mark.
£600 - £800

M11-0306
Limoges Mount
38mm
Bird motif.
£200 - £300

M12-0119
Strap End
90mm
See M12-0109 for similar example. This one has figure missing from the centre.

£60 - £80

M12-0105
Strap End with Bird
58mm
Smooth even patina. Good style. Complete.

£40 - £60

M12-0106
Strap End with Lettering
56mm
Letters engraved on the surface. Foliate design. Even patina.

£60 - £80

M12-0107
Strap End
60mm
Eagle in the centre. Good even patina.

£200 - £300

M12-0108
Strap End with Letter 'R'
70mm
Letter R on the plate. Even patina. Traces of silvering. Large size.
£100 - £150

M12-0109
Strap End St Christopher
90mm
St Christopher in the centre. Traces of silvering. Complete and undamaged. Rare.
£100 - £150

M12-0101
Strap End
85mm
Smooth even patina. Plain style.
£10 - £20

M12-0102
Strap End
102mm
Lacking patina. Large size.
£20 - £30

M12-0111
St Christopher
Strap End
60mm
Complete and
undamaged. Silvered
surface. Rare.
£200 - £300

M12-0112
Book clasp
110mm
Patina uneven. Surface
a little dented.
£40 - £60

M12-0113
Book clasp
65mm
50% of gilding
remaining.
Undamaged.
£100 - £150

M12-0114
Silver Book clasp
70mm
Much of the gilding
remaining. Complete.
£200 - £300

M12-0115
Strap End with Man
48mm
Even patina. Good detail.
Scarce type.
£300 - £400

M12-0116
Inscribed Strap End
65mm
Most gilding remaining.
Engraved. Undamaged.
£100 - £150

M12-0117
Inscribed Strap End
40mm
Surface a little rough. Some
gilding remaining. Engraved.
£40 - £60

M12-0415
Strap End
63mm
With mother and child
£100 - £150

M12-0201
Buckle with Hand & Arm
55mm
Even patina. Complete and
undamaged.
£10 - £20

M12-0202
Locking Buckle
30mm
Even patina. Working order.
£10 - £20

M12-0203
Buckle
40mm
Patina a little ragged.
£5 - £10

M12-0204
Buckle with Two Figures
65mm
Two figures standing on a
lion with their hands on each
other's head. Patina a little
patchy. Very rare.
£150 - £200

M12-0205
Buckle with Beasts
32mm
Traces of gilding. Two beasts
facing each other. Smooth even
surface.
£80 - £100

M12-0206
Beast Buckle
30mm
Beast biting its tail. Patina a little
patchy.
£40 - £60

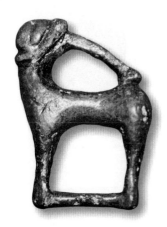

M12-0207
Lion Buckle
30mm
Beast biting its tail.
Good detail. Smooth,
even patina.
£80 - £100

M12-0208
Buckle with Crowned Head
28mm
Smooth, even surface.
Small size.
£20 - £30

M12-0209
Buckle with Crowned Head
38mm
Surface a little uneven.
Good size.
£20 - £30

M12-0210
Face Buckle
29mm
Surface a little pitted.
Small size.
£20 - £30

M12-0211
Face Buckle
30mm
Surface a little uneven.
£10 - £20

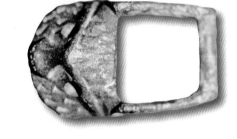

M12-0408
Buckle with Plate
Engraved
80mm
Even patina.
Engraved design on plate.
£10 - £20

M12-0409
Buckle with Plate
Gilded
60mm
Traces of gilding.
Pin missing.
£5 - £10

M12-0213
Buckle with Head
18mm
Patina a little patchy.
Small size.
£10 - £20

M12-0214
Buckle
58mm
Patina a little ragged.
Damage in places.
£10 - £20

M12-0215
Bird Buckle
49mm
Buckle in the form of a bird.
With its pin.
£5 - £10

M12-0301
Buckle Plate with Lion
40mm
Openwork design.
Even patina.
£60 - £80

M12-0302
Lion Buckle Plate
30mm
Openwork design.
Even patina.
£60 - £80

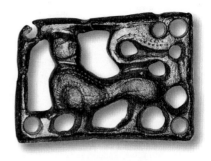

M12-0303
Beasts Buckle Plate
35mm
Traces of gilding.
Surface a little ragged.
£80 - £100

M12-0304
Dog Buckle Plate
58mm
Openwork design.
Detail fairly worn.
£80 - £100

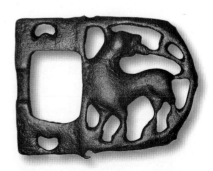

M12-0305
Buckle Plate with Dog
60mm
Openwork design.
Even patina. Good detail.
Some damage.
£120 - £180

M12-0306
Buckle Plate
40mm
Figure playing a harp. With
inscription. Silvered surface.
£100 - £150

M12-0307
Limoges Buckle Plate
31mm
Enamel intact but surface a
little ragged.
£40 - £60

M12-0401
Buckle with Plate
54mm
50% of gilding remaining.
Complete.
£40 - £60

M12-0402
Buckle with Plate
45mm
50% of gilding remaining.
Complete.
£200 - £300

M12-0403
Buckle with Plate
35mm
Basic design. Even patina.
£5 - £10

M12-0406
Zoomorphic Buckle
with Plate
65mm
Buckle in the form of a
beast. Dark, even patina.
£30 - £50

M12-0414
Buckle
80mm
Openwork design.
Silvered surface.
£60 - £80

M12-0415
Belt Plate
54mm
Sea lion regardant
motif.
£600 - £800

M12-0416
Buckle Plate
41mm
Cockatrice motif.
£200 - £300

M12-0417
Limoges Buckle Plate
36mm
With mounted knight motif.
£400 - £600

M12-0418
Belt Buckle
48mm
Enamelled design.
£200 - £300

M12-0419
Belt Plate
45mm
Lions rampant motif.
£600 - £800

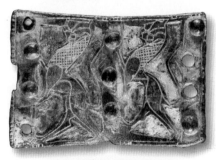

M12-0420
Belt Plate
43mm
Armed warrior motif.
£600 - £800

M15-0201
Norman Prick
Spur
150mm
Heavy construction
with acorn finial.
£80 - £100

M15-167014
Rowel Spur
180mm
Rowel with multiple
arms.
£100 - £150

M15-0202
Prick Spur
140mm
£80 - £100

M14-0101
Complete Mirror Case
45mm dia
Working condition. Surface a
little pitted.
£80 - £100

M14-0102
Complete Mirror Case
45mm dia
Working condition.
£80 - £100

M16-0112
Seal Matrix
35mm
Good surface. Lis in the
centre.
£30 - £40

M16-0101
Seal Matrix
34mm
Lis in centre. Weak in
places. Surface a little
scuffed.
£30 - £40

M16-0102
Seal Matrix
30mm
Lis in centre. Sharp detail.
Suspension loop intact.
£30 - £40

M16-0103
Seal Matrix
25mm
Petals in centre. Good, sharp
detail. Even surface.
£30 - £40

M16-0104
Seal Matrix
34mm
Sailing boat in centre. Sharp
detail. Rare type.
£40 - £60

M16-0105
Seal Matrix
36mm
Sharp detail. Large size.
£30 - £40

M16-0106
Seal Matrix
30mm
Lis in centre. Detail a little
weak. Surface ragged.
£20 - £30

M16-0107
Seal Matrix
32mm
Lis in centre. Sharp detail.
Even surface.
£30 - £40

M16-0108
Seal Matrix
27mm
Square and cross in the centre.
Suspension loop on back.
£30 - £40

M16-0109
Seal Matrix
41mm
Winged beast in the centre.
Surface a little rough.
£30 - £40

M16-0110
Seal Matrix
30mm
Petal design in the centre. Sharp
detail.
£30 - £40

M16-0111
Seal Matrix
32mm
Lion in the centre. Sharp detail.
£40 - £60

M16-0201
Seal Matrix
23mm
Letter 'B' in centre.
Even patina.
£50 - £80

M16-0202
Seal Matrix
22mm
Crowned letter I.
Patina a little patchy.
£40 - £60

M16-0203
Seal Matrix
20mm
Merchant's marks
within the shield.
Even patina.
£80 - £100

M16-0204
Seal Matrix
20mm
Figure blowing a horn and
seated on an animal. Sharp
detail. Even patina.
£150 - £200

M16-0205
Seal Matrix
22mm
Leaping stag.
Sharp detail.
Even patina.
£120 - £180

M16-0206
Seal Matrix
20mm
Monkey-like
animal. Detail a
little weak.
£100 - £150

M16-0207
Seal Matrix
19mm
Stag's head. Smooth
even patina. Sharp
detail.
£80 - £120

M16-0208
Seal Matrix
23mm
Bird in a tree together
with a human head.
Sharp detail. Even
surface and patina.
£100 - £150

M16-0209
Seal Matrix
20mm
Surface a little pitted.
Lis above clasped
hands. Weak detail in
places.
£80 - £120

M16-0210
Seal Matrix
27mm
Five leaves. Surface a little
uneven. Loop at top.
£80 - £120

M16-0211
Seal Matrix
22mm
Sacrificial lamb. Good, sharp
detail. Even patina.
£120 - £180

M16-0212
Seal Matrix
70mm
Very sharp detail. Good,
even surface. Complete and
undamaged. Large size. Rare.
From £10,000

M16-0213
Seal Matrix
28mm
St. Margaret spearing
a dragon. Sharp detail.
Even patina.
£200 - £300

M16-0214
Seal Matrix
33mm
Hawk on a glove.
Weak detail in places.
A little damage on the
edges.
£150 - £200

M16-0215
Seal Matrix
30mm
Bird with a worm in
its mouth. Good, sharp
detail. Even patina.
£180 - £240

M16-0216
Seal Matrix
31mm
Bird with a branch or twig in its mouth. Very sharp detail. Even patina. Personal name.
£180 - £240

M16-0217
Seal Matrix
31mm
Lion advancing. Very sharp detail. Complete and undamaged. Personal name.
£180 - £240

M16-0219
Seal Matrix
30mm
Sacrificial lamb. Sharp detail. Even patina. Personal name.
£120 - £180

M16-0222
Seal Matrix
40mm
Castle or abbey with lis above. Smooth surface. Large size. Personal name.
£200 - £300

M16-0223
Seal Matrix
30mm
Surface a little ragged. Personal name.
£100 - £150

M16-0221
Seal Matrix
26mm
Rampant lion. Sharp detail. Good, smooth patina.
£150 - £200

M16-0246
Seal Matrix
22mm
Flat with loop on the back. Head
in the centre. Motto around.
£120 - £180

M16-0247
Seal Matrix
32mm
Large, flat seal. Loop on the
back. Coat of arms in the
centre. Place name around.
Surface a little pitted.
£150 - £200

M16-0248
Seal Matrix
19mm
Flat with loop on back. Sharp
detail. Personal name around
(cleric).
£150 - £200

M16-0225
Seal Matrix
19mm
Four-leaf clover. Sharp
detail. Even patina.
£120 - £180

M16-0226
Seal Matrix
18mm
Smooth surface. Even
patina. Personal name.
Rare type.
£200 - £300

M16-0227
Seal Matrix
20mm
Even patina. Sleeping
lion in the centre, motto
around.
£100 - £150

M16-0228
Seal Matrix
31mm
Large personal seal.
Smooth, even surface.
Good patina.
From £500

M16-0229
Seal Matrix
20mm
Sharp detail. Surface a
little rough. Personal
name.
£150 - £200

M16-0230
Seal Matrix
18mm
Even patina. Head of St
John the Baptist. Motto
around.
£100 - £150

M16-0231
Seal Matrix
19mm
Smooth, even patina.
Depicting a bow and
arrow. Crescent and star
in field. Motto around.
Scarce type.
£150 - £200

M16-0232
Seal Matrix
20mm
Squirrel in the centre.
Personal name around.
£150 - £200

M16-0233
Seal Matrix
19mm
Smooth, rich patina.
Coat of arms in centre.
Personal name around.
£150 - £200

M16-0234
Seal Matrix
17mm
Head of St John the
Baptist in the centre.
Motto around.
£120 - £180

M16-0235
Seal Matrix
25mm
Implements or tools in the centre.
Personal name around.
Scarce type.
£200 - £300

M16-0236
Seal Matrix
25mm
Coat of arms in the
centre. No inscription.
£100 - £150

M16-0237
Seal Matrix
19mm
Small seal. Squirrel in
centre. Motto around.
£50 - £80

M16-0238
Seal Matrix
20mm
Hunting seal. Rabbit over
a dog. Motto around.
£100 - £150

M16-0239
Seal Matrix
25mm
Very sharp detail.
Smooth, even surface.
Lis in centre. Personal
name around.
£150 - £200

M16-0240
Seal Matrix
23mm
Patina a little patchy.
Bird in the centre.
Motto around.
£100 - £150

M16-0241
Seal Matrix
25mm
Smooth, even surface.
Coat of arms. Decoration
around.
£300 - £400

M16-0242
Seal Matrix
28mm
Three outwards facing
heads in the centre. Motto
around. Scarce type.
£200 - £300

M16-0249
Seal Matrix
22mm
Patina flaking in places. Flat with loop on back. Motto around.
£120 - £180

M16-0250
Seal Matrix
18mm
Hawk on a glove. Surface a little rough.
Personal name around.
£120 - £180

M16-0251
Seal Matrix with
St. Katherine
26mm
Large size. Sharp detail. St. Katherine in centre. Personal name around.
£200 - £300

M16-0244
Seal Matrix
18mm
Even patina. Clasped
hands. Motto around.
Sharp detail.
£100 - £150

M16-0252
Seal Matrix
28mm
Bird in the centre. Personal name
around. Smooth, even surface.
Sharp detail.
£180 - £240

M16-0254
Seal Matrix
32mm
Large size. Bird feeding its young
in the centre.
Personal name around.
£180 - £240

M16-0255
Seal Matrix
30mm
Pelican in her piety in the centre. Motto around.
£180 - £240

M16-0256
Seal Matrix
28mm
Bird feeding its young in the centre. Personal name around.
£180 - £240

M16-0257
Seal Matrix
42mm
Large size. Detail a little weak. Bull in the centre. Motto around.
£200 - £300

M16-0258
Seal Matrix
31mm
Sharp detail. Mary and child in a canopy. Figure praying beneath. Personal name around.

£300 - £400

M16-0259
Monastic Seal Matrix
49mm
Large priory seal. Slight damage at the bottom. Sharp detail.

From £1,000

M16-0260
Monastic Seal Matrix
50mm
Large monastic or abbey seal. Patina flaking in places.

From £1,000

M16-0301
Silver Seal Matrix
50mm
Virgin Mary with infant. Very sharp detail. Complete and undamaged. Large size. Rare.
From £3,000

M16-0302
Silver Seal Matrix
60mm
Bishop under a canopy, hand of God above. Detail a little weak. Large size. Rare.
From £3,000

M16-0303
Silver Seal Matrix
26mm
Silver seal with a Roman intaglio set in the centre. Motto around. Slight damage to the intaglio. Rare.
From £1,500

M16-0304
Seal Matrix
23mm
Madonna and
Child motif.
£100 - £150

M16-0305
Seal Matrix
27mm
Inscribed for St
Antimo Abbey,
Italy.
£400 - £600

M16 45516
Seal Matrix
23mm
'Isabelle of
Malling'.
£3,000 - £4,000

M16-0307
Seal Matrix
21mm
Rampant lion motif.
£150 - £200

M16-0308
Seal Matrix
20mm
Squirrel motif.
£150 - £200

M16-0309
Seal Matrix
24mm
With merchant's
mark.
£150 - £200

M16-0310
Seal Matrix
27mm
Unusual triangular shape.
£80 - £120

M16-0311
Seal Matrix
26mm
With hexafoil and
star.
£100 - £150

M16-0312
Seal Matrix
19mm
With portrait.
£100 - £150

M16-0313
Seal Matrix
24mm
With crowned R motif.
£100 - £150

M16-0314
Seal Matrix
19mm
With hexagonal bezel.
£100 - £150

M16-0315
Silver Seal Matrix
23mm
An angel holding a cross.
From £3,000

M16-0316
Heraldic Seal Matrix
39mm
Arms of Sir John
Bridsale.
From £2,000

M16-0317
Heraldic Seal
Matrix
33mm
Inscribed for
Renard of
Themericourt.
£800 - £1,000

M16-0318
Vesica Seal Matrix
59mm
Inscribed 'Of His Majesty The
King For Church Matters' for
the Bishop of Nottingham.
From £2,000

M16-0319
Vesica Seal Matrix
47mm
Heraldic design.
From £1,000

M16-0320
Seal Matrix
52mm
Inscribed for St Michael's
Monastery.
£300 - £400

M16-0321
Seal Matrix
32mm
Lion mask design. Inscription
reads 'SIGILLVM SECRET'
for 'a seal of secrecy'.
£400 - £600

M16-110522
Falconer's Seal Matrix
26mm
Legend to the border
' +S' RICARDI FIL'
SAMSVN' (seal
of Richard son of
Samson).
£400 - £600

M16-0323
Seal Matrix
30mm
Inscribed for Count
Goffridi (Geoffrey).
£1,000 - £1,500

M16-0324
Seal Matrix
25mm
Anchor motif,
chessman type.
£100 - £150

M16-0325
Silver-Gilt Seal
Matrix
19mm
Arms of Sir Richard
Wortley.
£400 - £600

M16-0326
Silver Seal Matrix
18mm
Inscribed 'SICILIE
de ASK' for Cecily
Herbert of Usk.
From £2,000

M16-0327
Seal Matrix
24mm
Inscribed for Alexander of Bergia.
£300 - £400

M16-0328
Crusader Seal Matrix
31mm
Inscribed for Stephen of Cyprus.
£150 - £200

M16-0329
Seal Matrix
21mm
Inscribed for
'Nicholas of
Stoneteli' with
manticore.
£150 - £200

M16-0330
Seal Matrix
36mm
Arms of Sir
William de Lisle
of Rougemont.
£600 - £800

M16-0331
Seal Matrix
65mm
From the Pope Urban V Papal
Office; attributable to Cardinal
Adam Easton.
From £4,000

M16-0332
Priory Seal
52mm
Inscribed for St. Victor of
Marseilles.
From £3,000

M16-0333
Silver-Gilt Seal Matrix
12mm
Inscribed 'Believe Me'.
£800 - £1,000

M16-0334
Seal Matrix
27mm
With heraldic design.
£150 - £200

M16-0335
Seal Matrix
23mm
Agnus Dei motif.
£100 - £150

M16-0336
Seal Matrix
20mm
With bird and
rabbit.
£100 - £150

M16-0401
Lead Papal
Bulla
35mm
Good detail.
Even colour.
£150 - £200

M16-0402
Lead Papal
Bulla
38mm
Even colour. A
few scuff marks.
Pierced in the
centre.
£150 - £200

M16-0403
Lead Papal
Bulla
39mm
One of the faces
scuffed. Sharp
lettering.
£200 - £300

M16-0404
Lead Papal
Bulla
38mm
Even colour. Sharp
detail on the faces.
£200 - £300

M16-0405
Lead Papal
Bulla
37mm
A little pitted on
the surface. Even
colour.
£150 - £200

M16-0406
Lead Papal Bulla
38mm
Scuffed in places.
Good detail.
£150 - £200

M16-0407
Lead Papal Bulla
40mm
Faces a little weak.
£150 - £200

M16-0408
Lead Papal Bulla
36mm
Scratches and scuffs over the surface.
£150 - £200

M16-0409
Papal Bulla
38mm
Perfect condition. Piece of original rope still running through the centre.
£300 - £400

M16-0501
Bag or Sack Seal
25mm
Crowned roses.
Complete.
£40 - £60

M16-0503
Wool Seal
44mm
Inscription reads 'Harlem
Alnager' in blackletter.
£60 - £80

M16-0601
Trial Piece
38mm
From a seal-maker's
workshop.
£120 - £180

M17-0117
Door Key
80mm
Even, green patina.
Surface a little uneven.
Unusual type.
£120 - £180

M17-0118
Door Key
80mm
Patina a little patchy in
places.
£80 - £120

M17-0119
Door Key
114mm
Large key. Surface
a little rough.
Typical style.
£100 - £150

M17-0120
Casket Key
47mm
Suspension loop at the top.
Simple style. Even patina.
£30 - £40

M17-0121
Barrel Lock Key
Smooth, even surface.
£30 - £40

M17-0105
Door Key
84mm
Even patina. Plain
style.
£80 - £100

M17-0106
Door Key
90mm
Surface a little
patchy. Plain style.
£80 - £100

M17-0107
Door Key
80mm
Good even patina.
Chunky size. Rare.
£200 - £300

M17-0108
Door Key
95mm
Smooth even patina.
Typical style.
£80 - £100

M17-0109
Door Key
88mm
Smooth even patina.
Complete and
undamaged.
£100 - £150

M17-0110
Door Key
85mm
Surface a little patchy.
Unusual style.
£80 - £120

M17-0111
Door Key
95mm
Even patina.
Complete.
£100 - £150

M17-0112
Door Key
90mm
Smooth even patina.
Handle well worn.
£80 - £100

M17-0113
Door Key
99mm
Even patina.
Unusual style.
£100 - £150

M17-0114
Door Key
90mm
Even patina.
Typical style.
£80 - £100

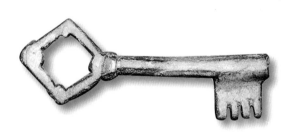

M17-0115
Door Key
85mm
Light green,
even patina.
Plain style.
£50 - £80

M17-0116
Door Key
85mm
Surface a little
rough. Plain
style.
£40 - £60

M17-0204
Iron Key
95mm
Good state of preservation.
Plain style.
£30 - £40

M17-0205
Iron Key
80mm
Complete. Very plain.
£10 - £20

M17-0206
Iron Keys
65mm
Good state of
preservation. Small
sizes.
£30 - £40 each

M17-0201
Iron Key
124mm
Good state of
preservation.
Large size.
£60 - £80

M17-0202
Iron Key
122mm
Good state of
preservation.
Large size.
Plain style.
£60 - £80

M17-0203
Iron Key
128mm
Good state of
preservation.
Plain style.
£30 - £40

M17-0104
Door Key
85mm
Surface a little patchy.
Complete.
£100 - £150

M17-0302
Casket Key
35mm
Smooth, even
surface and
patina.
£40 - £60

M17-0303
Casket Key
41mm
Trefoil bow type.
£20 - £30

M17-0401
Barrel Lock with Key
70mm
Surface a little ragged.
£40 - £60

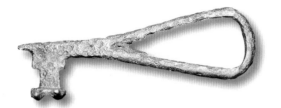

M17-0207
Iron Key
95mm
Good state of
preservation.
£30 - £40

M17-0208
Iron Key
97mm
Large iron key.
Good state of
preservation.
£30 - £40

M17-0209
Key
99mm
Trefoil head type.
£80 - £100

M17-0301
Casket Keys
Bronze
44mm
Undamaged.
Good even patina.
£10 - £20 each

M17 176578
Door Key
87mm
Lozenge-shaped
bow.
£80 - £100

M17-0505
Tudor Combination
Lock
32mm
Five-ring type.
£200 - £300

M17-0506
Tudor Combination
Lock
19mm
Five-ring type.
£150 - £200

M17-0501
Iron Ball Lock
30mm
Good state of
preservation.
Working order.
£40 - £60

M17-0502
Padlock
46mm
With incised
decoration.
£100 - £150

M18-0104
Gold Noble Coin Weight
19mm
Circular shape with sharp
detail. Even patina.
£20 - £30

M18-0203
Lead Trade Weight with
Three Lions
70mm
Fair detail. A few scuffs. Eight
ounce weight.
£40 - £60

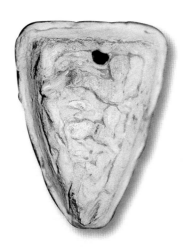

M18-0215
Lead Trade Weight with
Cross
60mm
Cross in the centre. Three
pellets around.
£20 - £30

M18-0204
Henry VII Trade Weight
70mm
Crowned 'H' stamped on the
surface. Even patina. Large
size.
£30 - £40

M18-0205
Steelyard Weight, Lead
Filled
70mm
Spherical with a suspension
loop. Four shields engraved
around the surface. Rare.
£400 - £600

M18-0206
Steelyard Weight, Lead
Filled
48mm
Spherical. Lead filled.
Depicting four lions.
Suspension loop missing.
From £500

M18-0207
Trade Weight (4oz)
60mm
Four ounce weight. Bronze.
Good patina. (Henry VII?)
£30 - £40

M18-0208
Elizabeth I Trade Weight
(2oz)
46mm
Scarce two ounce Elizabeth I
trade weight.
£40 - £60

M18-0209
Lead Trade Weight with
Three Lions
60mm
Eight ounce weight. A few
scuffs. Good detail.
£40 - £60

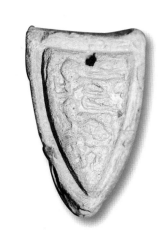

M18-0216
Lead Trade Weight, 1lb
78mm
Heavy pound weight. Possibly embossed with merchant's marks.
£30 - £40

M18-0217
Lead Trade Weight
35mm
Small weight. Weak detail.
£5 - £10

M18-0218
Lead Trade Weight, ½lb
55mm
Half pound weight.
'M' or 'W' in the centre.
£20 - £30

M18-0223
Trade Weight
69mm
Crown and Fleur-de-lys
type
£60 - £80

M18-0220
Lead Trade Weight
35mm
Four ounce weight. Lion in
centre. Weak detail.
£5 - £10

M18-0221
Lead Trade Weight
32mm
Small one ounce weight. Good
detailed lis in centre.
£10 - £20

M18-0401
Coin Weight
15mm
Antwerp Gold
Burgundian Ducat
1567.
£10 - £20

M18-0301
Nested Cup Weight
Set
41mm
Amsterdam issue type.
£100 - £150

M18-0502
Balance Arm
103mm
Nice, even patina.
Zoomorphic ends to the
arms.
£60 - £80

M18-0503
Tumbrel Coin Balance
85mm
Rare tumbrel. A little damage
on the balance arm. Full
museum report.
From £100

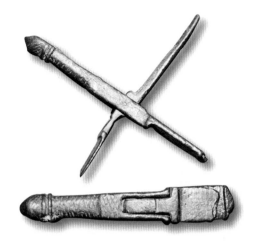

M18-0504
Tumbrel Coin Balance
89mm
£100 - £150

M21-0101
Pouring Spout
75mm
Good, smooth surface. Even
patina.
£30 - £40

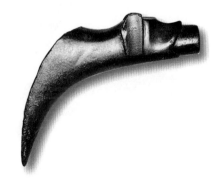

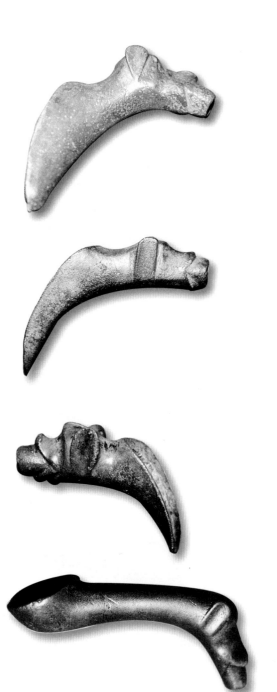

M21-0102
Pouring Spout
75mm
Surface a little pitted.
Patchy patina.
£30 - £40

M21-0103
Pouring Spout
75mm
Typical form. Surface
a little pitted. Patchy
patina.
£30 - £40

M21-0104
Pouring Spout
65mm
Good style. Even
patina.
£30 - £40

M21-0105
Pouring
Spout
120mm
Elongated neck.
Even patina.
£30 - £40

M21-0202
Spoon
174mm
Seal top. Tinned surface a
little patchy. Clear maker's
mark. Undamaged.
£120 - £180

M21-0203
Silver-Gilt Spoon
150mm
'Diamond point' finial.
From £1,000

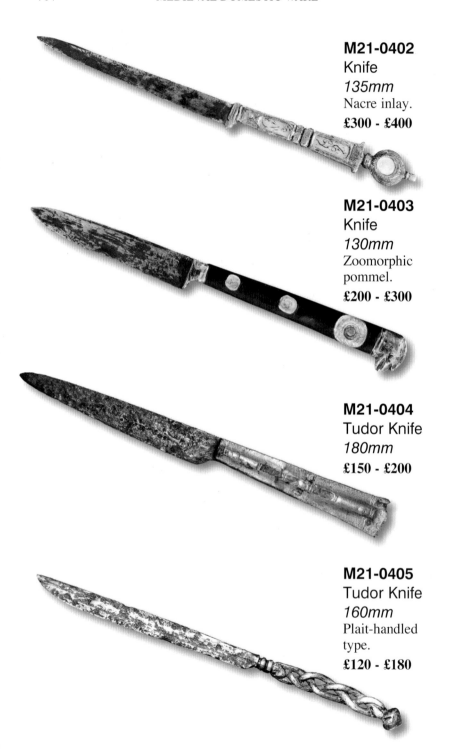

M21-0402
Knife
135mm
Nacre inlay.
£300 - £400

M21-0403
Knife
130mm
Zoomorphic
pommel.
£200 - £300

M21-0404
Tudor Knife
180mm
£150 - £200

M21-0405
Tudor Knife
160mm
Plait-handled
type.
£120 - £180

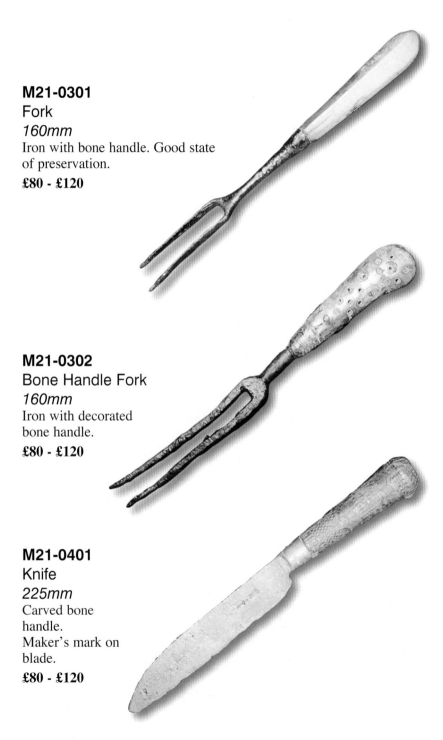

M21-0301
Fork
160mm
Iron with bone handle. Good state
of preservation.
£80 - £120

M21-0302
Bone Handle Fork
160mm
Iron with decorated
bone handle.
£80 - £120

M21-0401
Knife
225mm
Carved bone
handle.
Maker's mark on
blade.
£80 - £120

M23-0101
Jetton
25mm
Burgundian
steel and flints
type.
From £30

M23-0102
Jetton
25mm
Crown type.
From £10

M23-0103
Jetton
25mm
Dolphin type.
From £20

M23-0104
Jetton
25mm
Shield and lis
type.
From £15

M23-0105
Jetton
20mm
English. Crude
face type.
From £20

M23-0106
Jetton
17mm
English. Edward I
portrait type.
From £20

M23-0201
Boy Bishop
Token
28mm
Bishop's mitre.
Groat size.
£20 - £30

M23-0202
Boy Bishop
Token
25mm
Bishop's head.
Groat size.
£20 - £30

M23-0203
Boy Bishop
Token
15mm
Bishop's mitre.
Half groat size.
£10 - £20

M23-0204
Boy Bishop Token
28mm
Bishop's head. Groat
size. Sharp detail.
£30 - £40

M23-0205
Boy Bishop
Token
28mm
Groat size. Facing
bust. Sharp detail.
£30 - £40

M23-0207
Boy Bishop Token
28mm
Three crowns of Bury St
Edmunds. Groat size.
Slight damage.
£30 - £40

M23-0208
Boy Bishop Token
32mm
Large groat size.
Bishop's mitre.
£20 - £30

M23-0206
Boy Bishop
Token
28mm
Groat size.
Bishop's head.
£20 - £30

M24-162669
Pilgrim Badge
62mm
Dove with an olive branch
in its beak, with motto 'amor
uincit omia[sic]' ('love
conquers all').
£800 - £1,000

M24-0101
Pilgrim Badge
38mm
Virgin Mary badge with pin.
£100 - £150

M24-0102
Pilgrim Badge
35mm
Complete and undamaged
with pin.
£80 - £120

M24-0103
Tau Cross Pilgrim
Badge
38mm
Complete and undamaged
with pin.
£100 - £150

M24-0104
Virgin Mary Pilgrim
Badge
24mm
Associated with the shrine
at Walsingham. Undamaged
with pin.
£150 - £200

M24-0105
Virgin Mary Pilgrim
Badge
22mm
Associated with the shrine at
Walsingham. A little damage.
No pin.
£80 - £100

M24-0106
Virgin Mary Pilgrim
Badge
24mm
Associated with the shrine
at Walsingham. A little
damage. With pin.
£80 - £100

M24-0107
Axe Pilgrim Badge
67mm
Good example. Sharp
detail.
£200 - £300

M24-0108
Bromholm Pilgrim
Badge
44mm
Sacred hart badge with
pin intact.
£80 - £100

M24-0109
Scabbard Pilgrim Badge
58mm
Associated with Fitz Urse,
leader of the knights who
attacked Becket. Pin intact.
£150 - £200

M24-0110
Thomas Becket
Pilgrim Badge
88mm
Complete with pin. 'Thomas'
at the base. Large size.
From £500

M24-0111
St Leonard
Pilgrim Badge
50mm
Undamaged and complete with
pin. Of the finest quality.
From £800

M24-0112
St Leonard Pilgrim Badge
45mm
Complete with pin.
Slight damage.
Banner missing from base.
From £400

M24-0113
Pilgrim Badge
50mm
Scarce badge. Horse's front
legs missing. Pin intact.
£300 - £400

M24-0114
Pilgrim Badge
28mm
Sew-on type. A little damage.
£50 - £80

M24-162717
Pilgrim Badge
56mm
Three arches with St Maurice,
St Peter, Pope Boniface IX.
£800 - £1,000

M24-0116
Thomas Becket
Pilgrim Badge
55mm
Pewter badge. Good detail.
Most of pin remaining.
From £800

M24-0117
Badge
25mm
Small figure in the centre.
Flanked by another figure on
each side.
£40 - £60

M24-0118
Pilgrim Badge
55mm
Pewter bell suspended
from a chain.
£80 - £100

M24-162712
Pilgrim Badge
100mm
'Robe of the Virgin' type
from Aachen.
£800 - £1,000

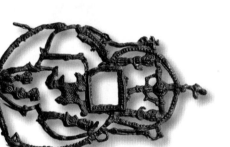

M24-162713
Pilgrim Badge
101mm
'Robe of the Virgin' type
from Aachen.
£800 - £1,000

M24-0121
Pilgrim Badge
56mm
Pewter crucifix. Sew on
badge.
£300 - £400

M24-0122
Pilgrim Badge
40mm
Advancing archer. Damaged in places.
£150 - £200

M24-177535
Pilgrim Badge
76mm
Three Gothic arches with figures.
£1,500 - £2,000

M24-0124
St George Pilgrim Badge
20mm
St George's cross. Badge with pin.
£40 - £60

M24-0125
Bellows Pilgrim Badge
22mm
Badge in the form of bellows.
With pin.
£50 - £80

M24-0126
Ostrich Feather Pilgrim Badge
58mm
A little ragged around the edges. Large size.
£80 - £120

M24-0127
Talbot Dog Retainer's badge
35mm
In the form of a talbot which was a hunting dog. With pin.
£80 - £100

M24-0128
Becket Pilgrim Badge
40mm
Openwork with Thomas
Becket's head in the centre.
Slight damage. With pin.
£400 - £600

M24-0129
Pilgrim Badge
55mm
Knight on horseback.
Badge with pin.
£120 - £180

M24-0130
Pilgrim Badge
48mm
Large badge.
'IHS' in the centre.
With pin.
£150 - £200

M24-0131
Phallic Pilgrim Badge
63mm
A walking phallus badge.
Surface a little ragged. Large
size.
£100 - £150

M24-0132
Poppinjay Pilgrim
Badge
48mm
Slight damage.
Feet missing. With pin.
£80 - £100

M24-0133
Pilgrim Badge
38mm
Badge in the form of a
crown. Small piece broken
at the top.
£80 - £100

M24-0135
Pilgrim Badge
40mm
Sew-on type openwork frame.
Mary and Child in the centre.
£150 - £200

M24-0136
Pilgrim Badge
34mm
Double-sided badge.
Probably worn as a
pendant.
£150 - £200

M24-0137
Walsingham Pilgrim
Badge
25mm
Virgin Mary and Child.
Complete with pin.
£120 - £180

M24-0138
Henry VI Pilgrim Badge
30mm
Badge associated with Henry
VI. Lozenge shape. Piece
missing at the top. With pin.
£150 - £200

M24-0139
Pilgrim Badge
22mm
In the form of a crossbow.
With pin.
£50 - £80

M24-0140
Punctured Heart
Pilgrim Badge
24mm
In the form of a punctured
heart. With pin.
£50 - £80

M24-0141
Lis Pilgrim Badge
22mm
Complete with pin.
£30 - £40

M24-0142
Gloves of Becket
Pilgrim Badge
19mm
Representing the gloves of
Thomas Becket. With pin.
£80 - £120

M24-0143
Gloves of Becket
Pilgrim Badge
18mm
Representing the gloves of
Thomas Becket. With pin.
£80 - £100

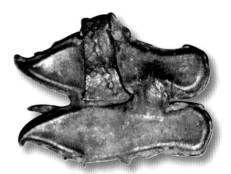

M24-0144
Walsingham Pilgrim Badge
20mm
Slippers associated with the shrine at Walsingham. With pin.
£80 - £100

M24-0145
Retainer's Badge
45mm
Lion passant. Large sew on type. One eyelet broken away.
£150 - £200

M24-0146
Pilgrim Badge
23mm
Bird feeding its young (pelican in piety). With pin.
£150 - £200

M24-0147
Fish Pilgrim Badge
61mm
Silvered surface. With pin. Scarce type.
£50 - £80

M24-0148
Pilgrim Badge
28mm
Seated Mary and Child within
a quatrefoil openwork frame.
With pin and undamaged.
£400 - £600

M24-0149
Pilgrim Badge
20mm
Petalled flower within an
openwork frame. With pin.
£50 - £80

M24-0150
Pilgrim Badge
25mm
Two figures standing
within a letter M with pin.
£200 - £300

M24-0151
Pilgrim Badge
27mm
Two figures standing within a letter M. With pin.
£100 - £150

M24-0152
Peter & Paul Pilgrim Badge
35mm
Depicting St Peter and St Paul. Good clear detail. Scarce type.
£300 - £400

M24-0153
Mount
49mm
A little damaged but sharp detail. Large size.
£400 - £600

M24-0154
Pilgrim Badge
38mm
Sew on type.
First class condition.
£500 - £700

M24-0155
Pilgrim Badge
23mm
Head within a frame.
Complete with pin.
£100 - £150

M24-0156
Pilgrim Badge
17mm
Head within a frame.
Inscription around.
With pin.
£100 - £150

M24-0157
St Leonard
Pilgrim Badge
42mm
Slight break in his crozier.
Apart from that a perfect
badge.
£800 - £1,000

M24-0158
Henry VI Pilgrim Badge
51mm
Good size. Slight damage.
With pin.
£100 - £150

M24-0159
John Schorn Pilgrim
Badge
42mm
Vicar John Schorn pulling the
devil out of a boot. With pin.
£200 - £300

M24-0160
Silver Pilgrim Badge
17mm
St George and the dragon
motif.
£200 - £300

M24-0161
Pewter Pilgrim Badge
15mm
A plough in profile with
openwork crown above, for
'Plough Monday'.
£150 - £200

M24-0162
King David Pilgrim
Badge
35mm
King David enthroned,
holding the head of
Goliath in one hand and
Goliath's sword in the
other.
£200 - £300

M24-0201
Pilgrim's Ampulla
34mm
Heraldic shields
design.
£150 - £200

M24-0202
Pilgrim's Ampulla
55mm
Cross and chevron
motifs.
£100 - £150

M24-0203
Pilgrim's Ampulla
48mm
St Thomas of
Canterbury type.
From £500

M24-0204
Pilgrim's Ampulla
28mm
Long Arrow of
Walsingham motif.
£50 - £80

M24-0205
Tin Pilgrim's Ampulla
23mm
One side shows Becket being beheaded. The other shows the head of Becket above a scallop. Small but complete. Rare.

£200 - £300

M24-0206
Tin Pilgrim's Ampulla
54mm
Scenes on each side. Reliquary-shaped. Rare.

From £500

M24-153703
Lead Pilgrim's Ampulla
58mm
Lead-alloy, raised 'H' motif.

£80 - £100

M24-0208
Lead Pilgrim's Ampulla
52mm
Both lugs present. Even shape.

£50 - £80

M24-0209
Lead Pilgrim's Ampulla
50mm
Both lugs present.
A little mis-shapen.
£60 - £80

M24-0210
Lead Pilgrim's Ampulla
48mm
Both lugs present.
Crude animal's head on one
side. A little mis-shapen.
£80 - £100

M24-0211
Lead Pilgrim's Ampulla
48mm
Both lugs present. Fairly even
shape.
£60 - £80

M24-0212
Lead Pilgrim's Ampulla
50mm
Lugs missing. Bag shaped.
Letters on one side.
£80 - £100

M24-0213
Lead Pilgrim's Ampulla
50mm
Both lugs present. Good even
shape.
£60 - £80

M24-0214
Lead Pilgrim's Ampulla
50mm
Both lugs present. Good even
shape.
£80 - £100

M24-0215
Lead Pilgrim's Ampulla
48mm
Both lugs present. A little ragged at the top.
£60 - £80

M24-0216
Lead Pilgrim's Ampulla
52mm
One lug damaged. Face on one side.
£60 - £80

M24-0217
Lead Pilgrim's Ampulla
45mm
Both lugs present. Good even shape.
£80 - £100

M24-0218
Lead Pilgrim's Ampulla
54mm
Both lugs present. Good even
shape. Letters on one side.
£100 - £150

M24-0219
Lead Pilgrim's Ampulla
53mm
Both lugs present. Even shape.
£60 - £80

M24-0220
Pilgrim's Ampulla
with Chain
58mm
Good even shape. Both lugs present.
Complete suspension chain. Very rare.
£400 - £600

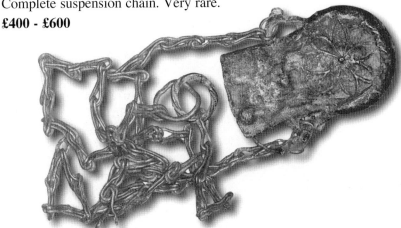

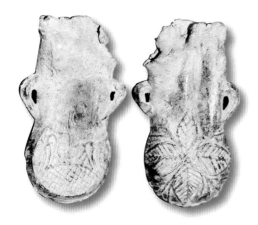

M24-0221
Lead Pilgrim's
Ampulla
55mm
A little damage.
Both lugs present.
£60 - £80

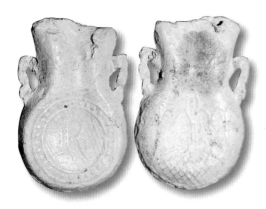

M24-0222
Lead Pilgrim's
Ampulla
47mm
Both lugs present.
Good, even colour.
£60 - £80

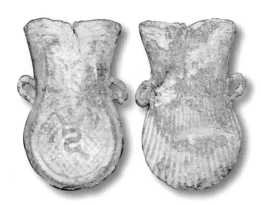

M24-0223
Lead Pilgrim's
Ampulla
48mm
Crowned reversed 'S'.
Both lugs present.
£80 - £100

M24-0224
Lead Pilgrim's
Ampulla
43mm
Letters on both sides.
A little scuffed
in places.
£150 - £200

M24-0225
Lead Pilgrim's
Ampulla
40mm
Coats of arms on
both sides.
Surface a little flaky.
£150 - £200

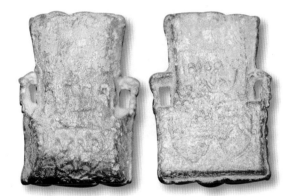

M24-0303
Silver Badge
18mm
Small retainer's badge
depicting an owl.
From £200

M24-0304
Silver Gilt
Retainer's Badge
28mm
Loop on the back.
George and dragon.
Detail a little worn.
£150 - £200

M24-0305
Pewter Hunting
Horn Badge
21mm
Hunting horn of St
Hubert motif with pin
to reverse.
£100 - £150

M24-0306
Pewter Jousting
Badge
31mm
A mounted horseman
with canted shield and
tilting helm. Rare.
£300 - £400

M24-130687
Agnus Dei
Roundel
55mm
'Lamb and Flag' motif.
£300 - £400

M24-135330
Papal Bulla Seal
40mm
Pope Clement V.
£150 - £200

M24-163733
Mount with Angel
47mm
Gilt bronze with
enamel cloisonné.
£2,000 - £3,000

M24-0310
Pilgrim's Whistle
39mm
Brass, St Catherine's
Wheel motif.
£50 - £80

M24-0311
Silver Cross
Pendant
33mm
£400 - £600

M24-0312
Silver-Gilt Cross
Pendant
36mm
£300 - £400

M24-0313
Silver-Gilt
Pendant
33mm
Religious text
"Thine Is The Power
Throughout Endless
Ages, O Lord".
From £2,000

M24-0314
Gold Pendant
46mm
Nativity motif.
From £10,000

M24-0315
Limoges Mount
40mm
£150 - £200

M24-0316
Large Limoges Cross
Mount
80mm
Most of the enamel and
gilding remaining.
From £1,000

M24-0317
Heraldic Bracteate
15mm
Knights of the Holy
Sepulchre.
£20 - £30

M24-167000
Corpus Christi
Fitting
*220mm incl
stand*
Limoges type,
gilded.
£2,000 - £3,000

M24-176326
Reliquary
35mm
Gilt-bronze reliquary
fragment, crowned
head of Christ.
£200 - £300

M24-176323
Reliquary Figure
79mm
Limoges type with
enamelled panels.

£200 - £300

M24-177519
Reliquary Figure
54mm
Limoges type with
enamelled panels.

£300 - £400

M24-0318
Openwork Fitting
26mm
Pommel or sceptre
finial.
£80 - £100

M24-0319
Laver Spout
62mm
With dog head.
£30 - £40

M24-0320
Leather Bible Bag
180mm
£300 - £400

M25-0101
Purse Bar
85mm
Fairly plain design.
Smooth, even patina.
£60 - £60

M25-0102
Purse Bar
90mm
Smooth, even
patina. Engraved
detail on the
surface.
£100 - £150

M25-0103
Purse Bar
90mm
Patina patchy. Silver inlaid
'IHS' in the centre.
£150 - £200

M25-0107
Purse Bar
146mm
With inscription.
£150 - £200

M25-0108
Purse Frame
205mm
With inscription.
£800 - £1,000

M25-0109
Purse Bar
59mm
With incised X-motif.
£50 - £80

M25-0202
Thimble
26mm
Even patina. Thick and
chunky style.
£30 - £40

M25-0203
Thimble
20mm
Chunky and heavy.
Patina a little patchy.
£20 - £30

M25-0207
Thimble
18mm
Smooth surface.
Even patina.
£25 - £30

M99-46624
Inscribed Silver Hawking Ring
9mm
Inscribed 'T M OF HITCHIN'.
£800 - £1,000

M99-0209
Silver Hawking Vervel
Ring
12mm
Inscribed for de Vere family.
From £1,200

M99-0210
Silver Hawking Vervel
Ring
16mm
Inscribed for 'Bourton on
Dunsmore'.
From £1,200

M99-0211
Silver Hawking
Vervel
15mm
Inscribed with
foliage and
blackletter text.
From £500

M99-0212
Silver Hawking
Vervel
9mm
Inscribed for 'Edmund
Plantagenet, Earl of
Rutland'.
From £1,000

M99-0213
Gold Seal Ring
22mm
Inscribed for Geoffrey Rudel de Blaye, intaglio with hawk.
From £3,000

M99-0402
Die Tester
80mm
Three repeated designs
from the same die.
£100 - £150

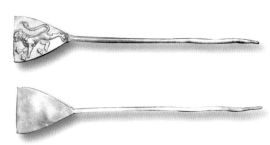

M99-0501
Silver-Gilt Pointer
94mm
Rampant lion. Super
detail. Book pointer or
marker.
£400 - £600

M99-0502
Page Marker
60mm
Rare page bookmark
with locking device.
Even patina.
£100 - £150

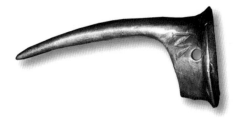

M99-0601
Silver Cockspur
28mm
Initialled WP.
£100 - £150

M99-0701
Sun Dial
29mm
Small but complete
pocket sundial.
From £500

M99-0301
Lead Casket Cover
Reliquary
70mm
Very slight traces of
enamel. Lion with right
paw on a shield. Scarce.
£300 - £400

M99-163730
Enamelled Fitting
86mm
Polychrome cloisonné
enamel ornament.
£800 - £1,000

M99-0802
Silver Bodkin
90mm
Has an ear scoop on the end.
With owner's initials and
maker's mark along its body.
£80 - £100

M99-0803
Silver Bodkin
88mm
Plain, undecorated.
£60 - £80

M99-0804
Silver Bodkin
120mm
Ear scoop on the end. Also
decorated along three quarters
of its length.
£80 - £100

M99-163746
Floor Tile
135mm
Spread eagle
motif on a heater
shield.
£300 - £400

M99-0902
Floor Tile
120mm
Part of a
four tile set
with heraldic
roundel.
£150 - £200

THE POST-MEDIEVAL PERIOD

The post-medieval period opens with the 17th century; most collectors assign it an end at the close of the Georgian era in 1837 although others lose interest after the Stuarts in 1688. Being still fairly recent by historical standards, the label 'post-medieval' may lack the lustre of antiquity conferred by 'Roman' or 'Bronze Age', but it encompasses the entire Commonwealth and the Restoration, Cavaliers and Roundheads, the secession of the American colonies and the transformation of Britain from a small island off the coast of northern Europe into a world-class power with ambitions around the globe.

The range of artefacts known from the period is truly staggering, with ephemera such as newspapers and advertising handbills surviving alongside masterpieces of jewellery, tableware, clothing, domestic items, ceramics and much else besides. The daily lives of the highest to the lowest can be reconstructed and interpreted from the remains available to us.

Advances in science and engineering allowed the development of chronometers, navigational aids, optical lenses, steam-powered machinery, printing presses, paper-mills, and new methods of creating materials such as spelter and brass.

With a greater access to literacy among the populace, inscriptions became very common – whether initials on the reverse of a spoon, a monogram on a seal, or a declaration of undying love written on the inner face of a posy ring – such rings with emotive texts became very collectible in recent years, and TimeLine Auctions recorded some very strong interest among collectors leading to high prices. Seals and tags became a popular means of identifying property – many of them produced in large numbers. This period saw the gradual but unstoppable rise of mechanisation and the mass-production of goods – household wares, belt-buckles, buttons, firearms, most of the small but important things on which human life depends.

P04-0101
Iron Knives
70mm
Pen-knife £40 - £60
Fixed blade £30 - £40

P04-0102
Iron Knife with Bone
Handle
200mm
Decorated handle. Good state
of preservation.
£80 - £100

P04-0103
Iron Knife with Silver
Handle
139mm
Silver decorated handle.
Good state of preservation.
£200 - £300

P04-0104
Folding Knife Handle
71mm
In the form of a squirrel or
beaver. Good detail.
£100 - £150

P04-153599
Rapier
940mm
Basket-hilt type with
side-guards.
£600 - £800

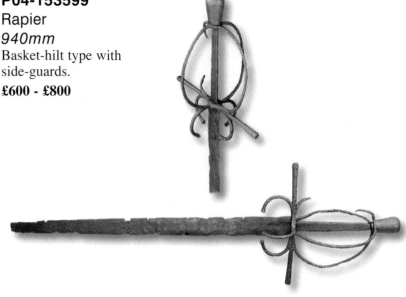

P04-0106
Iron Knife with
Inscription
85mm
Bronze handle. Iron blade
with inscription on both
sides.
£40 - £60

P05-0101
Iron Mace Head
164mm
Surface decorated. Four
fins around the shaft.
Rare.
£400 - £600

P08-0101
Silver Pendant
28mm
Engraved initials on
one side. Flower on
the other.
£100 - £150

P08-0102
Silver Pendant
28mm
Charles I royalist
badge or pendant.
Good detail.
From £400

P08-0103
Silver Pendant
31mm
With religious
inscription.
£100 - £150

P08-0201
Brass Badge
30mm
Figure standing by an altar.
Even patina. Fixing lug on
the back.

£30 - £50

P08-0202
Brass Bracteate Badge
38mm
Head in the centre
surrounded by an inscription.
A little damage.

£80 - £100

P08-139505
Military Reward
Badge
30mm
Badge of Robert
Devereux, 3rd Earl
of Essex.

£1,000 - £1,500

P06-0101
Silver-Gilt Pin
78mm
Openwork designed
head. Most of the
gilding remaining.
£100 - £150

P09-0101
Head Mount
65mm
Bearded man wearing a
cloth hat. Even patina.
£80 - £100

P09-0102
Heraldic Mount
48mm
Three fixing lugs on the
back. Good, even patina.
£80 - £100

P09-0105
Head Mount
63mm
Large mount in the
form of a gruesome
face.
£50 - £80

P09-0106
Pilgrim Mount
34mm
St John the Baptist
and Agnus Dei motifs.
£100 - £150

P09-0107
Stuart Mount
32mm
Double-eagle motif.
£40 - £60

P10-0101
Gold Posy Ring
20mm
Inscribed 'In Love
Love abide till death
devide'.
£800 - £1,000

P10-0102
Gold Posy Ring
22mm
Inscribed 'Hurt not
that (heart) whoes
Joy thou art'.
£1,000 - £1,500

P10-0103
Silver-Gilt Posy
Ring
18mm
Inscribed '-
CVMFORT ME'.
£300 - £400

P10-0104
Gold Posy Ring
20mm
Inscribed 'A true
Friends' gift'.
£600 - £800

P10-0105
Gold Posy Ring
19mm
Inscribed 'God
abouekeepe vs in
loue'.
£1,000 - £1,500

P10-0106
Gold Posy Ring
21mm
Inscribed 'As god
decreed so we
agreed'.
£800 - £1,000

P10-0107
Gold Posy Ring
17mm
Inscribed 'Heauens
perfect our intents'.
£1,000 - £1,500

P10-0108
Gold Posy Ring
20mm
Inscribed 'God's
Blessing Be On
Thee'.
£800 - £1,000

P10-0109
Gold Posy Ring
22mm
Inscribed 'be
Constant to the End'.
£800 - £1,000

P10-0110
Gold Posy Ring
22mm
Inscribed 'I like my
choyse to well to
change'.
From £2,000

P10-0111
Gold Posy Ring
17mm
Inscribed 'No gift to
true affection'.
£800 - £1,000

P10-0112
Gold Posy Ring
17mm
Inscribed 'Not a truer
frend aliue'.
From £1,500

P10-0113
Gold Posy Ring
22mm
Inscribed 'Seing god
hath made of two
but one - Let nothing
part but deth alone'.
From £2,000

P10-0114
Gold Posy Ring
22mm
Inscribed 'As God
decreed so we
agreed'.
£800 - £1,000

P10-177353
Gold Posy Ring
23mm
Inscribed '+ with love and joie i thynk of thee' (exterior); '+ loke on thys gyft and thynk of me'.
£6,000 - £8,000

P10-130962
Gold Posy Ring
19mm
P Incised 'Accept my good will x'.
£600 - £800

P10-134085
Gold Posy Ring
21mm
Incised '*I+like+my+choyse ".
£800 - £1,000

P10-131180
Gold Posy Ring
19mm
Inscription 'Vertue
Passeth Riches'.
£800 - £1,000

P10-153472
Gold Ring
22mm
Twelve inset table-
cut diamonds
surrounding a larger
similar diamond.
£3,000 - £4,000

P10-166456
Gold Ring
23mm
Inset table-cut and
polished facetted
rock crystal
gemstone.
£2,000 - £3,000

P10-167744
Gold Ring
22mm
Inset with carved
glass cabochon,
heraldic shield and
flower.
£2,000 - £3,000

P10-0205
Gold Memorial Ring
19mm
Heavy ring. Black enamel inlay. Maker's mark and date of 1671.
£800 - £1,000

P10-0206
Gold Memorial Ring
20mm
With skull motif and inscription.
£1,000 - £1,500

P10-0207
Gold Memorial Ring
20mm
Skull on an enamelled background.
£1,000 - £1,500

P10-0208
Gold Signet Ring
20mm
With large bezel.
From £4,000

P10-146451
Gold Ring
21mm
Inset table-cut diamond.
£4,000 - £6,000

P10-146452
Gold Ring
23mm
Three plaques each with an
inset table-cut diamond.
£3,000 - £4,000

P10-138805
Gold Memento Mori Ring
24mm
Inscribed 'R Dunn ob 28 Jan 1731
aet 46'.
£4,000 - £6,000

P10-141328
Gold Memento Mori
Ring
21mm
Inscribed 'In mem J. T. Bartt
obijt 28 feb 77'.
£600 - £800

P10-0209
Gold Signet Ring
20mm
Bunch of grapes motif.
From £6,000

P10-0210
Gold Ring
17mm
Inscribed 'BEFORE LYFE COMES DEATH'.
£800 - £1,000

P10-0211
Silver-Gilt Ring
24mm
Clasped hands motif.
£300 - £400

P10-0212
Gold Ring
21mm
Memento mori text.
£400 - £600

P10-0213
Gold Ring
21mm
Memento Moti
text.
£400 - £600

P10-0214
Gold Ring
21mm
With hunting dog intaglio.
£300 - £400

P10-0215
Gold Ring
23mm
With inset sapphire cabochon.
£800 - £1,000

P10-174779
Gold Ring
23mm
18th century ring with
inset Roman nicolo
intaglio of a horse
advancing.
£10,000 - £15,000

P11-0101
Staff Top
60mm
Bearded man wearing a hat. Silvered surface.
£50 - £80

P12-0103
Silver Buckle with Maker's Mark
40mm
Iron rivet still in situ. Prominent maker's mark.
£20 - £30

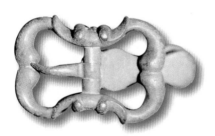

P12-0102
Buckle
38mm
Even patina. Decorative style.
£5 - £10

P12-0104
Gilded Buckle
57mm
Two opposing lions' heads.
£40 - £60

P13-131128
Silver Charles II Wedding Button
15mm
Associated with the marriage of Charles II and Catherine of Braganza in 1662.
£60 - £80

P13-0101
Button with Head Of Christ
25mm
Good detail. Even patina.
£10 - £20

P13-0102
Silver Cufflink or Button
16mm
Two crowned hearts.
£60 - £80

P15-0101
Bridle Boss
65mm
Cherub style head
in the centre. Heads
around the outside.
£50 - £80

P16-0101
Lead Bale Seal
40mm
A little scuffed
in places but
complete.
£30 - £40

P16-0102
Colchester
Lead Cloth Seal
48mm
Griffin on one side.
Three ships on the
other.
£60 - £80

P16-0103
Lead Bag or Bale Seal
50mm
Sharp detail.
£40 - £60

P16-0104
Lead Bag or Bale Seal
20mm
Small size. Complete.
£15 - £20

P16-0107
Lead Cloth Seal
64mm
Ascribed to the Swynford
family, inscribed 'Let the
Lord's will be Done'.
£50 - £80

P16-0106
Lead Bag or Bale Seal
23mm
Depiction of Queen Anne.
£20 - £30

P16-0108
Lead Bottle Seal
39mm
£40 - £60

P16-0201
Fob Seal
28mm
Some of the gilding remaining.
Good, undamaged stone.
£40 - £60

P16-0202
Silver Fob Seal with
Queen Anne
27mm
Seal gives a sharp impression.
Good silver.
£100 - £150

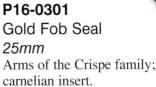

P16-0301
Gold Fob Seal
25mm
Arms of the Crispe family;
carnelian insert.
£200 - £300

P16-0403
Silver Seal
Matrix
23mm
With Queen Anne
portrait.
£100 - £150

P16-0404
Silver Seal
Matrix
27mm
Heraldic with
crowned shield.
£100 - £150

P16-0405
Seal Matrix
47mm
Ascribed to
Thomas Deas,
Bishop of Meath.
From £5,000

P17-0101
Casket Key
45mm
Openwork handle. Standard type.
£20 - £30

P17-0102
Casket Key
46mm
Openwork handle. Standard type. Smooth, even patina.
£20 - £30

P17-0103
Iron Latch Key
75mm
Good state of preservation.
£30 - £40

P17-0104
Iron Key
140mm
Good state of preservation. Large size.
£20 - £30

P18-0101
Queen Anne Lead Weight
48mm
Norwich. A few scuffs on the surface. Sharp marks.
£50 - £80

P18-0102
Bronze Weight
50mm
Large size. Even patina.
£5 - £10

P18-0105
Charles I Trade Weight
42mm
Even patina. Clear marks.
£10 - £20

P18-0106
Charles I Trade Weight
45mm
Surface a little battered. Four
ounce weight.

£30 - £40

P18-0107
Charles II Lead Weight
½ oz
23mm
Surface a little damaged.

£20 - £30

P18-0110
Crowned C
Lead weight
85mm
Large Charles I weight.

£30 - £40

P18-0118
Coin Weight
23mm
Charles I 'Silver Halfcrown' type.
£10 - £20

P19-0101
Horn Book
85mm
Used as a teaching aid. Some damage.
From £300

P19-0102
Lead Horn
Book
48mm
Good detail.
Undamaged. Rare.
Used as teaching
aid.
£200 - £300

P19-0103
Lead Horn
Book
48mm
Clear detail. Circular. Note letter
'T' comes after 'W'. Rare. Used as
teaching aid.
From £300

P19-0104
Lead Horn Book
30mm
Used as a teaching aid.
£150 - £200

P20-0101
Rumbler Bell
68mm
Very large size. Name
engraved on the bottom. Bell
rings.

£30 - £50

P20-0102
Rumbler Bell
60mm
Standard type. Large size.
Bell rings.

£20 - £30

P20-0103
Rumbler Bell
55mm
Standard type.
Clear markings. Large size.
£20 - £30

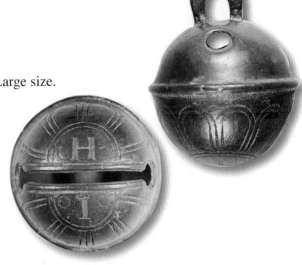

P20-0201
Decorated Bell
40mm
Good, even patina. Leaf design engraved
on the surface.
£40 - £60

P20-0301
Pewter Hawking
Whistle
48mm
Dog's head type.
£50 - £80

P20-0302
Pewter Hawking
Whistle
55mm
Dog's head. Suspension
loop underneath.
£50 - £80

P20-0303
Hawking Whistle
73mm
With bird of prey finkel.
£50 - £80

P20-0304
Silver Hawking Whistle
40mm
£200 - £300

P20-0305
Silver Whistle
48mm
£200 - £300

P20-0306
Silver Bosun's Whistle
40mm
£300 - £500

P21-0101
Bone Apple Corer
140mm
Bronze plate with a name
engraved.
£80 - £120

P21-0201
Iron Shears
88mm
Good state of preservation.
Working order.
£40 - £60

P21-0301
Barrel Tap
80mm
Zoomorphic. Even patina.
Undamaged.
£5 - £10

P21-0302
Silver-Gilt Bowl
Section
66mm
Fragment with Royal
Arms.
£400 - £600

P22-0101
Gold Love Token
15mm
George III '1762
Quarter Guinea' type.
£150 - £200

P22-0201
Norwich Trade Token
15mm
Good sharp detail. Even surface.
£20 - £30

P22-0202
Norwich Trade Token
15mm
Readable legend. Surface a
little ragged.
£15 - £20

P22-0203
Beccles Trade Token
15mm
Sharp detail. Even surface.
£30 - £40

P22-0204
Norwich Trade Token
15mm
Sharp detail. Even surface.
£15 - £20

P23-0201
Toy Cannon
90mm
Good working order.
£10 - £30

P23-0202
Toy Cannon Whistle
70mm
Even patina. Toy cannon
converted to a whistle.
£30 - £40

P23-0203
Toy Firearm
90mm
Trigger guard broken.
Decorated along the
barrel and butt.
£30 - £40

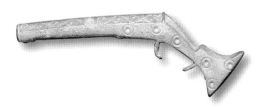

P23-0204
Toy Firearm
82mm
Ragged surface.
£20 - £30

P23-0205
Toy Firearm
65mm
Surface a little pitted. Small size.
£30 - £50

P23-0206
Toy Firearm
90mm
Surface a little uneven. Large size.
£50 - £80

P23-0207
Toy Firearm
77mm
Even patina.
Broken trigger guard.
£30 - £40

P23-0208
Toy Firearm with Curved Butt
75mm
Good, even surface. Scarce.
£50 - £80

P23-0209
Toy Firearm
78mm
Even patina. Complete.
£40 - £60

P23-0210
Toy Firearm
with Maker's Mark
95mm
Good, even patina. Maker's
mark stamped on the butt.
Large size. Rare.
£150 - £200

P23-0211
Toy Firearm
115mm
Good, even surface.
Ramrod in place. Very
large.
£150 - £200

P23-0212
Toy Firearm
76mm
Surface a little uneven.
Complete.
£40 - £60

P24-0101
Silver Reliquary
Cross
60mm
Hinged with suspension
loop. Rare.
£180 - £240

P26-0101
Pipe Tamper with
Four Heads
59mm
Turn upside down to view
another two heads. Even
patina. Complete.
£100 - £150

P24-0103
Candle Snuffer
40mm
£10 - £20

P25-0101
Charles I Silver Thimble
30mm
Oak tree on one side. King Charles' portrait on the other. Owner's initials engraved under the King's head. Rare.
From £1,200

P26-0102
Combination Ring, Pipe Tamper & Cork Screw
101mm
Even patina. Large size.
£40 - £60

P26-0101
Dragon Pipe Tamper
48mm
Even patina. Complete.
£30 - £40

P26-0102
Leg Pipe Tamper
50mm
Leg wearing a boot.
£10 - £20

P26-0103
Charles I Pipe
Tamper
70mm
Good detail. Crowned
Charles I on one side.
Weaker detail of his
wife on the other.
£150 - £200

P26-0104
Combination
Tamper Ring & Seal
55mm
Even patina.
£10 - £20

P26-0105
Erotic Pipe
Tamper
65mm
Good detail. Lack of
patina. Depicting a
couple copulating.
£100 - £150